SOUTHERN RAILWAY

SOUTHERN RAILWAY COMPANY

STATIONS IN CAPITAL LETTERS ARE INCLUDED IN THIS VOLUME

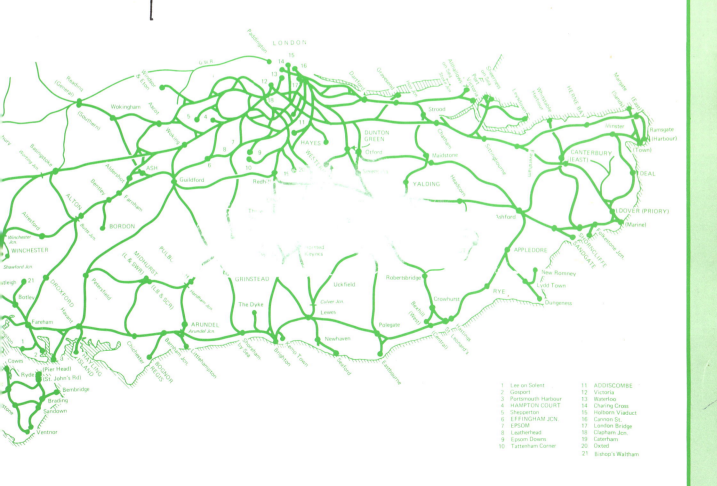

An Historical Survey of Selected

SOUTHERN STATIONS

VOLUME ONE

Wadhurst Station (SER), 1969.　　*photo: J. Scrace*

An Historical Survey of Selected

SOUTHERN STATIONS

LAYOUT AND ILLUSTRATIONS

VOLUME ONE

by

G. A. Pryer and G. J. Bowring

Oxford Publishing Co.

DEDICATION:
To the memory of Mary Anne Warwick—the last of the Great Victorians.

Acknowledgements

Publications covering the general history of a railway Company or branch line are quite numerous today, but detailed information on individual stations remains notoriously difficult to locate. The authors have therefore been obliged to enlist the help of so many people that there is not enough space to mention them all by name. Sincere thanks are offered to everyone who, over the last couple of years, has answered one of our enquiries, including the many Station Managers of the Southern Region who have willingly supplied interesting facts about the stations under their control. However, some officers of BR have gone to considerable trouble on our behalf, especially the Chief Civil Engineer (Croydon) and his staff in the Plan Arch at Waterloo, who supplied all the scale survey plans.

Information for the signalling diagrams has been drawn from a number of sources including the Public Records Office, Kew, and the extensive library of the Signalling Record Society. For dates and details of layout and signalling alterations we would like to thank Messrs. David Collins and J. M. Elms (both of the Signalling Record Society) and the staff of the Rules Section at the South-Western Divisional offices, Wimbledon. Other assistance with tracking down obscure dates has been received from Mr. A. J. Thomas (Totton), Mr. B. L. Jackson (Weymouth), and the late R. H. Clark, whose companion volumes on Great Western Stations are well known to all readers of railway literature. Mr. John Minnis has also rendered valuable assistance with the dating of buildings.

Amongst those who have helped with the more tedious tasks of production are Mrs. Jane Bunn of Salisbury, who has spent many hours labelling diagrams, and Mrs. C. Masterman of Southampton, who undertook some of the typing. There is no room here to mention all the photographers whose work enlivens the following pages, but one or two have been to special trouble in order to meet our needs, including B. L. Jackson, M. J. Tattershall, C. L. Caddy and R. C. Riley.

Lastly, but by no means least, mention must be made of our wives, who have put up with rooms full of "junk" and jobs around the house left undone for rather more than two years without undue complaint. Barbara Bowring also helped by doing some of the typing.

Bibliography

Many books have been consulted during the compilation of this volume, and readers who wish to know more about specific locations are advised to turn to the publications listed below. Certain official railway books are not available to the general public, but they can occasionally be purchased as collectors' items.

Regional History of the Railways of Great Britain: Vols. 1, 2 and 3.
Forgotten Railways—South East England. *H. P. White.*
The Railways of Southern England: Vols. 1, 2 and 3. *Edwin Course.*
Railways of Dorset. *J. H. Lucking.*
A Southern Region Chronology and Record. *R. H. Clark.*
Westerham Valley Railway. *David Gould.*
Plymouth, Devonport & South Western Junction Rly. *A. J. Cheesman.*
Sidmouth, Seaton and Lyme Regis Branches. *C. Maggs and P. Paye.*
The Railways of Purbeck. *R. W. Kidner.*
The Railways of Mid-Sussex. *Adrian Gray.*
The Oxted Line. *R. W. Kidner.*
The Railway Magazine. } Various articles.
Railway World.
Signalling Record Society Newsletter.
SR Appendix to the Working Timetables (1934). ⎫
Western Sectional Appendix (1960).   ⎬ BR Official books.
Central Sectional Appendix (1960).   ⎪
Eastern Sectional Appendix (1960).   ⎭
Track Layout Diagrams of the GWR and BR (WR). *R. A. Cooke.*

Introduction

Recent years have witnessed a great upsurge of interest in railways generally, and although locomotives continue to fascinate many people, they no longer hold the virtual monopoly of attention. When steam was King, the engines were studied in great detail and photographed from every conceivable angle, but with the introduction of modern and less photogenic forms of traction, cameras were focused on station buildings, old signals, and the whole range of railway structure and fittings. In many cases they were recorded just in time before the mass closures of the 1960s and modernisation schemes swept them away, but much was missed, and there are many locations which seem never to have been visited by photographers.

Railway enthusiasts have not been alone in their new awareness of stations. The last decade has seen a tremendous change in public taste, and to describe a building as "Victorian" or "Edwardian" no longer rates as automatic condemnation. Indeed, some stations of these periods are so cherished that preservation orders have been placed upon them, and almost every scheme to replace one with modern glass and concrete brings a storm of protest. Nostalgia has its part to play, of course, but it would be wrong to assume that this is the only reason for the appreciation of old stations. Modern man finds his architectural expression in the functional all-purpose building that could be anything from a church to a telephone exchange, and whilst it must be admitted that such structures are cheap to maintain and easy to keep clean, they have a regrettable sameness and lack of charm which makes the older and more decorative styles all the more appealing.

The foregoing remarks can be applied to Britain as a whole, but what can be said of Southern stations in particular? The South of England is fortunate in two ways, the first being that the policy of widespread electrification giving a regular interval service has succeeded in keeping many small stations open. One need only glance at a current railway map to see that stations are much thicker on the ground in Southern Region territory than they are, say, in Somerset or East Anglia, and what is more, they all enjoy a reasonably frequent service! Secondly, as the area was originally covered by four independent companies, followed by the Southern Railway, who had their own ideas on layout and design, there is a wide variety of architecture. Not all of it is good, some of it might even be called bad, but at least the very variety is a welcome break from a world rapidly becoming ever more standardised.

Of the pre-grouping companies, the LB & SCR was perhaps the most lavish builder of stations. They were executed in good-quality brick, and seldom was there evidence of the penny-pinching that sometimes became all too obvious on the other lines. The Company has a fondness for decoration, ornamental chimneys and gables being features of many "Brighton" stations, whilst the more important or prestigious establishments often sported a tower or turret, Tunbridge Wells West, Leatherhead and Groombridge being good surviving examples.

The L & SWR possessed a far-flung empire stretching from London to the remotest parts of North Cornwall, and consequently their architecture was diverse. As a general rule they preferred simple, rather spartan, stations, but the Company was capable of impressive building. The now-closed Southampton Terminus still stands as an excellent example of simple dignity, whilst the massive Bournemouth Central was obviously designed for the approbation of the genteel patrons of this high-class resort. Country stations were usually of the "Tudor Cottage" style, small and simple yet quite pleasing to the eye, but occasionally real parsimony resulted in buildings of corrugated iron like those at Andover Town.

Padstow (L & SWR) c. 1930, showing the fish station. *photo: Lens of Sutton*

Deal (SER) in SE & CR days. *photo: Lens of Sutton*

In the South-East the bitter competition between the SER and LC & DR impoverished both companies, and this lack of funds was often reflected in cheaply-built wooden structures. These were strictly functional in design and devoid of all ornamentation but were saved from disgrace by blending in with the clapboard tradition of the Kentish Weald. However, many better stations were built, the SER employing the architect William Tress to design stations for the Hastings Line. The result was a picturesque essay in Ecclesiastical Gothic for Battle, other pleasant Gothic buildings at Frant and Etchingham, and neat, restrained "Italianate" for Wadhurst. Gothic should surely have been the chosen style for Canterbury West, but here the Company erected a rather plain station fronted with columns of vaguely Classical appearance, not wholly in keeping with the character of the cathedral city.

The LC & DR also resisted any temptation to build a Gothic fantasy in Canterbury, their (East) station being plain to the point of severity. In fact plain simplicity was the Company's hallmark, but Malling and Borough Green survive as examples of better work.

At the Grouping of 1923 all these lines came into the fold of the newly-formed Southern Railway. Under the vigorous chairmanship of Sir Herbert Walker the policy of electrification was energetically pursued, and the resulting increase in traffic soon made it necessary to enlarge and rebuild many stations. For this work the Southern developed what is often called the "Odeon" style of architecture, so called because it reproduced in glass and concrete the rounded corners and other mannerisms associated with cinemas of the period. Changing fashions have made it appear curiously dated to modern critics, and some of the concrete has weathered badly, but some credit is due to the SR architects for taking a bold new approach to the problems of station design.

British Railways have continued the task of rebuilding, Chichester being a fine example, but in recent years they have tended to abandon architecture in favour of prefabricated structures which never succeed in looking permanent. There is also a modern tendency, typified by Crawley, to "redevelop" stations, the section dedicated to railway business being almost crowded out of existence by a mountain of office blocks let out to commercial firms. Regrettable as these trends are, they are also inevitable at a time when land values are soaring and the role of railways in society is changing. The Victorian station formed the hub of a town's industry and commerce and the gateway to the outside world, but in an age when most freight is moved by road and many of the younger generation have never travelled on a train, the railway's part in local affairs is, if still vital, much less significant, and a grand or elaborate building would be quite inappropriate.

In the many cases where stations of the older type still do duty today, the changing conditions under which they operate are emphasized by trackless goods yards and empty offices. Village stations are often completely unstaffed, or manned only at peak times of travel, and the spread of automatic signalling has even resulted in the removal of the signal box. At places which once carried a staff of perhaps a dozen men, it is now impossible to make an enquiry or send a parcel, but if all this sounds depressing, it should be noted on the credit side that to operate a station as cheaply as possible is often the only alternative to closure. The great pity is that the age of staff economies has coincided with the golden age of the vandal, and unattended stations quickly assume an aspect of complete dereliction, every wall liberally covered with mindless graffiti.

One thing is certain, as the traditional station receded further into memory, interest in its history, development and day-to-day working will increase. This book is designed to cater for that interest by bringing together an assortment of details for which the researcher would previously have been obliged to hunt through a wide variety of sources, whilst the scale layout plans should be of considerable value to the modeller. Selection of material has been difficult, the most interesting stations being much too large for satisfactory coverage in a book of this format. The authors sympathise with readers who feel that Ashford, Brighton or Salisbury should have been included, but point out that scale plans to cover such extensive layouts would have required so many cut sections that much of their appeal would have been lost. Branch line termini are ever popular, but the Southern system contained surprisingly few of these, many of their branches forming a link between two more important lines. Junctions are always worthy of study, and a fair sample of these is included, but many of the plans dealt with that type of station most common on the SR; the wayside main line variety. These were by no means all as straightforward as they sound, and one only has to look at Dorchester South with its odd arrangement of platforms, Deal with its middle siding and engine shed, or Tavistock North's curiously cramped goods yard, to find that many possessed features of considerable interest.

Isle of Wight stations are not included in the present volume, as the authors feel that this once extensive and self-contained system merits a book in its own right. The sundry "Light" railways of Southern England, some of which eventually became part of the Southern Railway or British Railways, (such as the Kent and East Sussex), and the narrow-gauge Lynton and Barnstaple, are also omitted. Otherwise the content ranges from Kent to Cornwall, and illustrates a reasonable cross-section of the small-to-moderate size stations found throughout the Southern system.

2-6-2 Standard Tank No. 82025 shunts coaching stock off a terminating service from Exeter at Budleigh Salterton.

photo: R. C. Riley

Notes on the use of plans and diagrams

SCALE PLANS This information is taken from official surveys, and care has been taken to copy them as faithfully as possible, but the amount of detail supplied by these is very variable. The more recent surveys tend to show the most detail, reflecting the use of aerial surveying techniques. Some concessions have had to be made to the much reduced scale of these drawings. Minor items, such as telegraph pole routes and drainage pits, are fine on plans drawn to such a large scale as 40 ft to the inch, but become very small and confusing when reproduced at a quarter of that size, and have therefore been omitted. For the same reason no attempt has been made to show the exact number of steps on footbridges etc, only the overall length of each flight being indicated.

Most features are clearly labelled, but where a drawing is likely to become over-congested certain standard items may be undescribed. Lamp posts on platforms are labelled "LP" where space permits, but are otherwise represented only by dots at regular intervals along the platform.

Main running signals which stand within the area covered by a scale plan are indicated by dots labelled "SP", but full details and configurations are generally reserved for the separate signalling diagram. Ground disc and other subsidiary signals are not normally shown on scale plans, except in a few cases where arrangements are very simple, when the entire signalling is given.

The stroke across the line at points represents exactly the tip of the switch blades.

SIGNALLING DIAGRAMS These are not drawn to scale, but whenever possible the distance (in yards) from each signal to the centre of the signal box is quoted.

Where the number of levers in a frame is given, this represents the TOTAL and not necessarily the number of working levers. In some cases there might appear to be more functions than there are levers to work them, but readers are reminded that most points are double-ended (both ends worked off the same lever) and that "push and pull" levers and selected signals can account for this discrepancy. Individual lever numbers are not quoted except for reference purposes, and track circuits, treadles, etc, are not shown.

Points operated from a lever frame are drawn to the "split line" format, the continuous line representing the route set when the lever is "Normal", viz

Hand operated points have no "Normal" or "Reverse" positions, and are shown in the same manner as on scale plans. The complete internal layouts of goods yards are not reproduced unless having some bearing on the signalling.

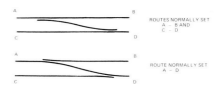

Two methods of ground disc (shunting signal) application can be found on the Southern, and these are as follows:—

1. The older (pre-Grouping) method, wherein a separate signal is provided for each available route.
2. The standard SR arrangement, which supplies only one signal to apply to all routes.

The two systems are never mixed on the same layout, and it is relatively simple to work out which one is in operation by comparing the number of discs with the number of possible routes. Generally speaking, a disc standing at every set of points, or the presence of double or triple discs, indicates that the older system applies. Ground disc signals are not normally workable for "straight back" movements in the wrong direction towards the Home Signal except in special circumstances, and where this is authorised a "Limit of Shunt" indicator is provided.

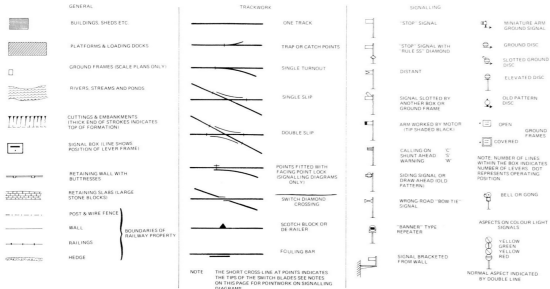

In the last days of Southern Region control BR "Standard" locomotives were drafted into the far West to replace the aged "T9s". Here 2-6-2 Tank No. 82023 shunts carriages into the bay platform at Bude before going into the yard for goods shunting.

photo: R.C. Riley

ADDISCOMBE

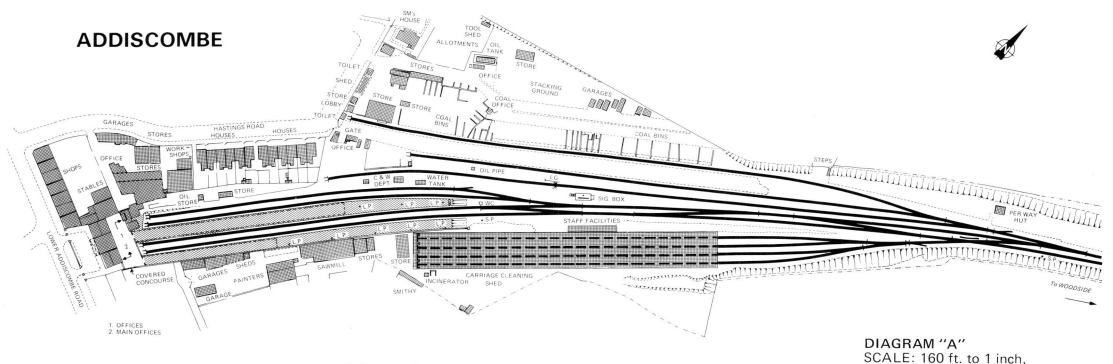

1. OFFICES
2. MAIN OFFICES

DIAGRAM "A"
SCALE: 160 ft. to 1 inch.
Survey Undated.

DIAGRAM "B"
Signalling—Not to scale.
Layout as in 1899, following partial reconstruction of station and provision of new signal box.

View from the buffer stops in the early 1950's.

photo: Lens of Sutton

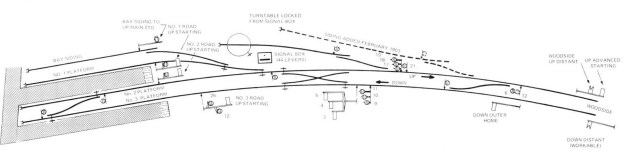

SIGNALS (LEVER NO's)

3 — TO NO. 3 PLATFORM DOWN INNER HOME
4 — TO NO. 2 PLATFORM DOWN INNER HOME
5 — TO NO. 1 PLATFORM DOWN INNER HOME
6 — SHUNT UP MAIN TO DOWN MAIN
9 — SHUNT DOWN MAIN TO NO. 3 PLATFORM
10 — SHUNT DOWN MAIN TO NO. 2 PLATFORM
11 — SHUNT DOWN MAIN TO NO. 1 PLATFORM

12 — SHUNT NO. 3 PLATFORM BACK TO DOWN MAIN
17 — SHUNT UP MAIN TO NO. 1 PLATFORM
18 — SHUNT UP MAIN TO NO. 2 PLATFORM
19 — SHUNT UP MAIN TO NO. 3 PLATFORM
21 — SHUNT UP MAIN TO TURNTABLE
26 — SHUNT NO. 3 PLATFORM TO UP MAIN
32 — SHUNT UP MAIN TO NEW SIDING

1

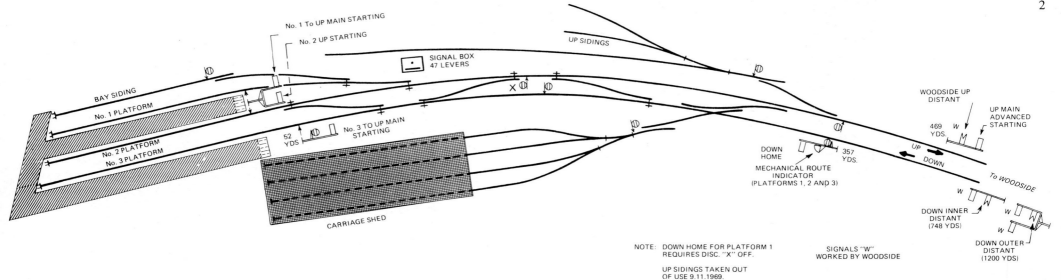

No. 1 To UP MAIN STARTING

No. 2 UP STARTING

UP SIDINGS

SIGNAL BOX
47 LEVERS

BAY SIDING

No. 1 PLATFORM

No. 2 PLATFORM

No. 3 PLATFORM

52
YDS.

No. 3 TO UP MAIN
STARTING

WOODSIDE UP
DISTANT

UP MAIN
ADVANCED
STARTING

469
YDS.   W

UP

DOWN

To WOODSIDE

DOWN
HOME   357
YDS.

MECHANICAL ROUTE
INDICATOR
(PLATFORMS 1, 2 AND 3)

W   W

DOWN INNER
DISTANT
(748 YDS)   W

CARRIAGE SHED

(748 YDS)

DOWN OUTER
DISTANT
(1200 YDS)

NOTE: DOWN HOME FOR PLATFORM 1
REQUIRES DISC. "X" OFF.

UP SIDINGS TAKEN OUT
OF USE 9.11.1969.

SIGNALS "W"
WORKED BY WOODSIDE

DIAGRAM "C"—Signalling
Not to Scale.
Date of Layout: 1950

Opened: 1.4.1864
Closed to goods: 17.6.1968
Electrified: 28.2.1926
Original Company: Mid-Kent Rly. amalgamated
with SER 1866.

ADDISCOMBE

This station was built as the terminus of a 3¼-mile extension from the Mid-Kent line at Beckenham. Although a local promotion, it was strongly supported by the SER from the outset, as it gave that Company access to Croydon (an LB & SCR stronghold) by the back door! The original station was a humble affair with a turntable at the platform end adjoining Lower Addiscombe Road, and there was a small engine shed.

Complete rebuilding was undertaken in 1899, the result being an excellent station with three platforms and a booking hall and offices in red brick. The sash windows and hipped slate roof were typical "South Eastern" touches of the period. The existing signal box (originally containing 44 levers, later increased to 47) was installed at this time, and the turntable was moved to a new site on the north side of the line. This layout is shown in diagram "B". There do not appear to have been any goods facilities, but an extra siding was provided in February 1903.

The next major alterations were made in 1925 in readiness for electrification. The crossover between platforms 2 and 3 was taken out of use (11-7-25) and those at the approach to the station rearranged to allow parallel working. Sidings and a new car shed were constructed on the Down side, and the turntable dismantled. Diagrams "A" and "C" show the station in this remodelled form.

In connection with the introduction of 10-car trains on the Mid-Kent lines in 1957 the island platform (1 and 2) was extended right up to the signal box, Platform 1 road being diverted behind the box. Platform 3 was demolished and the site used for an additional stabling siding.

Despite the spread of power signalling, Addiscombe remains fully mechanical at the time of writing (1979), the fringe box for London Bridge being Woodside. However, the layout has been greatly simplified, only one facing and one trailing crossover surviving (the latter being a single slip with the car sheds sidings). The station buildings are still intact and in good condition.

ALTON

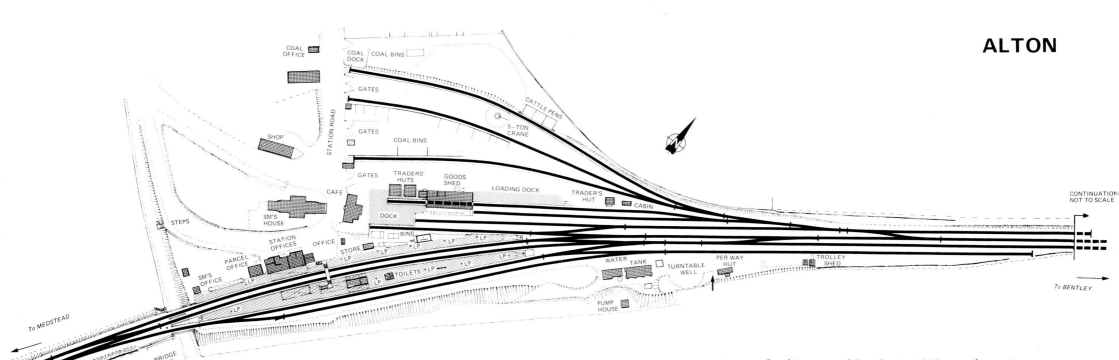

COAL
OFFICE

COAL | COAL BINS
DOCK

CATTLE PENS

5–TON
CRANE

GATES

SHOP

GATES

STATION ROAD

COAL BINS

TRADERS'
HUTS

GOODS
SHED

LOADING DOCK

TRADER'S
HUT

CABIN

CONTINUATION
NOT TO SCALE

CAFE

SM'S
HOUSE

DOCK

STEPS

STATION
OFFICES

OFFICE

STORE

BINS

LP

LP

LP

LP

LP

LP

LP

WATER
TANK

TURNTABLE
WELL

PER WAY
HUT

TROLLEY
SHED

To BENTLEY

PARCEL
OFFICE

SM'S
OFFICE

TOILETS

LP

LP

LP

LP

PUMP
HOUSE

To MEDSTEAD

BRIDGE
No. 46

To TISTED

Looking toward Bentley in 1967.   *photo: C.L. Caddy*

DIAGRAM "A"
SCALE: 160 ft. to 1 inch.
Date of Survey: 1955.

Opened: 28.7.1852 (Original Station).
Opened: 2.10.1865 (Present Station).
Electrified between Woking and Alton only: 4.7.1937
Closed: 6.1.1969 (Goods).
Original Company: L & SWR.

DIAGRAM "B"—Signalling
Layout as remodelled in 1903.
Not to Scale.

DOCK

SIGNAL BOX (39 LEVERS)

UP MAIN STARTING

GOODS YARD

UP MAIN

UP LOOP

56 YDS

UP LOOP STARTING

DOWN MAIN

69 YDS

DOWN SIDING WEST

DOWN HOME

134 YDS

332 YDS

UP ADVANCED STARTING

DOWN SIDING EAST

UP MAIN TO LOOP HOME

145 YDS

DOWN STARTING

UP MAIN HOME

292 YDS

1008 YDS

UP DISTANT

852 YDS

DOWN DISTANT

UP

DOWN

372 YDS

BUTTS JUNCTION

DOWN ADVANCED STARTING

PORTION OF DOWN LINE IN NO. 2 ROAD SHOWN THUS ⊢⊢⊢⊢ REMOVED 9.7.1967. BUFFER STOPS ERECTED AT BENTLEY END OF NO. 2 PLATFORM.

POINTS "A" OUT OF USE (2 pairs) 24.2.1969
POINTS "B" OUT OF USE 19.1.1970
POINTS "C" OUT OF USE 3.3.1970
POINTS "D" OUT OF USE 4.4.1970

DOCK

SIGNAL BOX (42 LEVERS)

UP SIDING NO. 2

53 YDS

37

YELLOW

A

UP SIDING NO. 1

NO. 1 ROAD DOWN STARTING

132 YDS

NO. 1 ROAD

NO. 2 ROAD

63 YDS

9

36

35

A

C

YELLOW

YELLOW

MEON VALLEY

DOWN SIDING

A

LINE TO MEDSTEAD OUT OF USE 5.2.1973 STOP BLOCKS FIXED HERE. APPROX. 672 YDS FROM SIGNAL BOX

UP MID HANTS TO NO. 2 ROAD HOME

UP MID HANTS TO NO. 1 ROAD HOME

135 YDS

B

3   14

15

13   12

D

DOWN SIDING

UP ADVANCED STARTING

620 YDS

UP

DOWN

472 YDS

DOWN MID HANTS UP

E

UP MEON VALLEY HOME

277 YDS

UP MID HANTS DISTANT

1579 YDS

MEDSTEAD

TISTED

SIDING TO FARRINGDON (FORMER MEON VALLEY LINE) OUT OF USE 6.1.1968. STOP BLOCKS FIXED HERE APPROX. 450 YDS FROM SIGNAL BOX

DOWN MEON VALLEY UP

UP MEON VALLEY DISTANT

1579 YDS

37 — NO. 1 ROAD UP STARTING
36 — NO. 2 ROAD UP STARTING
35 — MEON VALLEY UP STARTING
9 — MEON VALLEY TO DOWN SIDING SHUNT

3 — NO. 2 ROAD TO MID HANTS DOWN STARTING
15 — NO. 2 ROAD TO MEON VALLEY DOWN STARTING
13 — MEON VALLEY DOWN STARTING
14 — NO. 2 ROAD TO MEON VALLEY SHUNT AHEAD
12 — MEON VALLEY SHUNT AHEAD

2 — TO NO. 2 ROAD DOWN HOME
4 — TO MEON VALLEY DOWN HOME
42 — TO NO. 1 ROAD DOWN HOME

42

2

4

675 YDS

BENTLEY

DOWN DISTANT

1575 YDS

DIAGRAM "C"—Signalling
Revised layout for electrification, 1937.
Not to Scale.

ALTON

For a station of its size, Alton has had a very complicated and varied history. The original station served as the terminus of an extension from Farnham, and had a rather quaint building of local stone with steep gables. It survived as the Station Master's house into the late 1950s, but was then demolished and the site taken in as part of a new car park.

When the Mid-Hants line to Winchester was constructed the junction at Alton fell a few chains east of the existing station, and it was therefore decided to erect a new one. Fortunately it was possible to leave the goods yard in its original position. The new station was opened on the same day as services to Winchester commenced—2nd October, 1865. It was much plainer in style than the 1852 structure, being a brick single-storey building with a small entrance hall flanked by two rectangular wings.

At this stage Alton was nothing more than a crossing station on a rather unimportant single line, but it must have benefited considerably from the opening of the line between Pirbright Junction and Farnham Junction (via Aldershot) in 1870, the distance to London being somewhat reduced. There matters rested until 1901, when the line was doubled from Farnham to a new signal box at Butts Junction (just over one mile west of Alton), at which point the light railway to Basingstoke diverged. Services to Basingstoke commenced on 1st June, 1901.

Widespread changes took place in 1903 in readiness for the opening of the Meon Valley line to Fareham, which also joined the existing railway at Butts Junction and opened on 1st June that year. The Down platform was rebuilt as an island, the Down line being diverted to the outer face and the former Down line becoming an Up Loop, Diagram "B" shows the layout in this form. It was necessary to reconstruct the road underbridge at the west end of the station to carry an extra track, and other work included a new 39-lever signal box, additional toilets and waiting rooms on the island platform, and demolition of the small engine shed.

Alton now enjoyed three services in a westerly direction and the line became quite busy, although there was less shunting in the station area than might be expected as the Basingstoke branch was worked by push-and-pull trains from 1904 and most Meon Valley services ran through from Farnham and beyond. The Basingstoke and Alton Light Railway was closed between 1917 and 1924, the passenger service being finally withdrawn on 12th September, 1932 followed by goods in 1936. Butts Junction box was then abolished and the double line from there to Alton converted into two parallel single lines as part of the electrification scheme then taking place. Other works in connection with this project included lengthening the Up platform (compare diagrams "B" and "C") and some revision of the layout and signalling to facilitate reversible working through all three platforms, although, somewhat oddly, platform 2 was not electrified. The lever frame in the signal box was extended by three levers. Electrification brought a vastly improved service to London, but to the West things remained much as before until 7th February, 1955, when the

Meon Valley trains ceased. The line was retained for goods as far as Farringdon Siding until 1968, after which it was removed (see Diagram "C"). On a brighter note, the Mid-Hants line was dieselised in 1957 and given an hourly service. During 1968/69 the track layout was greatly simplified, Platform 2 becoming a dead-end bay for the use of Winchester trains. Full details are shown on Diagram "C".

The Mid-Hants line was closed completely on 5th February, 1973, and Alton reverted to its original terminal status. The only trains are now the Waterloo electrics, which run a half-hourly service throughout the day with additions at peak hours. No berthing sidings are necessary as all stock is stabled at a large depot at Farnham. Most trains use No. 1 platform, No. 3 being pressed into service only during rush hours. The goods yard has been completely obliterated by a car show room, and the "Gents" on the island platform has been demolished. However, it is not all gloom; the Mid-Hants Railway, currently operating a preserved length of line between Alresford and Ropley, plans to connect with the BR system at Alton again in the fairly near future.

Looking west towards Medstead in the early 1960's. *photo: B.L. Jackson*

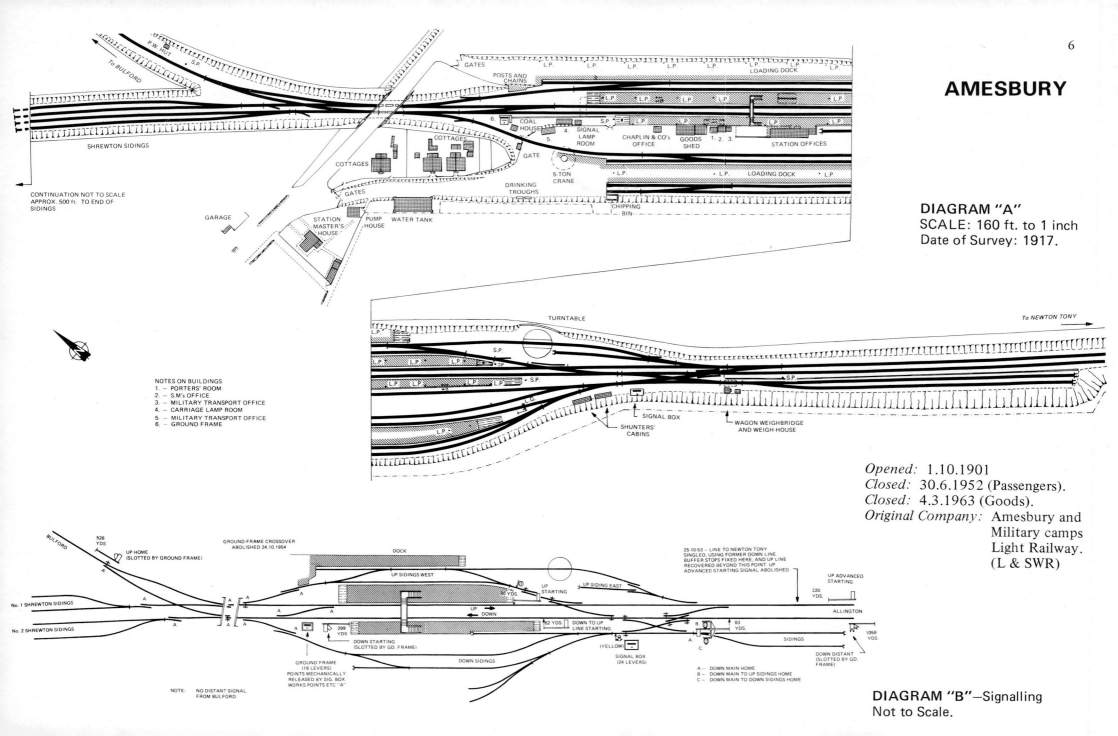

AMESBURY

DIAGRAM "A"
SCALE: 160 ft. to 1 inch
Date of Survey: 1917.

DIAGRAM "B"—Signalling
Not to Scale.

Opened: 1.10.1901
Closed: 30.6.1952 (Passengers).
Closed: 4.3.1963 (Goods).
Original Company: Amesbury and Military camps Light Railway. (L & SWR)

AMESBURY

The lonely southern slopes of Salisbury Plain had little attraction for nineteenth-century railway promoters, and Amesbury would almost certainly have been left without rail connection had not the Government set up large military camps in the area.

Construction of the branch commenced in 1899. It was classified as a "Light" railway, formidable gradients being tolerated to economise on earthworks, and opened as a single line with Amesbury as the terminus. Two platforms faces were designated as being for "ordinary" traffic, the three long loading dock lines being reserved for military purposes. The Board of Trade agreed that troop trains could be started from any line by hand signals under special instructions. The line terminated in a headshunt with run-round connections operated from a 3-lever ground frame bolt locked from the signal box.

Military traffic soon became so heavy that doubling was carried out in 1904, and at the same time a burrowing junction with the main line was constructed to permit through running in the direction of Salisbury. Thereafter most of the regular passenger trains used this route, the east-facing curve being retained for troop trains and goods traffic. The single line extension to Bulford Camp opened on 1st June, 1906, and a much larger ground frame was opened at the Bulford end of the station to control the additional connections. The Bulford extension was never doubled.

Good bus services and increasing car ownership quickly robbed the line of its non-military traffic. Amesbury station stood on the extreme edge of the town, and once reached, the train journey to Salisbury was circuitous indeed compared with the direct main road taken by the buses. Freight remained at a reasonable level after the withdrawal of the passenger service, but the run-down of the armed forces eventually resulted in all military goods being concentrated on Ludgershall. During its final years the track had again been singled throughout (see diagram "B"), the tablet section being Grateley to Amesbury, with "No Signalman" Key token working between Amesbury and Bulford.

The station was rather a bleak place, but typical of several to be found in the military area. The chief feature was the spaciousness of the platforms, ideal for drawing up a battalion of men with all their equipment. Little remains today, the site having been redeveloped.

View from the road overbridge in 1964, over a year since the last train had run. Everything is still in position, including the signals. The 18 lever ground frame is on the right.

photo: B.L. Jackson

ANDOVER TOWN

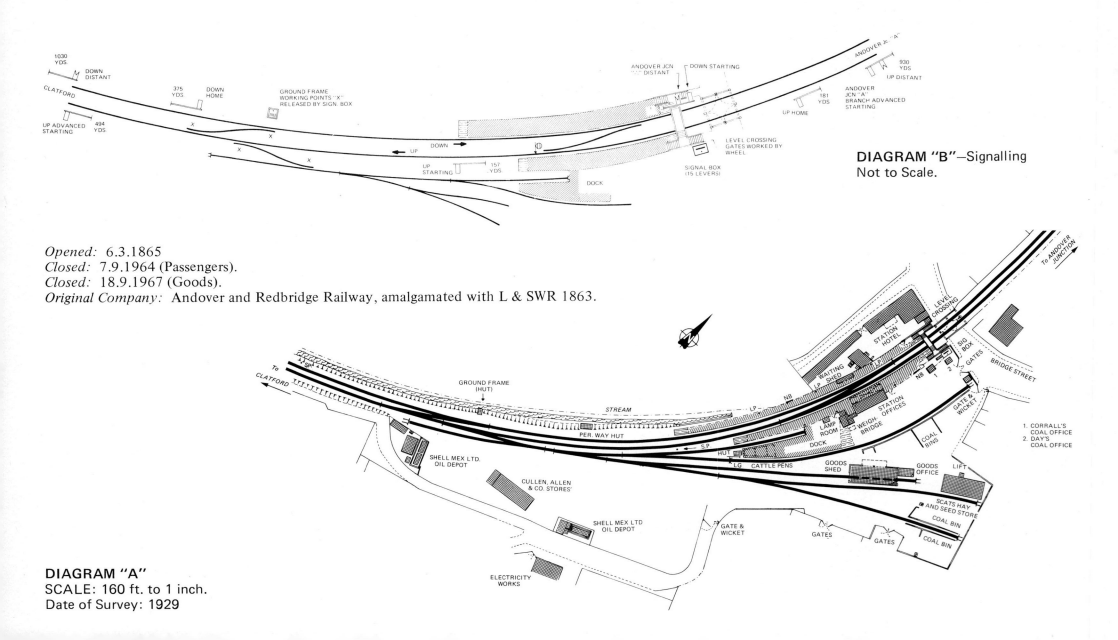

1030
YDS.

DOWN
DISTANT

CLATFORD

375
YDS.

DOWN
HOME

GROUND FRAME
WORKING POINTS "X"
RELEASED BY SIGN. BOX

ANDOVER JCN
"C" DISTANT

DOWN STARTING

ANDOVER Jc "A"

930
YDS.

UP DISTANT

UP ADVANCED
STARTING

494
YDS.

ANDOVER
JCN "A"
BRANCH ADVANCED
STARTING

181
YDS.

UP HOME

X

X

DOWN

UP

LEVEL CROSSING
GATES WORKED BY
WHEEL

X

X

UP
STARTING

157
YDS.

SIGNAL BOX
(15 LEVERS)

DOCK

DIAGRAM "B"—Signalling
Not to Scale.

Opened: 6.3.1865
Closed: 7.9.1964 (Passengers).
Closed: 18.9.1967 (Goods).
Original Company: Andover and Redbridge Railway, amalgamated with L & SWR 1863.

To
CLATFORD

SP

GROUND FRAME
(HUT)

STREAM

PER. WAY HUT

SHELL MEX LTD.
OIL DEPOT

CULLEN, ALLEN
& CO. STORES'

SHELL MEX LTD
OIL DEPOT

ELECTRICITY
WORKS

GATE &
WICKET

To ANDOVER
JUNCTION

LEVEL
CROSSING

STATION
HOTEL

SIG
BOX

GATES

BRIDGE STREET

WAITING
SHED

LP

LP

NB

NB

1   2

GATE &
WICKET

LP

NB

LAMP
ROOM

STATION
OFFICES

WEIGH-
BRIDGE

COAL
BINS

SP

HUT

DOCK

S.P.

LG   CATTLE PENS

GOODS
SHED

GOODS
OFFICE

LIFT

SCATS HAY
AND SEED STORE

COAL BIN

GATES

GATES

COAL BIN

1. CORRALL'S
   COAL OFFICE
2. DAY'S
   COAL OFFICE

DIAGRAM "A"
SCALE: 160 ft. to 1 inch.
Date of Survey: 1929

ANDOVER TOWN

Despite its convenient position in the centre of the town, this was very much the "poor relation" to the Junction station on the main line. The train service in steam days consisted mostly of non-too-frequent local workings between Andover Junction and Eastleigh or Southampton, the only through traffic coming off the old M & SWJ line from the direction of Cheltenham. This was vastly improved in 1957 with the introduction of diesel-electric multiple units on an hourly interval basis, although by this time the Cheltenham service had shrunk to one train per day in each direction. The Andover By-pass was still a thing of the future, and the crossing gates were a constant source of delay to traffic on the busy "A303", and the main reason for the town's reputation as a traffic jam black spot!

The line was originally single track, and as there was no crossing place at Andover Town, the station had only one platform. The level crossing was under the control of a "Gateman". In 1882 the section of line up to the Junction station was doubled, the second platform and signal box being provided at this time. The line remained single towards Clatford until 1884.

An unusual feature of the track layout was the crossover between the platforms, and it is interesting to note that it was placed in this position on the insistence of the Board of Trade inspector. The point had at first been laid well clear of the level crossing on the Junction side, but the inspector considered that this would give rise to continual shunting across the public highway, and ordered its repositioning. He was also critical of the daring attempt to operate the points at the Clatford end mechanically from the signal box, and required a ground frame to be placed there for the purpose. These matters had been attended to by May 1883.

Goods traffic was heavy and outlived the passenger service by three years. With the withdrawal of the latter the line was closed completely south of Andover Town, and a stop block was erected in the Up line 300 yds on the Clatford side of the goods yard points. Part of the Down line was removed, and the ground frame dismantled. The signal box was retained to work the crossing gates, but all points were converted to hand operation. The Up line between the crossover in the platform and Andover Junction was also severed, the former Down line providing the only access. All this work took place on 29th September, 1964. Two signals remained to protect the gates — the Down Starting and the Up Home.

The station and yard were derelict for some time after complete closure, but the site has now been redeveloped.

OPERATING NOTE: Bogie coaches prohibited from passing alongside loading dock.

Above: Nineteenth-century view of Andover Town, looking north towards Andover Junction.
photo: Lens of Sutton

Right: A similar view in the 1960's. Many changes are apparent, including the replacement concrete footbridge and simplified canopy on the Down waiting shelter.
photo: B.L. Jackson

APPLEDORE (KENT)

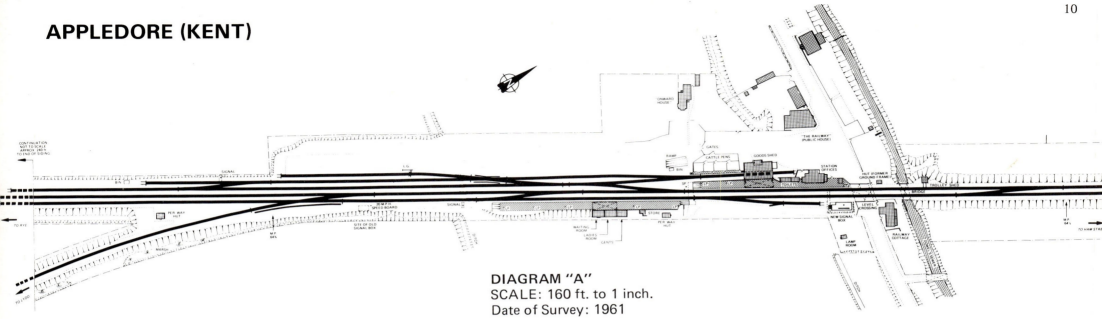

DIAGRAM "A"
SCALE: 160 ft. to 1 inch.
Date of Survey: 1961

Looking towards Rye about 1930.　　　*photo: Lens of Sutton*　　　Looking from the Down platform towards Ham Street in 1974.　　　*photo: J.R. Minnis*

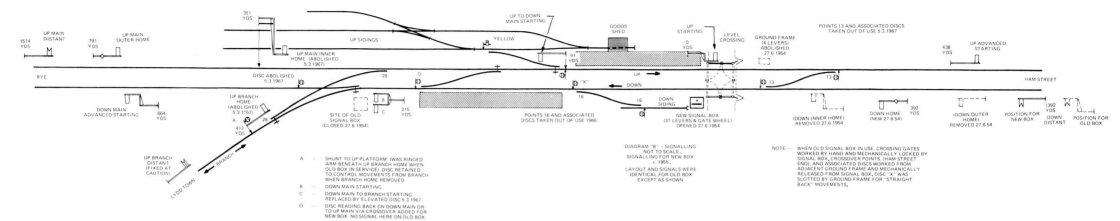

A — SHUNT TO UP PLATFORM. (WAS RINGED ARM BENEATH UP BRANCH HOME WHEN OLD BOX IN SERVICE). DISC RETAINED TO CONTROL MOVEMENTS FROM BRANCH WHEN BRANCH HOME REMOVED.

B — DOWN MAIN STARTING.

C — DOWN MAIN TO BRANCH STARTING. REPLACED BY ELEVATED DISC 5.3.1967.

D — DISC READING BACK ON DOWN MAIN OR TO UP MAIN VIA CROSSOVER ADDED FOR NEW BOX. NO SIGNAL HERE ON OLD BOX.

NOTE:— WHEN OLD SIGNAL BOX IN USE, CROSSING GATES WORKED BY HAND AND MECHANICALLY LOCKED BY SIGNAL BOX. CROSSOVER POINTS, (HAM STREET END), AND ASSOCIATED DISCS WORKED FROM ADJACENT GROUND FRAME AND MECHANICALLY RELEASED FROM SIGNAL BOX. DISC "X" WAS SLOTTED BY GROUND FRAME FOR "STRAIGHT BACK" MOVEMENTS.

Opened: 13.2.1851
Closed: 27.5.1963 (Goods).
Original Company: South Eastern Railway

DIAGRAM "B"—Signalling
Not to Scale
Shows arrangements for new signal
box c. 1965. Layout and signals identical
for old box except where shown.

APPLEDORE (Kent)

Standing over a mile from the village whose name it bears on a lonely site in the flat expanse of Romney Marsh, Appledore survives to the present day as an excellent example of a "South Eastern" country station. Fortunately it dates from before that Company's "poor" period, and the main office block is a neat structure in a vaguely Classical style. The shelter on the Down platform is of hipped roof timber construction, typically SER in style but distinguished by an unusually large canopy. There has never been a footbridge or subway, the platform originally being connected by means of a board crossing, but in recent years this has been dispensed with in favour of a new footpath from the road to the Down platform running behind the signal box and along the site of the short Down Siding.

On 7th December, 1881 it became a junction station with the opening of the branch to Lydd and Dungeness, but no separate bay platform was provided to cater for this traffic. Some branch trains ran through to Ashford, but those terminating were quickly shunted into the goods yard, where the layout allowed running round to take place without interfering with the main lines. Once the connecting Up service had departed, the branch stock was propelled into the Up platform. The signalling permitted branch trains to re-start from that point via the crossover.

Until the new signal box was opened the crossing gates were under the control of a "Gateman", the old box being situated at the opposite end of the station near the junction. Passenger services on the branch were withdrawn on 6th March, 1967 and this, coupled with the loss of freight facilities in 1963, was the cue for much rationalisation of the track layout (see diagram "B"). However, the branch remains in use as a goods line serving the ARC stone terminal at Lydd and the Dungeness nuclear power station.

For some years the future of the passenger service was in doubt, but on 30th September, 1979, the line between Appledore and Ore (Hastings) was reduced to single track, and the resulting economies make retention more likely.

11

ARUNDEL

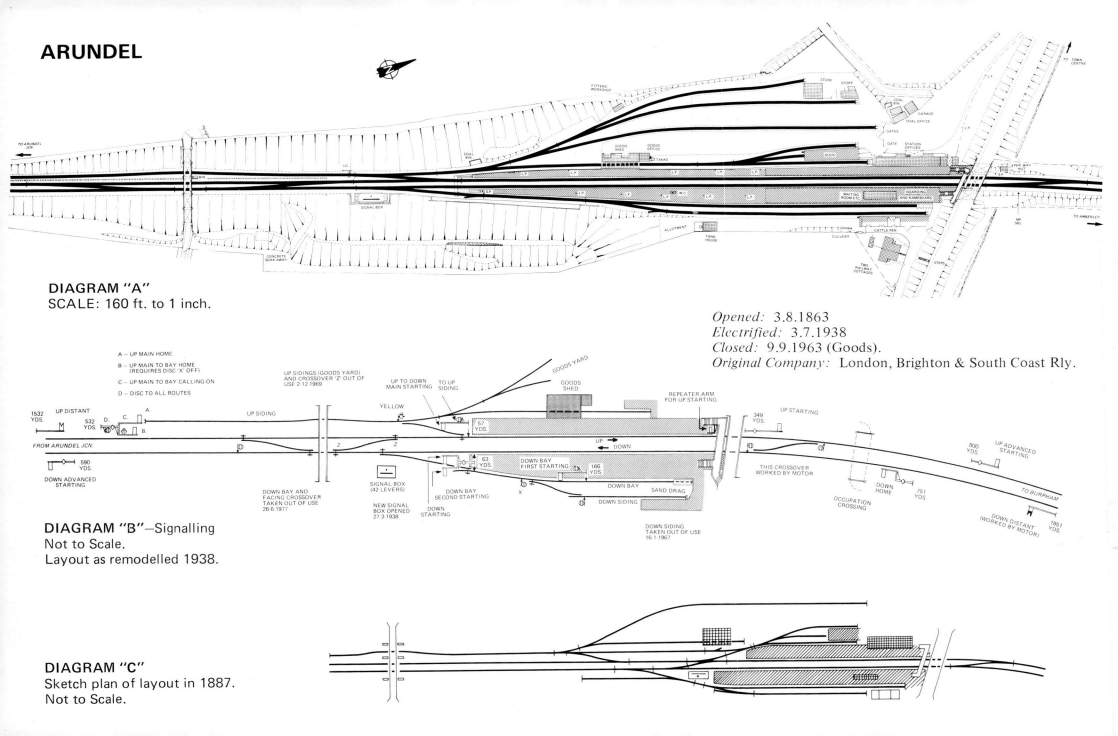

DIAGRAM "A"
SCALE: 160 ft. to 1 inch.

Opened: 3.8.1863
Electrified: 3.7.1938
Closed: 9.9.1963 (Goods).
Original Company: London, Brighton & South Coast Rly.

A — UP MAIN HOME
B — UP MAIN TO BAY HOME
(REQUIRES DISC 'X' OFF)
C — UP MAIN TO BAY CALLING-ON
D — DISC TO ALL ROUTES

DIAGRAM "B"—Signalling
Not to Scale.
Layout as remodelled 1938.

DIAGRAM "C"
Sketch plan of layout in 1887.
Not to Scale.

View from buffer stops of Down bay platform, pre 1923. The old signal box is visible in the background.
photo: Lens of Sutton

Looking north along the main line platforms in 1969. The extra length of canopy erected by the SR in 1938 is obvious.
photo: J. Scrace

ARUNDEL

The main office building and large goods shed are original, but there have been later additions on the North wing of the former, and the Up side canopy was extended to the South around the same time—c.1906. The signal box which appears in the early photograph dated from 1876, but it was extended ten years later to accommodate a 31-lever frame when the station was enlarged to cater for a shuttle service over the new Littlehampton Direct line.

Littlehampton trains could use the Up Bay for both arrival and departure, but the Down Bay was for departure only. The Down platform and buildings were reconstructed at that time (1886). A major rebuilding took place in 1937/8 when the platforms were extended to a length of 820 ft. in readiness for electrification. The extension was carried out at the South end to save reconstruction of the road bridge, but this involved rearrangement of the goods yard connections. A new "Glasshouse"-style signal box was brought into use on 27th March, 1938 to control the new layout, which included a facing crossover to provide direct access to the Down Bay. This facility allowed the old Up Bay to be abolished, and its site was incorporated into the goods yard. A new length of canopy was provided on the Down side, utterly hideous when compared with the original LB & SCR canopies which still survive!

The South Coast timetable was completely reorganised in 1972 and the shuttle service to Littlehampton ceased, although the bay remained in use for a time to cater for a few peak-hour workings, to Chichester for example. Most of the layout has now been removed (for dates see diagram "B"), and indeed only the crossover at the North end remains connected to the box. The station itself, however, survives in good condition, and has a healthy passenger traffic.

13

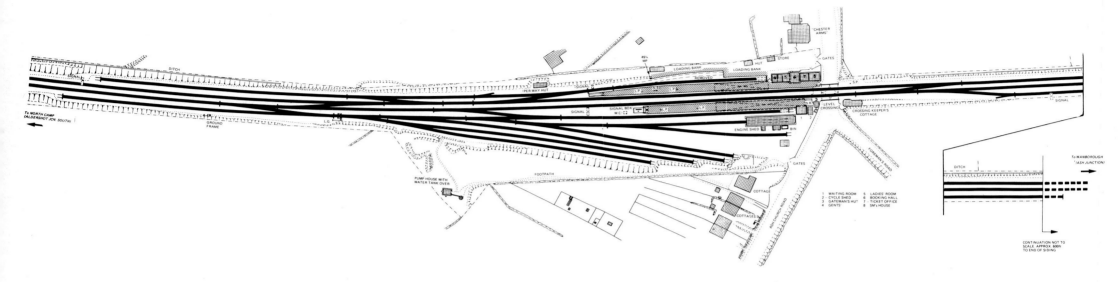

DIAGRAM "A"
SCALE: 160 ft. to 1 inch.
Survey Undated, but shows position
c. 1959.

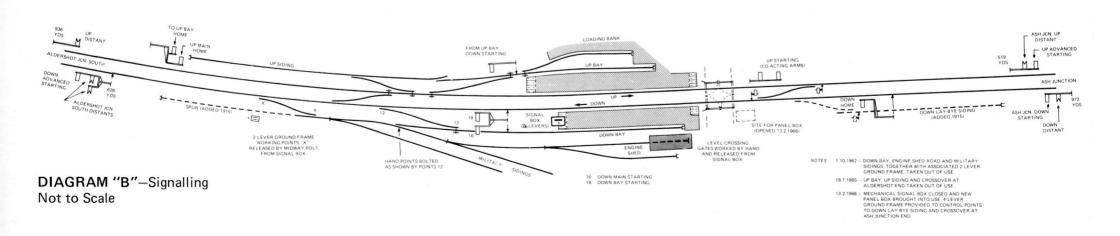

DIAGRAM "B"—Signalling
Not to Scale

NOTES 1.10.1962 — DOWN BAY, ENGINE SHED ROAD AND MILITARY
SIDINGS, TOGETHER WITH ASSOCIATED 2-LEVER
GROUND FRAME, TAKEN OUT OF USE.

18.7.1965 — UP BAY, UP SIDING AND CROSSOVER AT
ALDERSHOT END TAKEN OUT OF USE.

13.2.1966 — MECHANICAL SIGNAL BOX CLOSED AND NEW
PANEL BOX BROUGHT INTO USE. 4-LEVER
GROUND FRAME PROVIDED TO CONTROL POINTS
TO DOWN LAY BYE SIDING AND CROSSOVER AT
ASH JUNCTION END.

Looking toward Wanborough in the 1950's. The engine shed, in its altered form following demolition of that part of the building formerly used as a goods shed, can be seen behind the Down platform. Particularly noteworthy is the Saxby & Farmer type signal box—very rare on the SER.

photo: Lens of Sutton

Opened: 20.8.1849
Electrified: 1.1.1939
Closed: 7.11.1960 (Goods).
Original Company: Reading, Guildford and Reigate Railway, amalgamated with SER 1852.

ASH

When the RG & R line was built Aldershot was but an insignificant village which the railway made no attempt to serve. Its subsequent development as a Military centre played havoc with the established transport pattern of the area and changed Ash from a little wayside station into a junction of considerable local importance.

A spur line (between Aldershot Junctions North and South) linking the SER and L & SWR was opened in 1879, and as this gave direct access to Aldershot station, the South Eastern introduced a shuttle service to connect with Reading line trains. The two Bay platforms and signal box were added the same year. From 1882 the shuttle was augmented by a new L & SWR service between Aldershot and Guildford, Ash then dealing with the trains of both Companies. This arrangement lasted until electrification in 1939, when the shuttle was replaced by regular electric trains from Waterloo to Guildford via Ascot and Aldershot. The bay lines were seldom used thereafter, but the layout remained remarkably intact until the early 1960s (see diagram "B").

The offices and Station Master's house on the Up side date from the opening of the line, although minor extensions of later date have tended to obscure their original appearance. The waiting room on the Down platform and an extra length of canopy are luxuries provided in Southern Railway days. There has never been a footbridge or subway, passengers making use of the road level crossing. Originally a large double building was erected in the yard, one side being an engine shed and the other a goods shed. The goods side was demolished by 1905, but the section used by the Motive Power Department remained in use until about 1946. It is now used as a store.

The main building on the Up platform in April 1979, as viewed from the level crossing.

photo: G. Bowring

15

ASHBURY

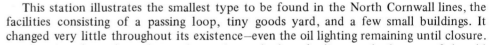

UP DISTANT

UP HOME

SIGNAL BOX (12 LEVERS)

WAITING SHED

UP STARTING

DOWN HOME

To MELDON JCN. AND OKEHAMPTON

To HALWILL JUNCTION

OCCUPATION LEVEL CROSSING

DOWN STARTING

TROLLEY SHED

DOCK

CATTLE PEN

GOODS SHED

STATION OFFICES

BRIDGE No. 12

DOWN DISTANT

FEED STORE

ASH BIN

WEST DEVON FARMERS' UNION STORES

GATE

SCALE: 160ft = 1 inch

SHUNTING SPUR AND SHORT DOCK SIDING REMOVED 28·3·1964.

NOTE: BOTH DISTANT SIGNALS ARE WORKABLE

Opened: 20.1.1879
Closed: 7.9.1964 (Goods).
Closed: 30.10.1966 (Passengers).
Original Company: L & SWR.

ASHBURY

This station illustrates the smallest type to be found in the North Cornwall lines, the facilities consisting of a passing loop, tiny goods yard, and a few small buildings. It changed very little throughout its existence—even the oil lighting remaining until closure.

The plan shows how the road was diverted when the line was built, part of the old route being clearly indicated. As can be seen in the photograph, platforms and bridges in the area were built of stone, as were the station offices, although the rendering makes this less obvious. The architecture was undistinguished, but the buildings provided ample accommodation for any traffic that could be obtained in such a thinly-populated district. No footbridge was provided, but the flight of steps on each side of the road bridge allowed passengers to use the latter for crossing between the platforms.

The goods shed was small, and had a short canopy over the loading points on each side—a common feature West of Okehampton. Signalling was already well established when this line was opened, so the 12-lever signal box forms part of the original fittings. In the early days traffic was controlled by Train Staff and Ticket, but this was later changed to Electric Tablet—probably when the line was extended from Holsworthy to Bude in 1898. The loop was lengthened slightly at the Okehampton end (probably during the Second World War); latterly it held 34 wagons, engine and brake van. The only other alterations are noted on the plan.

All lines in the area were transferred to the Western Region in January 1963, and the subsequent decline in the train service is detailed in the feature on Bude.

Looking toward Okehampton c.1905. The shrubs and flower beds along the front of the building were features which disappeared in BR days.
photo: Lens of Sutton

AXMINSTER

Opened: 19.7.1860
Closed: 18.4.1966 (Goods).
Original Company: L & SWR

DIAGRAM "A"
SCALE: 160 ft. to 1 inch.
Date of Survey: 1903.
Shows complete signalling for that
period. Later arrangements appear on
Diagram "B".

Axminster in the 1930's with one of the Lyme Regis branch tank engines standing in the Up platform.   *photo: Lens of Sutton*

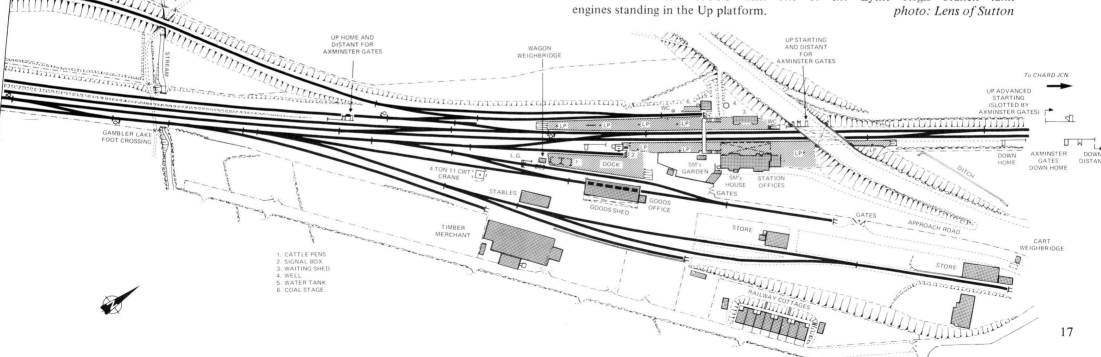

1. CATTLE PENS
2. SIGNAL BOX
3. WAITING SHED
4. WELL
5. WATER TANK
6. COAL STAGE

AXMINSTER (Cont.)

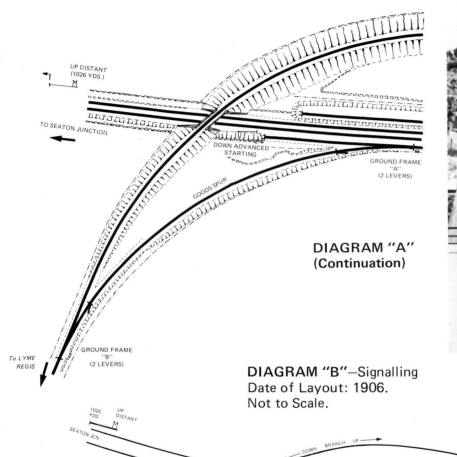

UP DISTANT
(1026 YDS.)

M

TO SEATON JUNCTION

DOWN ADVANCED
STARTING

GOODS SPUR

GROUND FRAME
"A"
(2 LEVERS)

DIAGRAM "A"
(Continuation)

To LYME
REGIS

GROUND FRAME
"B"
(2 LEVERS)

DIAGRAM "B"—Signalling
Date of Layout: 1906.
Not to Scale.

Looking toward Chard Junction in October 1963. The bay platform for Lyme Regis trains is on the extreme left.

photo: B.L. Jackson

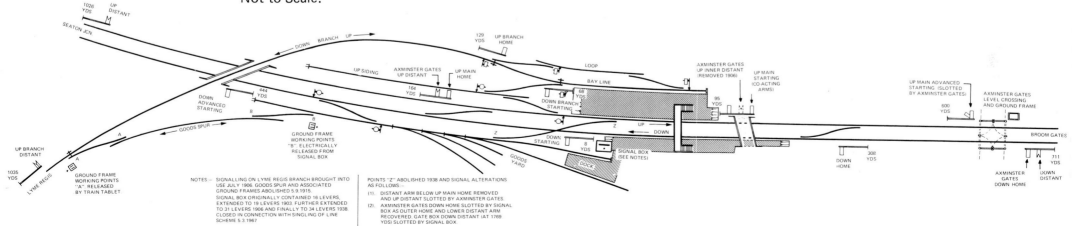

1026
YDS

UP
DISTANT

M

SEATON JCN.

DOWN BRANCH UP

129
YDS

UP BRANCH
HOME

UP SIDING

AXMINSTER GATES
UP DISTANT

UP MAIN
HOME

LOOP

BAY LINE

AXMINSTER GATES
UP INNER DISTANT
(REMOVED 1906)

UP MAIN
STARTING
(CO-ACTING
ARMS)

UP MAIN ADVANCED
STARTING (SLOTTED
BY AXMINSTER GATES)

AXMINSTER GATES
LEVEL CROSSING
AND GROUND FRAME

164
YDS

M

DOWN
ADVANCED
STARTING

444
YDS

B

B

68
YDS

DOWN BRANCH
STARTING

95
YDS

600
YDS

GROUND FRAME
WORKING POINTS
"B" ELECTRICALLY
RELEASED FROM
SIGNAL BOX

Z

Z

UP

DOWN

BROOM GATES

UP BRANCH
DISTANT

A

GOODS SPUR

A

Z

DOWN
STARTING

8
YDS

SIGNAL BOX
(SEE NOTES)

DOWN
HOME

308
YDS

711
YDS

1035
YDS

M

LYME REGIS

GROUND FRAME
WORKING POINTS
"A" RELEASED
BY TRAIN TABLET

GOODS
YARD

DOCK

AXMINSTER
GATES
DOWN HOME

W

DOWN
DISTANT

NOTES:— SIGNALLING ON LYME REGIS BRANCH BROUGHT INTO
USE JULY 1906. GOODS SPUR AND ASSOCIATED
GROUND FRAMES ABOLISHED 5.9.1915.
SIGNAL BOX ORIGINALLY CONTAINED 16 LEVERS,
EXTENDED TO 19 LEVERS 1903. FURTHER EXTENDED
TO 31 LEVERS 1906 AND FINALLY TO 34 LEVERS 1938.
CLOSED IN CONNECTION WITH SINGLING OF LINE
SCHEME 5.3.1967

POINTS "Z" ABOLISHED 1938 AND SIGNAL ALTERATIONS
AS FOLLOWS:—

(1). DISTANT ARM BELOW UP MAIN HOME REMOVED
AND UP DISTANT SLOTTED BY AXMINSTER GATES.

(2). AXMINSTER GATES DOWN HOME SLOTTED BY SIGNAL
BOX AS OUTER HOME AND LOWER DISTANT ARM
RECOVERED. GATE BOX DOWN DISTANT (AT 1769
YDS) SLOTTED BY SIGNAL BOX.

SIGNALLING ON BRANCH RECOVERED 20.7.1965.
BRANCH, BAY LINE AND LOOP TAKEN OUT OF USE
29.11.1965.

AXMINSTER

When first opened this station was just another intermediate stop between Salisbury and Exeter, although it always ranked as one of the more important stations as it served a wide area including the coastal town of Lyme Regis. The main offices and Station Master's house were erected on the Down platform. The architect was Sir William Tite, and his prominent gables and large chimney stacks were features shared by many other stations on the line.

Axminster almost became a junction in 1864 when a line to Bridport was proposed, and a scheme for a Lyme Regis branch was drawn up the following year, but both these plans lapsed, and it had to wait until the twentieth century to achieve junction status. The Light Railway to Lyme eventually opened on 24th August, 1903.

A glance at the plans will show the layout to be a curious one. The branch crossed the main line by a girder bridge on concrete abutments, then descended to a bay behind the Up platform by a gradient of 1-in-80. This arrangement had the advantage of leaving the original goods facilities undisturbed, the only alteration on the Down side being a new goods connecting spur. At first the branch was operated under "One Engine in Steam" regulations, and as no signals were provided, it was only necessary to extend the original lever frame in the signal box by three levers (see diagram "B"). Tablet working with full signalling was introduced in 1906, and for this the frame was extended to 31 levers.

On the face of it, the goods connecting spur was a most useful feature which allowed branch freights direct access to the yard without interfering with traffic on the main lines. However, in reality it was an operational embarrassment, as trains had to stop twice in order that the ground frames could be worked, and re-starting Down trains on the 1-in-40 gradient was no easy matter! The train crews showed an understandable preference for shunting across to the bay and starting from there, so the Goods Spur was an early casualty, being abolished in 1915 (see diagram "B"). Thereafter the only access to the branch was via the Up Siding, but despite the difficult layout of the junction through carriages between Waterloo and Lyme Regis were operated for many years—only ceasing in November 1963.

The station altered little for many years, although the Down platform was lengthened in the 'thirties to accommodate eight coaches. Transfer to the Western Region in January 1963 soon brought changes, the first being that the Lyme Regis branch reverted to its original method of working. All branch signals were removed, and two ground frames installed to control the points of the run-round loop. Only a few months later—on 29th November, 1965—the branch was closed completely. It was then decided to single the main line, and as part of the preparatory work Axminster signal box was taken out of use on 5th March, 1967, all sidings being abolished. The crossing ground frame at Axminster Gates was temporarily up-graded to a block post, remaining as such until returning to ground frame status with the introduction of single line working on 11th June,

Adams' "Radial" tank No. 30583 in the Lyme Regis bay at Axminster, August 1959. Note the large water tank at the end of the platform. *photo: B.L. Jackson*

1967. Thereafter all trains used the former Down platform, and the covered footbridge and waiting shed on the Up platform were demolished. In view of Axminster's importance, it seems odd that no sidings or crossing facilities were retained!

There was a final alteration on 16th December, 1973, when Axminster Gates ground frame was closed and full lifting barriers provided at the crossing. These are controlled from the station office with the aid of closed circuit television.

All booked trains continue to call at Axminster, which now serves as the railhead for the whole of West Dorset and East Devon. It therefore has a good long-distance passenger traffic, and there is considerable commuting business with Exeter.

Victorian view of the station forecourt at Axminster. The gothic style and prominent chimneys of Sir William Tite's design were, with slight variations, standard features of the Salisbury–Exeter line.

photo: Lens of Sutton

Legend:
1. PARCELS OFFICE
2. TICKET OFFICE
3. BOOKING HALL
4. HAIRDRESSER
5. LADIES WAITING ROOM
5a. LOBBY TO S.M.s HOUSE (HOUSE IN UPPER STOREY)
7. LADIES TOILET
8. BUFFET
9. KITCHEN
10. GENTS
11. OFFICE
12. MESS ROOMS
13. OIL STORE
14. STAFF TOILETS
15. STORES
16. CYCLE SHEDS
17. S.M.s OFFICE
18. STAFF ROOMS

DIAGRAM "A"
SCALE: 160 ft. to 1 inch.
Date of Survey: 1960.

The station frontage in 1972.

photo: J.R. Minnis

21

Looking towards Barnham along platforms 2 and 3 in 1963.   *photo: R.T.H. Platt*

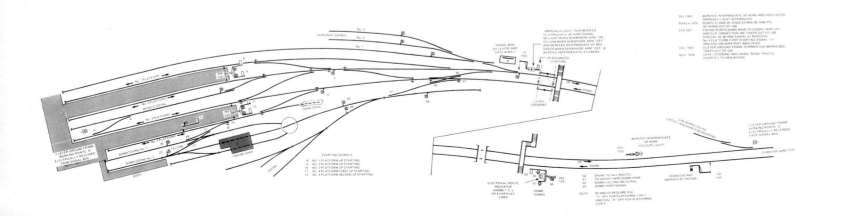

DIAGRAM "B"—Signalling
Not to Scale.
Shows layout from the electrification
and details of subsequent alterations.

BOGNOR REGIS

As can be seen from Diagram "C", the original station was small and decidedly simple. It also seems to have been accident-prone! The roof was lost in a gale in 1897 and the whole building destroyed by fire in September 1899, a temporary station being hurriedly erected. This lasted until the new and greatly enlarged station illustrated here was completed in 1902.

The layout had expanded gradually during the Nineteenth Century, additional sidings appearing in 1878 and 1885, but the rebuilt station was laid out in a much grander fashion. Like its predecessor it was called plain "Bognor" until King George V's convalescence in the town in 1929, when "Regis" was added. The terminal building was executed in red brick, and contained a large booking hall, offices, a refreshment room and a first-floor residence for the Station Master. Three wide platforms, well endowed with canopies, were provided, and the goods yard was laid out on a new site on the Down side. A two-road engine shed (also in red brick) was erected close to the site of the original one. The old signal box was closed, and a new "Station" box with 80 levers brought into use, the line being doubled thence to Bersted Crossing to facilitate shunting in the station area. The existing Bersted Crossing box was retained with a re-locked frame. The remainder of the line to Barnham Junction was doubled in July 1911.

Several changes were made in connection with electrification in 1938. The three existing platforms were extended to a length of 820 ft, and a fourth platform capable of holding an eight-car train was provided by converting a siding on the Down side. Three berthing sidings were added on the Up side, and the whole layout placed under the control

Opened: 1.6.1864
Electrified: 22.5.1938
Closed: 3.5.1971 (Goods).
Original Company: Bognor Railway, amalgamated with LB & SCR 1864.

of a new signal box adjacent to Bersted Crossing (see Diagram "B"). The narrow "platforms" shown on Diagram "A" between the berthing sidings are in fact concrete stages for the use of carriage cleaners.

The engine shed closed in 1953 and was largely demolished in 1956, an engine siding alongside the shed being removed at the same time. The scale plan shows the station in this condition. Following withdrawal of freight services the sidings in the goods yard were removed, but the massive goods shed has been taken over by a local firm. Dates of recent layout alterations are given on Diagram "B".

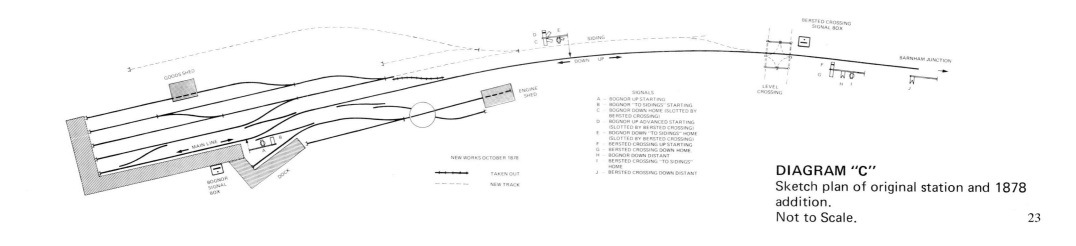

SIGNALS

A — BOGNOR UP STARTING
B — BOGNOR "TO SIDINGS" STARTING
C — BOGNOR DOWN HOME (SLOTTED BY BERSTED CROSSING)
D — BOGNOR UP ADVANCED STARTING (SLOTTED BY BERSTED CROSSING)
E — BOGNOR DOWN "TO SIDINGS" HOME (SLOTTED BY BERSTED CROSSING)
F — BERSTED CROSSING UP STARTING
G — BERSTED CROSSING DOWN HOME
H — BOGNOR DOWN DISTANT
I — BERSTED CROSSING "TO SIDINGS" HOME
J — BERSTED CROSSING DOWN DISTANT

NEW WORKS OCTOBER 1878

━━━━━━ TAKEN OUT

---------- NEW TRACK

DIAGRAM "C"
Sketch plan of original station and 1878 addition.
Not to Scale.

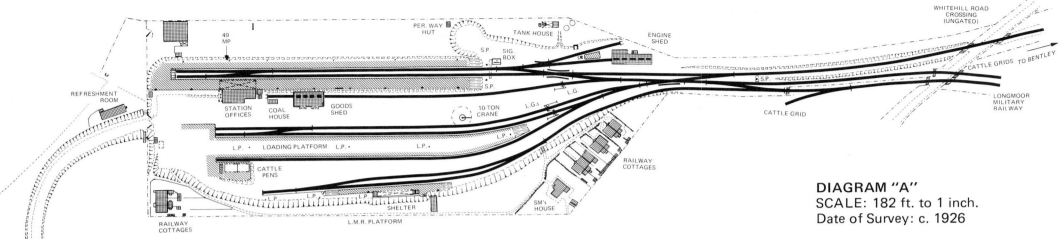

PER. WAY
HUT

TANK HOUSE

ENGINE
SHED

WHITEHILL ROAD
CROSSING
(UNGATED)

49
MP

S.P.

SIG.
BOX

CATTLE GRIDS   TO BENTLEY

REFRESHMENT
ROOM

S.P.

L.G.

S.P.

LONGMOOR
MILITARY
RAILWAY

STATION
OFFICES

COAL
HOUSE

GOODS
SHED

10-TON
CRANE

L.G.s

CATTLE GRID

RAILWAY
COTTAGES

L.P. •   LOADING PLATFORM   L.P. •

L.P.

L.P.

DIAGRAM "A"
SCALE: 182 ft. to 1 inch.
Date of Survey: c. 1926

CATTLE
PENS

L.P.   L.P.

SM's
HOUSE

RAILWAY
COTTAGES

SHELTER

L.M.R. PLATFORM

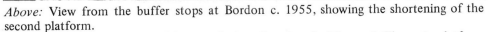

Above: View from the buffer stops at Bordon c. 1955, showing the shortening of the second platform.
Right: The ground level signal box, with site of engine shed beyond. The main platform starting signal is of the L & SWR type whilst the other is a SR "rail-built" structure.

photos: Lens of Sutton

BORDON (Cont.)

DIAGRAM "B"
Signalling.
Not to Scale.

Opened: 11.12.1905
Closed: 16.9.1957 (To regular passenger trains).
Closed: 4.4.1966 (Completely).
Original Company: Bordon Light Railway (L & SWR).

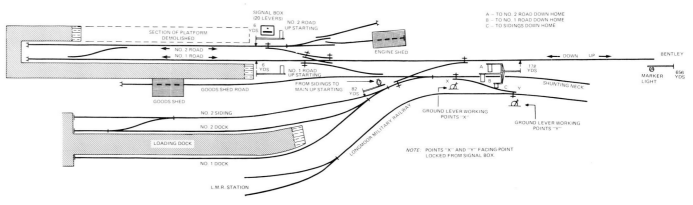

BORDON

Although legally a Light Railway, the Bordon branch operated for much of its life as a conventional line, the one concession to its official status being three ungated level crossings. It was constructed to serve one of the many Army camps erected to accommodate troops returning from the Boer War, and Military traffic was always the mainstay of the line. In fact, Bordon station was a long way from the village of that name and public patronage was slight.

The Longmoor Military Railway (known as the Woolmer Instructional Railway until 1935, and wholly War Department property) was opened between Bordon and Longmoor in 1907, and thereafter most of the traffic conveyed over the branch was exchanged with the Military line. Troop trains working through changed engines at Bordon station, WD locomotives working all traffic on to Longmoor.

Bordon is typical of stations found in the Military area (compare Amesbury), having spacious sidings and loading docks sufficient to deal with tremendous surges of traffic. Two long platforms were originally provided, but the North one was seldom used and was converted into a short loading dock by the Southern Railway, who also refaced the surviving platform with standard concrete panels. An engine shed was erected to house the branch locomotive, but it seems to have been little used and was abandoned altogether in 1951. Earthworks for a turntable were prepared, but this facility never materialised.

The signal box was of the ground-level type and had a chequered career. When first opened the line was worked under "One Engine in Steam" regulations, but this quickly proved inadequate and Tablet Working was introduced. Traffic declined between the wars and the box was reduced to Ground Frame status in 1927, but again there were second thoughts, and the SR Appendix for 1934 lists it as a "Temporary Block Post". This "Temporary" arrangement lasted until the end of the line! Although the track layout on the Military Railway side has been altered on a number of occasions, that on the "Southern" side has always been much the same.

An early view of the station forecourt at Bordon.   *photo: Lens of Sutton*

Military traffic declined after the Second World War, although there was sufficient freight tonnage to maintain the branch for almost nine years after the demise of the passenger service. Some troop trains also visited Bordon during this period, but complete closure came in 1966. Access to the Military line was maintained via Liss, the Bordon end of the system being torn up.

Bordon Station

BRENTOR

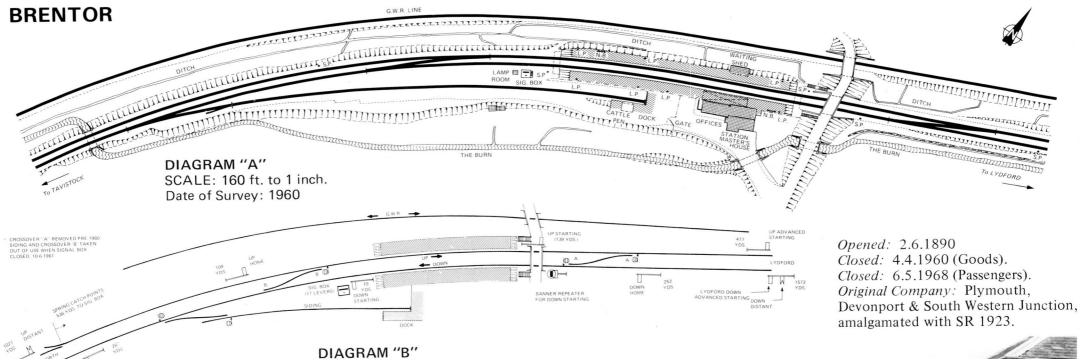

DIAGRAM "A"
SCALE: 160 ft. to 1 inch.
Date of Survey: 1960

DIAGRAM "B"
Signalling.
Not to Scale.

CROSSOVER "A" REMOVED PRE-1960 SIDING AND CROSSOVER "B" TAKEN OUT OF USE WHEN SIGNAL BOX CLOSED: 10-6 1961

Opened: 2.6.1890
Closed: 4.4.1960 (Goods).
Closed: 6.5.1968 (Passengers).
Original Company: Plymouth, Devonport & South Western Junction, amalgamated with SR 1923.

BRENTOR

Like all stations on the PD & SWJ line, Brentor was a well-built structure of local stone incorporating a house for the station master, and for many years served as the terminus for a local service from Plymouth. The track layout was very simple, but it was considered to be worth including to illustrate the way in which the two rival Companies followed each other down the valley of the little River Burn on their way between Lydford and Tavistock. For the historical background to this seemingly wasteful arrangement, see "Tavistock North".

As is obvious from diagram "A", there were no facilities for GWR trains, that Company preferring to serve their own station at Mary Tavy about 1½ miles further down the valley. Goods accommodation was minimal, although originally there were two sidings behind the signal box, the one nearest to the main line being taken out in the 1950's. A goods shed was never provided, "smalls" traffic being handled at Tavistock.

The signal box was opened for several short periods each day to deal with the pick-up goods and terminating "locals". Its proximity to Lydford rendered it superfluous at other times, and it was therefore switched out of circuit. It was taken out of use in 1961 (see diagram "B"), the block section becoming Lydford—Tavistock North.

Since complete closure of the line in 1968, the station buildings have been converted into a private house and remain in good condition to the present day.

Brentor station looking toward Lydford. The train at the Up platform is one of the terminating locals from Plymouth, and the engine has just run round in readiness to shunt the stock across to the Down side for the return journey. *photo: J.H. Aston*

BRIDESTOWE

Diagram "A" labels:

RAILWAY COTTAGES

RAILWAY COTTAGES

GATE

STATION OFFICES

SM'S HOUSE

CATTLE PEN

L.G.

GOODS SHED

DOCK

PER WAY HUT

SIGNAL BOX

SP.

To MELDON JCN (OKEHAMPTON)

To LYDFORD

BRIDGE No. 628

WAITING SHED

RAILWAY COTTAGES

TROLLEY SHEDS

SHEDS

12" PIPE

DRY STONE WALL

SP.

GATES

CULVERT No. 727A

DRY STONE WALL

RATTLEBROOK PEAT RAILWAY TO NODDEN GATE

DIAGRAM "A"
SCALE: 160 ft. to 1 inch.
Survey Undated.

Opened: 12.10.1874
Closed: 5.6.1961 (Goods).
Closed: 6.5.1968 (Passengers).
Original Company: L & SWR.

BRIDESTOWE

Looking toward Lydford in 1964, only a few weeks after the closure of the signal box.
photo: C.L. Caddy

27

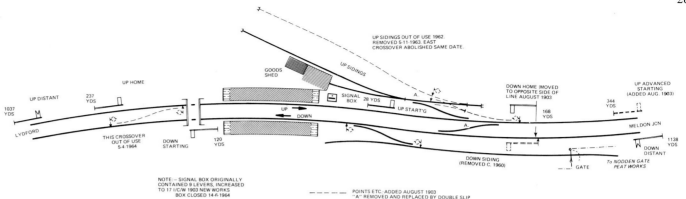

DIAGRAM "B"—Signalling
Not to Scale.
Shows new works of 1903.
Note: All ground discs added August 1903.

BRIDESTOWE

The village of Bridestowe was separated from its railway station by about 1½ miles of steeply-climbing road, and consequently passengers were never very numerous. Rabbits were of much greater importance, and before the War when warrening was a considerable industry on Dartmoor, hundreds of boxes of them were forwarded by passenger train, mostly in the "Up" direction!

Originally facilities were of the utmost simplicity, the signal box containing only nine levers, but in 1880 the West of England Peat Company started operations in a very remote spot on the moor known as Nodden Gate, and constructed a railway seven miles long to enable their wares to reach the main line. The L & SWR laid in the Down Siding in June of that year, forming an end-on junction with the peat works line. Traffic was exchanged at the boundary gate, horses supplying the motive power on the steeply-graded branch. The peat railway had ceased to carry traffic by 1925 and the rails were removed in 1932, buffer stops being erected on the railway side of the gate.

There had been further expansion in August 1903, when an additional siding was provided in the goods yard. The signalling was modernised at the same time, and Diagram "B" shows the extent of this work, which necessitated enlargement of the lever frame in the signal box.

The Second World War brought a burst of activity, an American Army Camp being established adjacent to the station and many refugees from the Plymouth bombing seeking sanctuary in this remote countryside, but thereafter a steady decline set in, and latterly the station did little business. Following the withdrawal of freight facilities the signal box opened only occasionally as required, and was finally abolished on 14th June, 1964, the block section becoming Meldon Junction—Lydford.

OPERATING NOTE:— Rattlebrook Peat Railway. This line was operated by the authorities of the Duchy of Cornwall, and engines were prohibited from passing beyond the boundary gate.

Details of the main buildings on the Up side as they appeared in 1962.

photo: R.T.H. Platt

BROAD CLYST

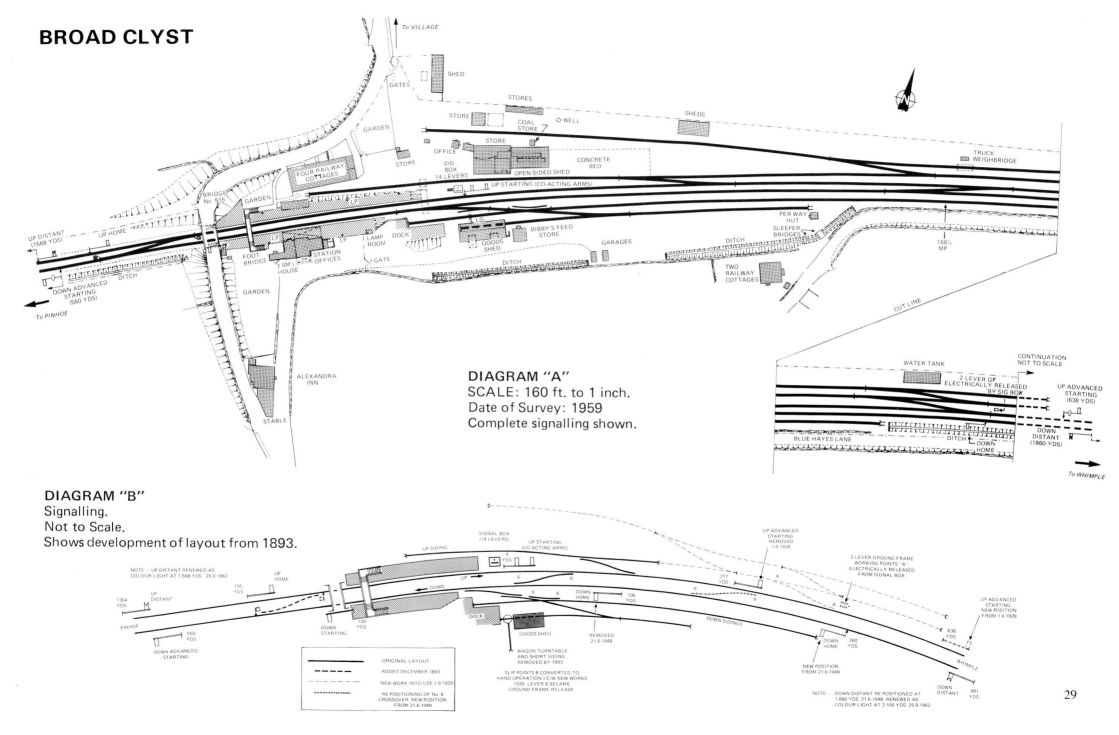

To VILLAGE

GATES

SHED

STORES

STORE

SHEDS

COAL STORE

WELL

STORE

OFFICE

TRUCK WEIGHBRIDGE

CONCRETE BED

SIG BOX 14 LEVERS

OPEN-SIDED SHED

UP STARTING (CO-ACTING ARMS)

FOUR RAILWAY COTTAGES

GARDEN

STORE

PER WAY HUT

SLEEPER BRIDGES

166½ MP

BRIDGE No. 515

GARDEN

LP

LG

BIBBY'S FEED STORE

DITCH

UP DISTANT (1568 YDS)

UP HOME

LAMP ROOM

DOCK

GOODS SHED

GARAGES

DITCH

FOOT-BRIDGE

LP

TWO RAILWAY COTTAGES

SM's HOUSE

STATION OFFICES

GATE

DITCH

DOWN ADVANCED STARTING (550 YDS)

GARDEN

To PINHOE

DITCH

CUT LINE

ALEXANDRA INN

STABLE

DIAGRAM "A"
SCALE: 160 ft. to 1 inch.
Date of Survey: 1959
Complete signalling shown.

WATER TANK

CONTINUATION NOT TO SCALE

2 LEVER GF ELECTRICALLY RELEASED BY SIG BOX

UP ADVANCED STARTING (638 YDS)

DOWN DISTANT (1860 YDS)

BLUE HAYES LANE

DITCH

DOWN HOME

To WHIMPLE

DIAGRAM "B"
Signalling.
Not to Scale.
Shows development of layout from 1893.

SIGNAL BOX (14 LEVERS)

UP SIDING

UP STARTING (CO-ACTING ARMS)

UP ADVANCED STARTING REMOVED 1-9-1929

2 LEVER GROUND FRAME WORKING POINTS "A" ELECTRICALLY RELEASED FROM SIGNAL BOX

4 YDS

NOTE — UP DISTANT RENEWED AS COLOUR LIGHT AT 1,568 YDS. 25-9-1962

195 YDS

UP HOME

DOWN

UP

6

6

277 YDS

A

1364 YDS

UP DISTANT

8

8

6

6

A

DOWN HOME

105 YDS

UP ADVANCED STARTING NEW POSITION FROM 1-9-1929

PINHOE

550 YDS

DOWN STARTING

120 YDS

DOCK

DOWN SIDINGS

638 YDS

DOWN ADVANCED STARTING

GOODS SHED

REMOVED 21-6-1948

DOWN HOME

360 YDS

WHIMPLE

WAGON TURNTABLE AND SHORT SIDING REMOVED BY 1893

NEW POSITION FROM 21-6-1948

DOWN DISTANT

981 YDS

	ORIGINAL LAYOUT
	ADDED DECEMBER 1893
	NEW WORK INTO USE 1-9-1929
	RE-POSITIONING OF No. 6 CROSSOVER. NEW POSITION FROM 21-6-1948

SLIP POINTS 8 CONVERTED TO HAND OPERATION I/C/W NEW WORKS 1929. LEVER 8 BECAME GROUND FRAME RELEASE

NOTE — DOWN DISTANT RE-POSITIONED AT 1,860 YDS. 21-6-1948. RENEWED AS COLOUR LIGHT AT 2,100 YDS. 25-9-1962

29

Opened: 19.7.1860
Closed: 6.9.1965 (Goods).
Closed: 7.3.1966 (Passengers).
Original Company: L & SWR

BROAD CLYST

The village of "Broadclyst" was well over a mile from the station and latterly the only passenger traffic came from the small Victorian settlement that had grown up around the station. The name was a constant source of argument, the Post Office insisting on one word and the railway on two!

Like all intermediate stations between Salisbury and Exeter, Broad Clyst was constructed to the vaguely Gothic designs of Sir William Tite. The platforms were shorter than average, the Up one accommodating four carriages and the Down only three, but as it was only served by local trains no extensions were ever made. Indeed, the station changed little in its 106 years of public service, the only significant alteration being the shortening of the canopy on the Down platform. Lighting was by oil lamps right up to closure, and water for the toilets was supplied from a well via the large tank in the engineers' yard.

The Chief Civil Engineers' depot on the Up side made a modest start in 1896, but it was greatly extended in 1929, additional sidings being laid in. The ground frame and East connection to the Up Sidings were brought into service on 1st September that year. Developments in permanent way technology later made it a "pre-assembly" yard, and to facilitate running round long trains loaded with track sections, the East crossover was moved in 1948 (see diagram "B"). The depot always boasted its own small departmental engine for shunting, the last one being DS 1169, a diminutive four-wheeled diesel which replaced an older engine in 1959. It had previously seen service in Folkestone Warren.

Public goods traffic was light for many years, the station being slightly unusual in not possessing a resident coal merchant, but in the early 1960s a steady outwards traffic in three-wheel invalid cars developed. These were manufactured locally and driven to the station under their own power, there to be placed on "LOWFIT" wagons in the loading dock. During the summer of 1964 these vehicles were being despatched in such quantity that a wooden ramp was constructed into the long-disused goods shed to enable scotching and roping to be carried out in the dry. At about the same time the Signal & Telegraph Department began using the yard as a dump, and wagons containing scrap lever frames and old signals became regular arrivals. Steel mineral wagons of sugar beet were also despatched in the season.

The line passed into Western Region control in January 1963 and the new administration soon decided to close the engineers' yard. Materials were dispersed to Taunton (Fairwater Yard) and Yeovil Junction, the depot closing at the end of 1964. Goods traffic was concentrated on Exeter the following year, and thereafter the signal box was opened only as required. By this time plans to single the line were well advanced, and as a prelude to this the local stopping service was withdrawn. The last train called on the evening of Saturday 5th March, 1966, there being no Sunday service at that time of year.

OPERATING NOTE:— Engines prohibited from entering goods shed.

Broad Clyst in Western Region days. A 3 car DMU departs on a Yeovil to Exeter Central stopping service, 13th September, 1964.

photo: C.L. Caddy

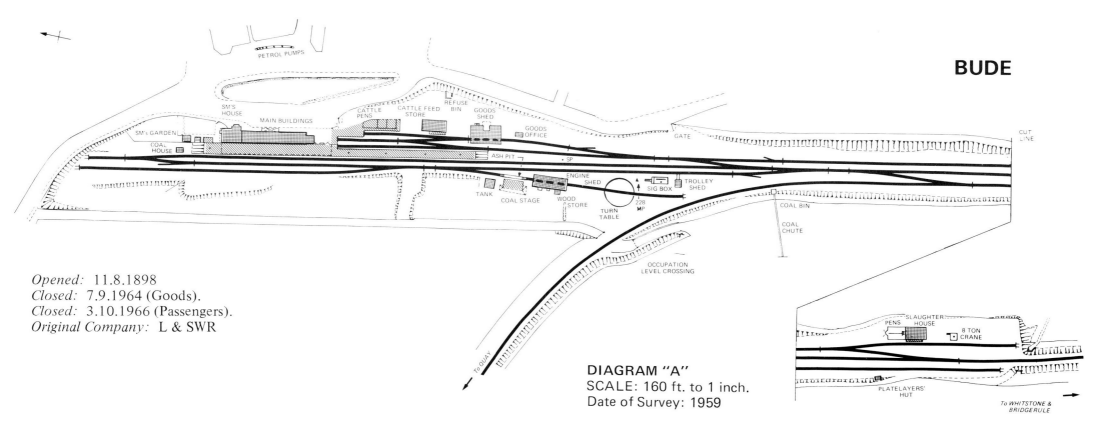

BUDE

Opened: 11.8.1898
Closed: 7.9.1964 (Goods).
Closed: 3.10.1966 (Passengers).
Original Company: L & SWR

DIAGRAM "A"
SCALE: 160 ft. to 1 inch.
Date of Survey: 1959

BUDE

Bude received its station rather late in the Railway Age—although the L & SWR had operated a smart coach service from their railhead at Holsworthy since January 1879— and when it did arrive it was deliberately sited on the outskirts of the town to please the residents of near-by Stratton. Despite this fault, there was nothing skimpy about the station itself. The offices were solidly constructed of local stone, and there was a refreshment room and a large bay-windowed house for the Station Master.

Much of the soil of North Devon and Cornwall is poor, and greatly improved by the liberal application of sand such as that obtained from the beach at Bude. Mainly to tap this traffic, and also to a lesser extent to allow coal imported in sloops from South Wales to be distributed by rail, a branch was built to the canal basin. Traffic was heavy in the early years, but the introduction of chemical fertilizers and competition from road transport reduced it considerably between the Wars, and although the branch lasted until withdrawal of freight services in 1964 there was little business latterly. Other freight was very much of a general nature, although there was a regular traffic in meat for London. The "Coal Chute" shown on Diagram "A" led into the gas works.

The station itself changed hardly at all during its life, but the track layout was remodelled in April/May 1939 (see diagrams "B" and "C").

The train service was never very frequent, but it was useful. There were several daily through portions to and from Waterloo—and whole trains at Summer weekends! This changed somewhat following transfer to the Western Region from 1st January, 1963. The service became more local in nature, and DMUs were introduced in September 1964, the engine shed at Bude being closed. In the Summer of 1965 the Saturday through trains from London were diverted from Waterloo to Paddington (reversing at Exeter St. David's), but for the final few months there was nothing except "locals" operating a shuttle service from Bude to Okehampton.

Motive power experts will perhaps remember the line best as the last stronghold of the famous "T9" 4-4-0s. Bulleid Pacifics were permitted from the end of April 1962, but these appeared mainly on excursions and the through week-end trains, the bulk of the service being in the capable hands of the "N" class until dieselisation.

Closure in 1966 was a blow for Bude and the surrounding district, the railhead at Okehampton being thirty miles away! This situation became even worse in January 1972 with the closure of Okehampton, visitors to the resort thereafter having to make their own way from Exeter.

31

Above: The main platform at Bude, looking towards the buffer stops.
photo: Oxford Publishing Co. collection

Above: View from the platform towards Whitstone & Bridgerule, showing engine shed (with gas works beyond) and signal box.
photo: Oxford Publishing Co. collection

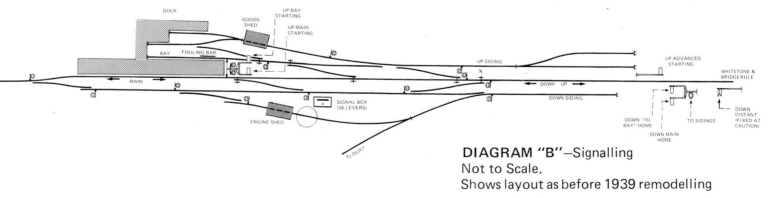

DIAGRAM "B"—Signalling
Not to Scale.
Shows layout as before 1939 remodelling

Note re Ground Disc Signals:
Discs "X" (2) and "Z" are "running dummies", and lead Down Homes thus:—
1. "To BAY HOME" requires both discs "X" & Disc "Z" off.
2. "Down MAIN HOME" requires both discs "X" off.

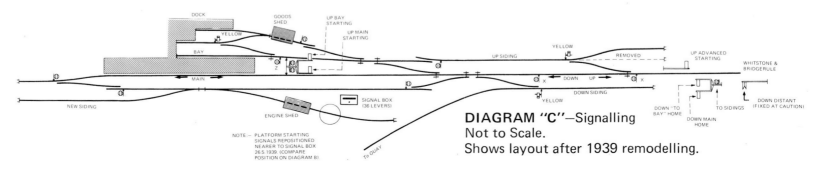

DIAGRAM "C"—Signalling
Not to Scale.
Shows layout after 1939 remodelling.

NOTE:— PLATFORM STARTING SIGNALS REPOSITIONED NEARER TO SIGNAL BOX 26.5.1939. (COMPARE POSITION ON DIAGRAM B)

BUDLEIGH SALTERTON

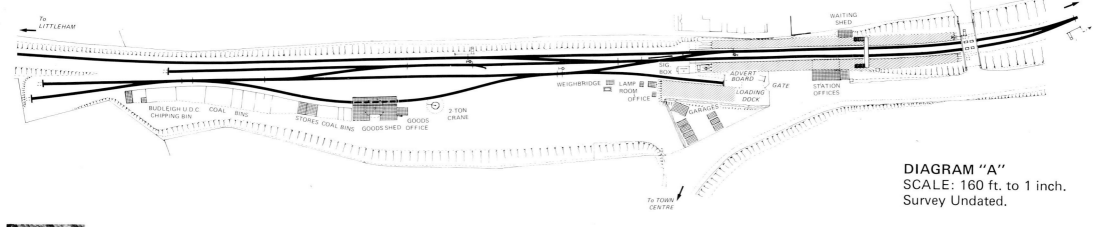

To LITTLEHAM

To TIPTON ST. JOHN

WAITING SHED

BUDLEIGH U.D.C. CHIPPING BIN

COAL BINS

STORES COAL BINS

GOODS SHED

GOODS OFFICE

2 TON CRANE

WEIGHBRIDGE

LAMP ROOM OFFICE

SIG. BOX

ADVERT BOARD

LOADING DOCK

GATE

GARAGES

STATION OFFICES

To TOWN CENTRE

DIAGRAM "A"
SCALE: 160 ft. to 1 inch.
Survey Undated.

General view, looking towards Littleham, c. 1955.

photo: Lens of Sutton

Looking towards Tipton St. John's, c. 1955. The well-kept flower beds on the platform were a feature of so many branch line stations in the pre-Beeching era.

photo: Lens of Sutton

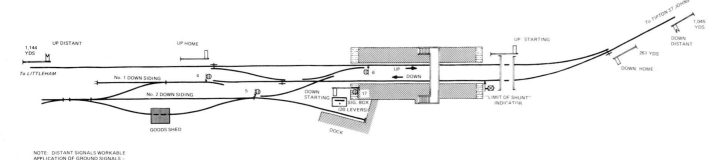

UP DISTANT   UP HOME   To TIPTON ST JOHNS

1,144
YDS

1,045
YDS

UP STARTING

DOWN
DISTANT

To LITTLEHAM

261 YDS

DOWN
DISTANT

No. 1 DOWN SIDING   4

DOWN HOME

UP

No. 2 DOWN SIDING   5

DOWN

6

17

DOWN
STARTING

"LIMIT OF SHUNT"
INDICATOR

SIG. BOX
(20 LEVERS)

GOODS SHED

DOCK

NOTE: DISTANT SIGNALS WORKABLE
APPLICATION OF GROUND SIGNALS –
4 — TO UP OR DOWN LOOPS
5 — TO UP LOOP ONLY
6 — TO No. 1 OR No. 2 SIDINGS
17 — TO No. 1 DOWN SIDING

DIAGRAM "B"—Signalling
Not to Scale.

34

Opened: 15.5.1897 (as Terminus).
Opened: 1.6.1903 (Extension to Exmouth).
Closed: 27.1.1964 (Goods).
Closed: 6.3.1967 (Passengers).
Original Company: Budleigh Salterton Rly.

BUDLEIGH SALTERTON

When opened as the terminus of the line from Tipton St. Johns the station possessed a single platform only (later to become the "Down" platform). The neat, brick, single-storey building is believed to be original, but other facilities were fairly basic in the early days. Goods sidings were provided, but there was never a turntable as at many branch termini, and the line was worked under "One Engine in Steam" regulations using a wooden train staff fitted with a key for unlocking the various ground frames. The Board of Trade ruled that only small tank engines were to be used, and that all trains were to call at the intermediate station (East Budleigh).

Considerable improvements were carried out in connection with the Exmouth extension of 1903. The second (Up) platform and footbridge were added, and a ground-level signal box containing a 20-lever "knee" frame was installed. The station was then fully signalled, electric tablet working being introduced.

Budleigh then settled down to a long period of peaceful existence, the only alteration of note being the provision of the 2-ton yard crane in 1938. A small crane inside the goods shed which had been part of the original fittings was then removed. Summer Saturdays could be quite busy by branch line standards, several through trains between Waterloo and Exmouth running via this line, and from 1960 to 1962 a cross-country service from Cleethorpes to Exmouth further enlivened the scene. All through workings ceased after the Summer season of 1966.

There has never been any industrial development in the district, and goods traffic was correspondingly light. Following the withdrawal of freight service all sidings were taken out of use in February 1964, and from then until closure the track layout was that of a basic crossing station.

Looking towards Exmouth from the road over-bridge.   *photo: R.C. Riley*

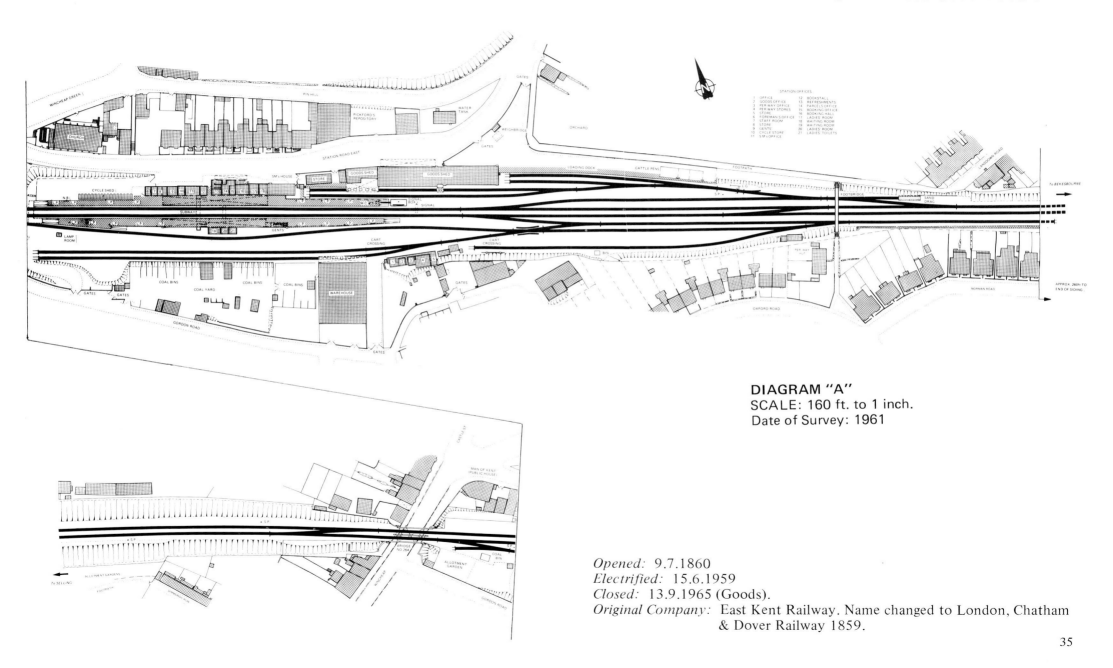

STATION OFFICES
1	OFFICE	12	BOOKSTALL
2	GOODS OFFICE	13	REFRESHMENTS
3	PER WAY OFFICE	14	PARCELS OFFICE
4	PER WAY STORES	15	BOOKING OFFICE
5	STORE	16	BOOKING HALL
6	FOREMAN'S OFFICE	17	LADIES ROOM
7	STAFF ROOM	18	WAITING ROOM
8	STORE	19	WAITING ROOM
9	GENTS	20	LADIES ROOM
10	CYCLE STORE	21	LADIES TOILETS
11	S.M.'s OFFICE		

DIAGRAM "A"
SCALE: 160 ft. to 1 inch.
Date of Survey: 1961

Opened: 9.7.1860
Electrified: 15.6.1959
Closed: 13.9.1965 (Goods).
Original Company: East Kent Railway. Name changed to London, Chatham
& Dover Railway 1859.

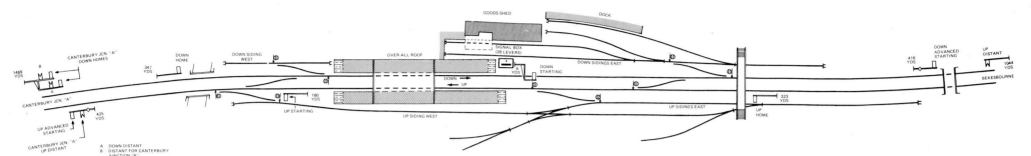

DIAGRAM "B"—Signalling
Layout as in 1950.
Not to Scale.

CANTERBURY EAST

Although initially the terminus of the line from Faversham, this station was laid out for through running in anticipation of the extension to Dover, which opened on 22nd July, 1861.

The buildings are quite large and offer most of the facilities usually provided at the more important stations, but they have none of the architectural flourish one might expect in such a historic city. As can be seen from the older photograph, an overall roof formed part of the original structure, but even this prominent feature was plain to the point of ugliness!

For many years there was a small engine shed on the Up side, Faversham end of the station, but this has long been closed and virtually no trace survives—although the scale plan shows what could well have been the earthworks surrounding the turntable. Apart from the demolition of this engine shed there were few changes until commencement of the preparatory work for electrification. In the Autumn of 1958 the Down Siding West was abolished and the crossover at the Selling end of the station repositioned to allow the platforms to be extended, this being done early the following year. Also in 1959 the

layout of the Down yard was altered (compare diagrams "B" and "C"), and a short Passenger Loop provided. This is of sufficient length to hold a four-car EMU, the idea being to "Loop" stopping trains so that boat traffic bound for Dover could enjoy a clear run. The overall roof was also taken down and replaced with a second-hand canopy recovered from the unopened station at Lullingstone.

In 1965 goods traffic was concentrated on Canterbury West, and most of the sidings have since been removed (see diagram "C" for dates). However, on 3rd May, 1971 the large goods shed received a new lease of life as a parcels concentration depot, but no sidings were relaid in connection with this traffic. Parcel vans are conveyed on through services, and are unloaded in the station platforms.

It is worth drawing attention to the signal box. The building itself is a fairly standard LC & DR edifice, but it is elevated on a framework of girders. In these days of widespread track circuiting the object of tall signal boxes has been lost, but the original idea was to provide the signalman with a clear view of that section of his layout on the other side of the overall roof.

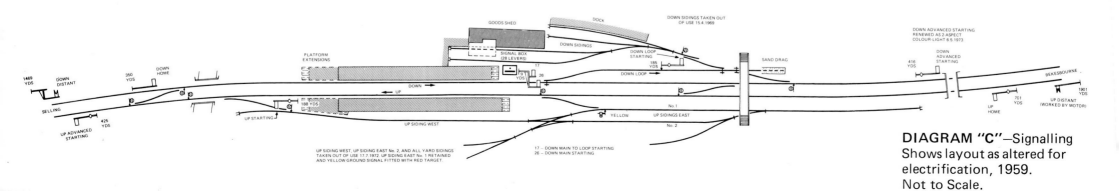

DIAGRAM "C"—Signalling
Shows layout as altered for electrification, 1959.
Not to Scale.

Looking towards Selling c. 1915, showing the original overall roof. Note the old SECR pattern ground signal in the foreground.   *photo: Lens of Sutton*

A similar view in 1976. The rather temporary looking canopies were salvaged from the station at Lullingstone, which had never been opened for traffic because housing development failed to take place in the area.   *photo: B.L. Jackson*

CREDITON

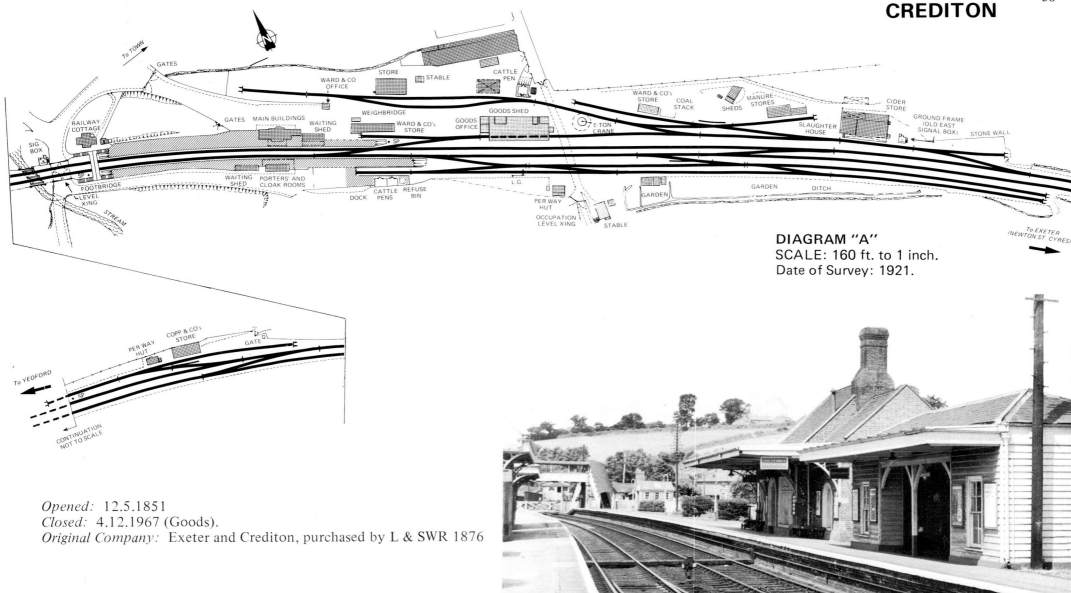

To TOWN

GATES

RAILWAY COTTAGE

GATES

SIG BOX

FOOTBRIDGE

LEVEL XING

STREAM

MAIN BUILDINGS

WAITING SHED

WAITING SHED

PORTERS' AND CLOAK ROOMS

WARD & CO OFFICE

STORE

STABLE

CATTLE PEN

WEIGHBRIDGE

WARD & CO's STORE

GOODS OFFICE

GOODS SHED

6-TON CRANE

DOCK CATTLE PENS

REFUSE BIN

L.G.

PER WAY HUT

OCCUPATION LEVEL XING

STABLE

WARD & CO's STORE

COAL STACK

SHEDS

MANURE STORES

SLAUGHTER HOUSE

GARDEN

GARDEN DITCH

CIDER STORE

GROUND FRAME (OLD EAST SIGNAL BOX)

STONE WALL

To EXETER (NEWTON ST CYRES)

DIAGRAM "A"
SCALE: 160 ft. to 1 inch.
Date of Survey: 1921.

To YEOFORD

PER WAY HUT

COPP & CO's STORE

GATE

CONTINUATION NOT TO SCALE

Opened: 12.5.1851
Closed: 4.12.1967 (Goods).
Original Company: Exeter and Crediton, purchased by L & SWR 1876

The main office block on the Up platform, dating from the broad gauge days of the Exeter and Crediton Railway. The wooden waiting shelter is a later addition.

photo: Lens of Sutton

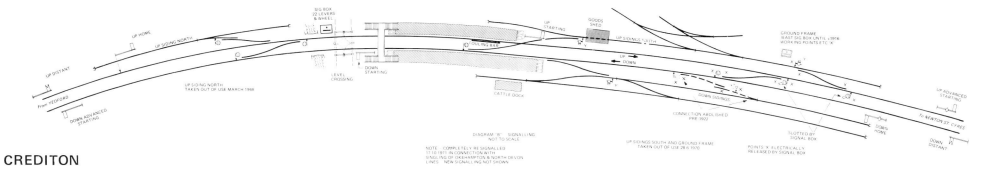

CREDITON

The early history of this station is somewhat complicated, as originally it formed the terminus of a Broad Gauge branch allied to the Bristol & Exeter Railway. As such, it should have been drawn into the fold of the GWR, but Waterloo had other ideas, Crediton being viewed as a valuable jumping-off point for the L & SWR drive into the far West. By some very dubious dealings in shares (which caused quite a scandal at the time) the latter Company eventually gained complete control.

The station illustrated here is actually the second one to be erected in Crediton, the old terminus having been replaced for the opening of the Taw Vale line to Fremington on 1st August, 1854. Mixed gauge was provided in 1863. Further traffic was added in November 1865 with the opening of the line from Coleford Junction to North Tawton, and in May 1876 this became a through link with Plymouth, placing Crediton firmly on an important trunk line.

Although the GWR were undoubtedly the losers in this story their influence took a long time to die. The Company retained freight rights at Crediton until 1903, their daily goods train being broad gauge until 1892, after which the "Broad" rails were taken out.

Being served by both Plymouth and North Devon services there was no shortage of trains and the station enjoyed a long period of moderate prosperity, but in the Motor Age much local business was lost to road transport, as it was sited on the extreme edge of the town. Despite the lack of heavy industry in the district, freight traffic was well maintained until recent years, coal, livestock and agricultural supplies making up a considerable tonnage. When all Southern lines in the area passed to the Western Region for the last time in January 1963 the proverbial writing was on the wall, and services were gradually reduced. General goods facilities were withdrawn on 6th September, 1965, the yard handling coal traffic only until this too was discontinued in December 1967. The service to Plymouth was cut back to terminate at Okehampton on 6th May, 1968 and withdrawn altogether on 5th June, 1972, leaving Crediton with only the few North Devon trains, but the Okehampton line remains in use to provide access to Meldon Quarry. The line is still double between Cowley Bridge Junction (Exeter) and Crediton, but singling has been carried out west of the station (see diagram "B" for dates).

Although the station has been unstaffed for some time some of the buildings of 1854 still survive. The offices on the Up platform have much in common with those at "Bristol & Exeter" stations, but no other structures so obviously of "Broad Gauge" origin can be seen. However, it is interesting to observe on diagram "A" that, once clear of the platforms, the two running lines spread out to give a much wider "six-foot" than usual, another legacy of Brunel's gauge being spacious track formations.

DIAGRAM "B"—Signalling
Not to Scale.

General view of Crediton station, looking towards Exeter.

photo: Lens of Sutton

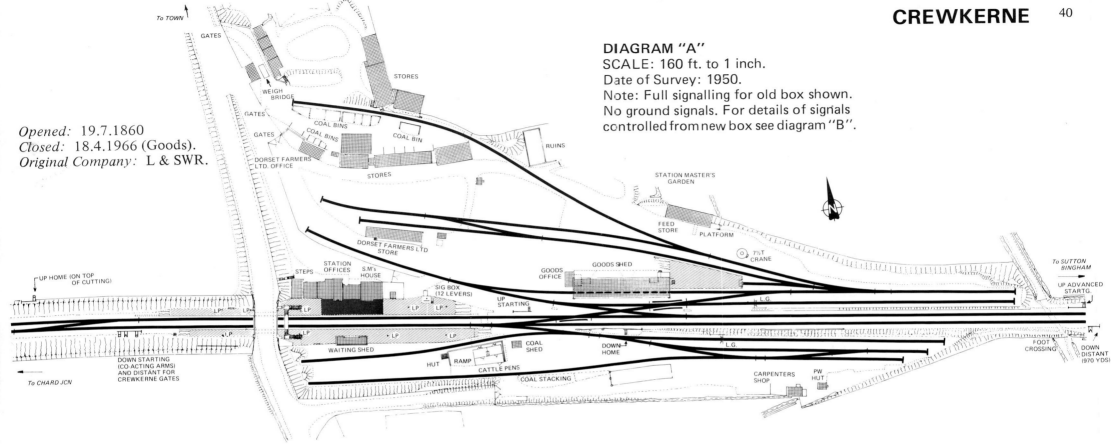

Opened: 19.7.1860
Closed: 18.4.1966 (Goods).
Original Company: L & SWR.

DIAGRAM "A"
SCALE: 160 ft. to 1 inch.
Date of Survey: 1950.
Note: Full signalling for old box shown.
No ground signals. For details of signals
controlled from new box see diagram "B".

DIAGRAM "B"— Signalling (new box)
Not to Scale.

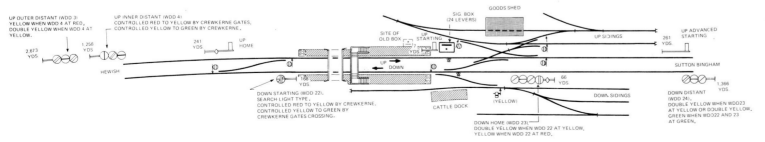

Notes:

24.10.1960 — New signal box brought into use
and original one closed. Ground
discs introduced, but running
signals remained as indicated on
diagram "A".

16/17.12.1962 — Colour-light signals brought into
use, and signal box given prefix
"WDD".

26.2.1967 — Signal box closed and all points
taken out of use.

7.5.1967 — Line singled, all traffic passing
over former Up road.

CREWKERNE

Crewkerne station stands on the former main line between Salisbury and Exeter and serves a small market town of that name. The original offices and striking, gabled Station Master's house remain in use to this day, although the canopy dates from the early days of BR and replaces a rather more ornate one which was destroyed by a flying locomotive crankpin! The Southern Railway made its mark with a pre-cast concrete footbridge and fencing panels—products of their works at Exmouth Junction.

The goods yard was quite large, although diagram "A" does not do it justice as there had been some simplification prior to 1950. In the 1930s it was one of the last strongholds of the shunting horse, the layout containing several wagon turntables. The complicated tangle of pointwork near the goods shed (incorporating a scissors crossing and both double and single slips) was very unusual for a small station on the L & SWR, but made necessary in this instance by the restricted nature of the site. Main line and sidings were on different levels, and all connections had therefore to be packed into the short length where they coincided.

The old signal box in the photograph dated from around 1875. It contained a 12-lever frame, and was too small to allow for additional levers for the operation of ground signals. In some places this difficulty was overcome by fitting "Push-and-Pull" or "Russell" levers, but at Crewkerne all shunting movements were controlled by hand signals until the opening of the new box (see diagram "B" for dates).

The station was transferred to the Western Region in January 1963, and is now a mere shadow of its former self. The line was reduced to single track in May 1967, the Down platform then becoming disused. Traffic is now controlled by Western Region Tokenless Block, but there are no sidings or crossing facilities at Crewkerne, the section being Yeovil Junction to Chard Junction.

The Up platform at Crewkerne in 1960, showing the old signal box. The tall gabled section of the station building is the Station Master's house. *photo: B.L. Jackson*

Looking through the road bridge towards Yeovil in 1961. The new signal box is in the background. *photo: Lens of Sutton*

Looking West, with Up train bound for Waterloo arriving. The tall Down Starter with lower Distant for Crewkerne Gates can be seen over the road bridge. *photo: R.C. Riley*

DEAL

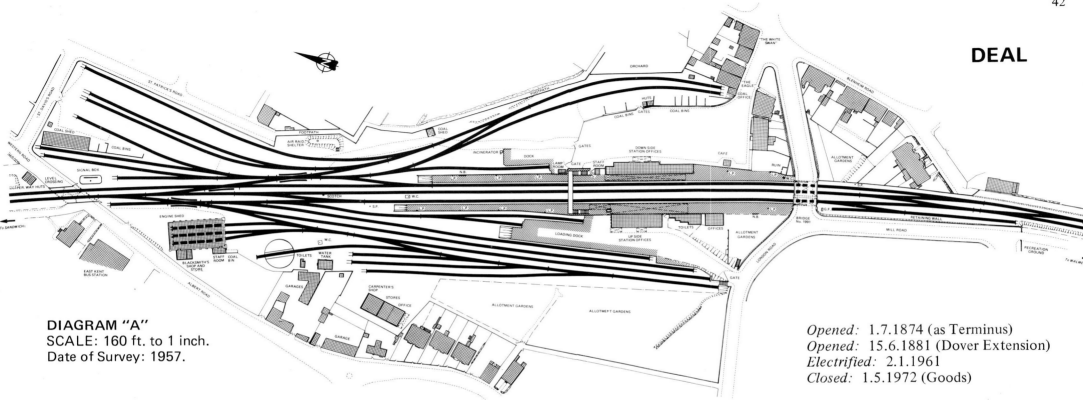

DIAGRAM "A"
SCALE: 160 ft. to 1 inch.
Date of Survey: 1957.

Opened: 1.7.1874 (as Terminus)
Opened: 15.6.1881 (Dover Extension)
Electrified: 2.1.1961
Closed: 1.5.1972 (Goods)

DEAL

It is rather surprising that Deal enjoyed status for so long; after all, there was no direct link between Dover and Ramsgate until the line was extended from Deal. The "Up" and "Down" will be referred to according to current train workings: "Down" being towards Ramsgate and "Up" towards Dover.

The Up side buildings are certainly of a very early date, and could well go back to the opening of the line (there is a similar structure at Sandwich). The canopy was of the "Train Shed" type, spanning the platform line and middle road. The other platform might be original, as the layout of two platform lines separated by a central engine release siding was common on the SER, but the office buildings on that side are certainly a later addition.

Despite the fact that the extension to Dover was a joint enterprise with the LC & DR there is no visual evidence of any "Chatham" influence. The engine shed was closed in 1930 following the provision of new sheds at Dover. It was converted for use as a goods shed, and survived for that purpose into the 1960s, when it was demolished. By some miracle the turntable (50 ft 1 inch in diameter) also survived.

Resignalling in 1939 brought some changes. The old SER gate box at the crossing was abolished and the points at the Dover end of the station were rearranged, thus enabling the platforms to be extended right up to the road bridge. All passenger trains were booked to call at Deal, so the centre track was never classified as a through line but always a siding, and this arrangement was perpetuated with the new signal box. The old goods shed, a large brick structure in the Up Sidings (on a siding near the coal bins behind the loading dock) was demolished around the time of the Second World War, the "spread" between the two lines giving a good clue as to its position. Thereafter the yard on this side of the line was devoted to coal traffic. The "Train Shed" canopy was taken down around 1947.

Track rationalisation started in the 1960s with the elimination of the former loco shed and turntable, and other connections were severed from time to time as traffic declined. Dates are given on diagram "B". There was a brief resurgence of freight traffic early in 1979, when a temporary aggregate dump was established in the Down Sidings in connection with the Thames Flood Barrier project.

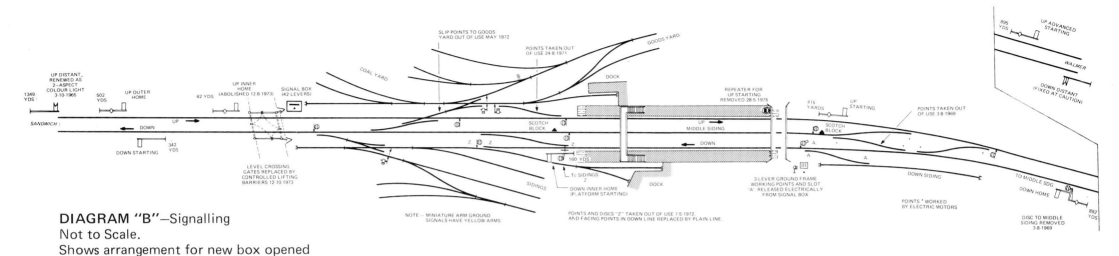

DIAGRAM "B"—Signalling
Not to Scale.
Shows arrangement for new box opened
14th May, 1939.

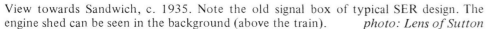

View towards Sandwich, c. 1935. Note the old signal box of typical SER design. The engine shed can be seen in the background (above the train). *photo: Lens of Sutton*

General view of station from the road overbridge, c. 1935. The original terminal building is on the right. *photo: Lens of Sutton*

CATTLE MARKET

MARKET

RAILWAY COTTAGE (BUNGALOW)

WEYMOUTH AVENUE

GATES

SIX RAILWAY COTTAGES

STATION APPROACH

ADVERT BOARD

S.M.'s HOUSE

SUMMER HOUSE

SHED

COAL OFFICE

T. BURT & SON'S COAL OFFICE

LORRY WEIGHBRIDGE

GATE

CYCLE SHED

LAMP ROOM

FISH PEN

CYCLE SHED

COAL BIN

ASH BIN

STATION OFFICES

SUBWAY RAMP

SUBWAY

SUBWAY RAMP

BUILDER'S YARD

DORSET COUNTY POLICE HEADQUARTERS

RAMP

TO DORCHESTER JUNCTION AND WEYMOUTH

LIMIT OF SCALE PLAN. 90 ft. TO END OF SIDING.

'BUS DEPOT

HOUSES

ALFRED ROAD

COAL STACK

SIGNAL BOX

WATER TANK

SITE OF LOCO SIDINGS (REMOVED)

SITE OF TURNTABLE

ASH PIT

ENGINE SHED (DISUSED)

ENGINE SHED EXTENSION

(DEMOLISHED)

SITE FOR NEW SIGNAL BOX

GROUND FRAME (HUT)

ALLOTMENTS

TWO RAILWAY COTTAGES

FOUR RAILWAY COTTAGES

FOOTPATH

WELFARE HUT

FOWL RUN

ELDRIDGE, POPE & CO. DORCHESTER BREWERY

OVERHEAD PIPE

OVERHEAD PIPE

BREWERY BUILDINGS

TANKS

COAL PENS

COAL PEN

STORE

COAL PENS

STORE

COAL BINS

CATTLE ROAD

GATE

CATTLE ROAD

CATTLE PENS

CATTLE DOCK

GOODS OFFICE

GOODS SHED

FEED STORES

SHUNTERS CABIN

CHIPPING

TANK TRAPS

FOOTPATH

TWO RAILWAY COTTAGES

TWO RAILWAY COTTAGES

TWO RAILWAY COTTAGES

TWO RAILWAY COTTAGES

ALLOTMENTS

PER. WAY HUT

7½-TON CRANE

DIAGRAM "A"

SCALE: 160 ft. to 1 inch.
Date of Survey: 1957.

Opened: 1.6.1847
Original Company: Southampton & Dorchester Rly.
Amalgamated with L & SWR 1848.

GATE

HUT

LOADING DOCK

3-ARCH BRIDGE NO. 120

COAL YARD

GATE

BARNES WAY

HOUSES

HOUSES

MONMOUTH ROAD

TANK TRAPS

PRINCE OF WALES ROAD

RAILWAY COTTAGE

RAILWAY COTTAGES

CONCRETE TANK TRAPS

BRIDGE NO. 119

135¾ M.P.

EDISON STEAM ROLLING CO. "MANSFIELD SIDING"

TO MORETON

CONTINUATION NOT TO SCALE

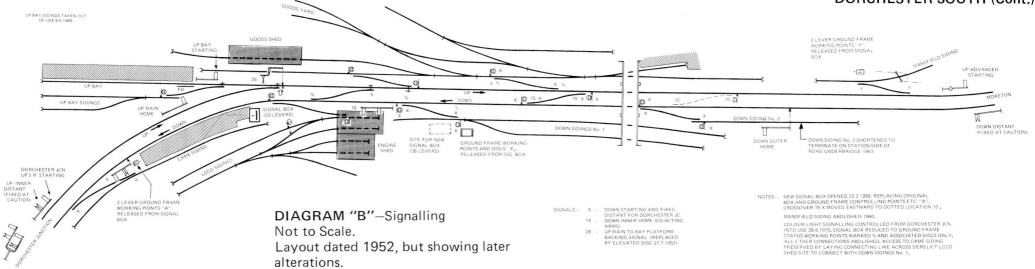

UP BAY SIDINGS TAKEN OUT OF USE 6.5.1969.

GOODS YARD

UP BAY STARTING

GOODS SHED

2 LEVER GROUND FRAME WORKING POINTS "Y" RELEASED FROM SIGNAL BOX

MANSFIELD SIDING

UP ADVANCED STARTING

UP BAY

28

UP BAY SIDINGS

FB

UP

DOWN

UP MAIN HOME

DOWN

UP

19

SIGNAL BOX (33 LEVERS)

CAME SIDING

ENGINE SHED

LOCO SIDINGS

SITE FOR NEW SIGNAL BOX (36 LEVERS)

GROUND FRAME WORKING POINTS AND DISCS X, RELEASED FROM SIG BOX

DOWN SIDINGS No. 1

15

15

10

10

MORETON

DOWN SIDING No. 2

DOWN DISTANT (FIXED AT CAUTION)

DOWN OUTER HOME

DOWN SIDING No. 2 SHORTENED TO TERMINATE ON STATION SIDE OF ROAD UNDERBRIDGE 1963

DORCHESTER JCN UP S.R. STARTING

UP INNER DISTANT (FIXED AT CAUTION)

2 LEVER GROUND FRAME WORKING POINTS "A" RELEASED FROM SIGNAL BOX.

DORCHESTER JUNCTION

DIAGRAM "B"—Signalling
Not to Scale.
Layout dated 1952, but showing later alterations.

SIGNALS:—
5 — DOWN STARTING AND FIXED DISTANT FOR DORCHESTER JC
19 — DOWN INNER HOME (CO-ACTING ARMS)
28 — UP MAIN TO BAY PLATFORM BACKING SIGNAL. (REPLACED BY ELEVATED DISC 27.7.1952).

NOTES:— NEW SIGNAL BOX OPENED 22.2.1959, REPLACING ORIGINAL BOX AND GROUND FRAME CONTROLLING POINTS ETC. "X", CROSSOVER 15 X MOVED EASTWARD TO DOTTED LOCATION 10.

MANSFIELD SIDING ABOLISHED 1960.

COLOUR LIGHT SIGNALLING CONTROLLED FROM DORCHESTER JCN. INTO USE 28.6.1970. SIGNAL BOX REDUCED TO GROUND FRAME STATUS WORKING POINTS MARKED % AND ASSOCIATED DISCS ONLY. ALL OTHER CONNECTIONS ABOLISHED, ACCESS TO CAME SIDING PRESERVED BY LAYING CONNECTING LINE ACROSS DERELICT LOCO SHED SITE TO CONNECT WITH DOWN SIDINGS No. 1.

The Up platform as it appeared in October 1931, before removal of the overall roof. Note the disused "Island" platform, and the Down platform curving away in the left foreground.
photo: H.C. Casserley

. . . and as it appeared on 10th July 1956, with No. 30787 approaching with an Up train from Weymouth. This view was taken from the old signal box.
photo: R.C. Riley

DORCHESTER SOUTH

In any competition to find the oddest station in Britain, Dorchester South must be a serious contender. Originally it formed the terminus of the line from Southampton and was worked as a "one-sided" station, Up trains being handled at the Moreton end of the solitary platform, and Down trains at the end nearest the buffer stops. A crossover was provided half-way along the platform to admit Down trains. Later a very short platform was added opposite the original one, but this was not (as might be expected) for Down traffic, but served as an occasional alternative departure point for Up trains.

The station had not been laid out as a conventional terminus, there being great hopes that the line would eventually be extended to Exeter. These came to nothing, and in January 1857 the GWR settled the matter by opening their line to Weymouth, cutting off the line of advance in a westerly direction. Instead, a single track curve was laid connecting with the GWR, L & SWR trains running through to Weymouth from 20th January, 1857. The curve connected with the Up line only, and as no platform existed to cater for through traffic, protracted and complicated shunting was necessary. This unsatisfactory arrangement culminated in a collision between two passenger trains in November 1877, and the harsh words of the Board of Trade inspecting officer caused improvements to be made. On 5th May, 1879 the curved Down platform was brought into use, the connecting line being doubled, but strangely no corresponding Up platform was built, Up trains continuing to reverse into the old terminus for another ninety-one years!

A two-road engine shed existed from the earliest days, but it soon became over-crowded and an extension covering another two lines was added. At one time Down trains usually changed engines, and to permit this to be done in the platform a new siding behind the Down platform and its associated ground frame was added in July 1883. This practice had ceased by 1910, the points at the engine shed end being taken out, but the siding and ground frame were retained for stabling loco coal. The layout of the engine shed was far from convenient, the only access being via No. 1 shed road. In effect, this left only three roads available for their intended purpose.

Around 1938 the Southern Railway carried out limited modernisation, the most noticeable feature being the removal of the train-shed type roof on the Up side, but even then nothing was done to eliminate the reversal. The short (and long-disused) island platform was also demolished at this time.

Until nationalisation the station was plain "Dorchester", the "South" being added in November 1949. Revision of regional boundaries brought all lines in Dorset under Southern control from 2nd April, 1950, and this was the cue for some rationalisation of facilities. Cattle traffic was concentrated on Dorchester West, but this was balanced by all sundries traffic being transferred to South. One shunting engine was also made to serve both yards, transfer trips via the junction being worked as required.

The engine shed closed on 17th June, 1957, the allocation of locos being transferred to Weymouth, and two years later the lofty signal box on the end of the Down platform was replaced by a new one (see diagram "B").

The old signal box at Dorchester South, which was replaced by a modern box in 1959. The lever frame was "end-on" to traffic instead of the more conventional arrangements of along the front or back of the building.   *photo: B.L. Jackson*

Goods traffic was once heavy, coal in particular being much in evidence. In 1963 the derelict engine shed site became a coal dump, but in recent years this business has declined. The goods shed closed on 1st March, 1965, sundries being concentrated on Weymouth, and at the time of writing (1979) the yard is visited by only two freight trains per week.

The interval service of "push-and-pull" diesel trains was fully implemented on 10th July, 1967, but Up trains continued to reverse until the new platform was commissioned on 28th June, 1970. At the same time the signal box was reduced to ground frame status and the semaphores replaced by colour-lights under the control of Dorchester Junction. The goods shed has since been demolished.

OPERATING NOTE: Eldridge, Pope & Co's Brewery.

The overhead pipe-line between the Malt House and Bonded Store, which crosses the main siding 10 feet from the buffer stops, is only 12 ft. 9 in. above rail level, and engines and covered wagons must not pass to the extremity of this siding.

DOVER PRIORY

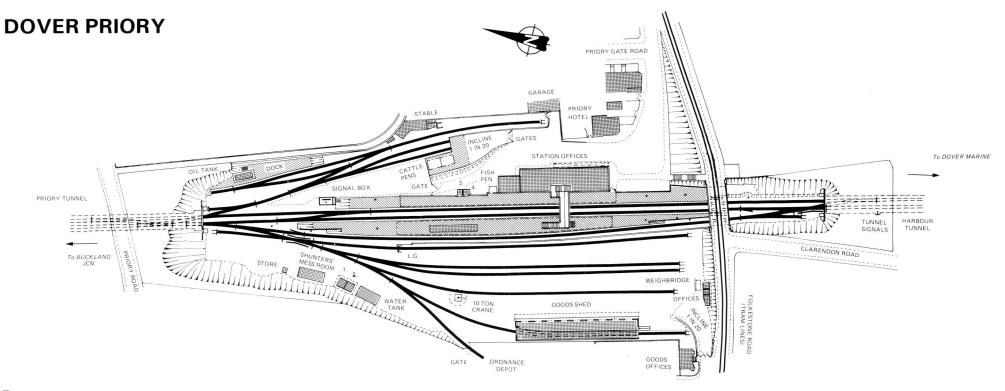

PRIORY GATE ROAD

GARAGE

PRIORY HOTEL

STABLE

INCLINE 1 IN 20

GATES

STATION OFFICES

To Dover Marine

OIL TANK

DOCK

CATTLE PENS

GATE

FISH PEN

Priory Tunnel

SIGNAL BOX

3.

4.

TUNNEL SIGNALS

HARBOUR TUNNEL

To Buckland JCN.

PRIORY ROAD

SHUNTERS' MESS ROOM

1. 2.

L.G.

CLARENDON ROAD

STORE

WEIGHBRIDGE

OFFICES

WATER TANK

10-TON CRANE

GOODS SHED

FOLKESTONE ROAD (TRAM LINES)

INCLINE 1 IN 20

GATE

ORDNANCE DEPOT

GOODS OFFICES

DIAGRAM "A"
SCALE: 160 ft. to 1 inch.
Date of Survey: 1932.

Opened: 22.7.1861
Electrified: 15.6.1959
Closed: 3.7.1961 (Goods).
Original Company: London Chatham and Dover Railway

Looking north towards Buckland Junction, c. 1961.

photo: Lens of Sutton

This station is ideal for the modeller, as it enables him to construct an important station with interesting traffic working in a very limited space.

At first it was called "Dover Town", but was given its present name in July 1863. For a few months it was a terminus, the line to the harbour being opened on 1st November, 1861. The station was reconstructed by the Southern Railway in 1932, and it is this version which is illustrated by the two plans.

The layout of the original station was rather different. There were only two platforms linked by an overall roof in the manner of Canterbury East, and there was an engine shed on the Up side. A loop line ran behind the Up platform to provide access to the shed for engines arriving from the Harbour direction, and as the platforms were considerably shorter, there was room for a refuge siding on the Down side between the mouth of Priory Tunnel and the station.

Work on remodelling actually started in 1930, the Down Refuge siding being taken out of use on 10th May that year to enable the platforms to be extended. On 16th November, 1930 the existing signal box replaced the old LC & DR installation. During the next two years the overall roof was taken down and the back of the Up platform opened out to form a useful reversible loop. The old engine shed was also swept away, and the site laid out as additional goods sidings complete with a large goods shed. The old Victorian buildings were demolished and replaced by typical SR structures. The station was badly damaged during World War Two, but has since been restored.

Minor alterations took place in connection with electrification. The Down platform was lengthened at the North end, and the crossover points at that end moved back into Priory Tunnel and signalled so that Up trains could depart from the Down platform. Later alterations have been few, and are shown on diagram "B". Despite the withdrawal of freight in 1961, only the Down Sidings have been removed. Those on the Up side are still in use for berthing parcel vans and spare passenger stock.

OPERATING NOTE: GAS WORKS SIDINGS. To ensure trains standing clear of the spring points in the Up Line, no train having work to perform at these sidings was permitted to exceed 35 vehicles.

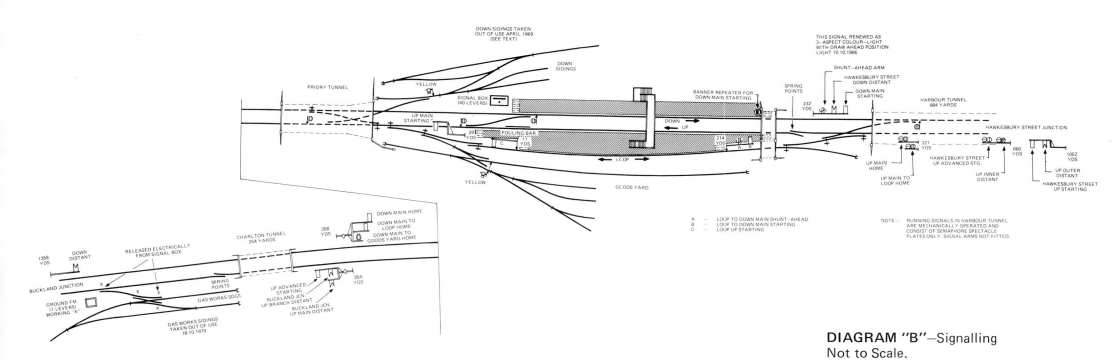

DIAGRAM "B"—Signalling
Not to Scale.

DROXFORD

DIAGRAM "A"

SCALE: 160 ft to 1 inch.
Date of Survey: 1939.
Full Signalling shown.

Opened: 1.6.1903
Closed: 7.2.1955 (Passengers).
Closed: April 1962 (Completely).
Original Company: L & SWR.

DROXFORD

Droxford was situated on one of the last cross-country lines to be built by the constituents of the Southern Railway. Known as the "Meon Valley Line", it ran from Butts Junction, Alton, to Knowle Junction, near Fareham. Throughout its length it possessed an undeniably rural character which prevailed all through its comparatively short working life.

Despite the slight traffic potential in such a thinly-peopled area, the whole branch was laid out on a lavish scale. It had been planned as an alternative through route to Gosport in a bid to keep the GWR out of the Portsmouth area, and although a double track was never required, the bridges and other major works were constructed with this in mind. The five stations at Wickham, Droxford, West Meon, Privett and Tisted were very similar in style and track layout, except that Wickham had a slightly larger goods yard with a siding passing through the goods shed. At Droxford the yard was on the Up side, the three sidings converging on a short head-shunt. A lengthy refuge siding was also provided, and local instructions insisted that the rear portions of all Up goods trains were placed therein before shunting commenced because of the severe gradient in the direction of Wickham. The goods shed was small, with a short canopy over the doorway on each side. The Up platform sported a neat brick shelter with a window in each end, the design exactly matching that of the main building opposite. A standard all-brick signal box containing 24 levers (5 spare) controlled the layout.

The station nameboard read "Droxford for Hambledon"—a statement not without a touch of optimism since Droxford itself was about a mile away, and the sleepy Hampshire village of Hambledon nearer four miles!

As will be seen from the photographs, the main building was quite a picturesque affair. The side facing the platform was obscured by an ample canopy running the full length of the building, but the architecture could be better appreciated from the forecourt. It was still in good condition in 1976, having found a new role as a training centre for heavy goods vehicle drivers.

Traffic was generally light, but the service operated was not typical of country branch lines, some through workings between Gosport and Waterloo being provided in the early days. It never really caught on as a through route, and electrification of the Portsmouth Direct Line ended any pretentions in that respect. With the withdrawal of the passenger service the line was closed completely between Droxford and Farringdon, the remaining freight traffic being worked via Fareham. After abandonment by BR in 1962, the line from Knowle Junction to Droxford was leased by a Mr. Charles Ashby, and used for conducting experiments with the "Sadler Rail Coach". His lease later expired, and the track was removed.

Above left: Looking northwards, c. 1952.   *photo: Lens of Sutton*

Above right: The dismal scene after closure to passengers. The signal box has gone but one signal (minus its arm) has survived.   *photo: Lens of Sutton*

Right: Roadside view of booking hall and station entrance as at 27th May, 1976.
photo: G.J. Bowring

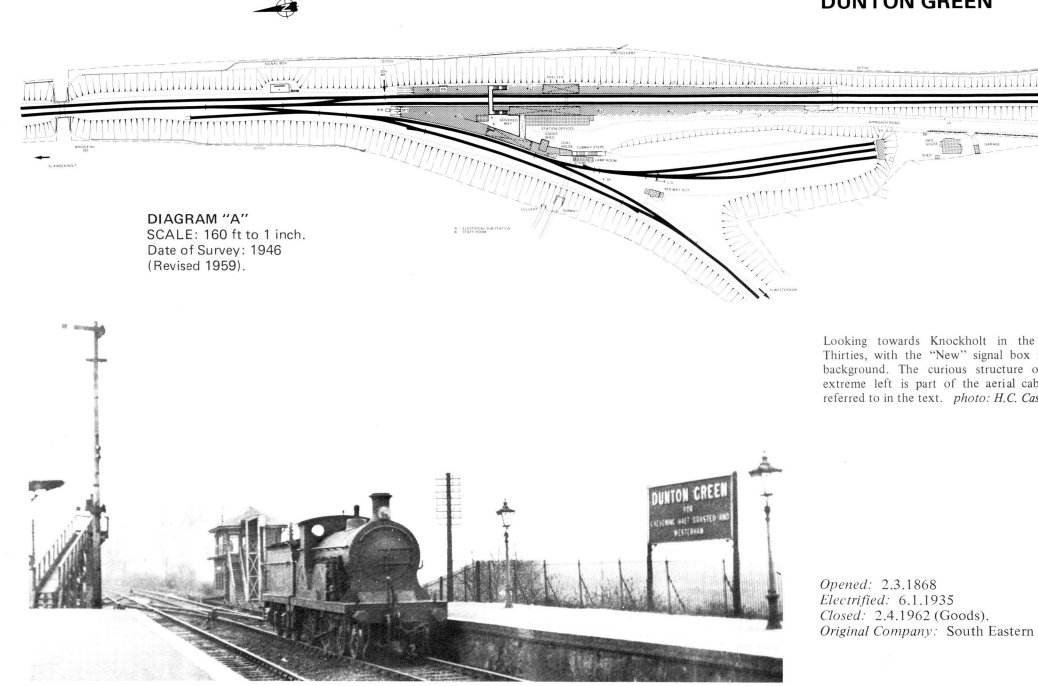

DUNTON GREEN

DIAGRAM "A"
SCALE: 160 ft to 1 inch.
Date of Survey: 1946
(Revised 1959).

A — ELECTRICAL SUB STATION
B — STAFF ROOM

Looking towards Knockholt in the early Thirties, with the "New" signal box in the background. The curious structure on the extreme left is part of the aerial cableway referred to in the text.   *photo: H.C. Casserley*

Opened: 2.3.1868
Electrified: 6.1.1935
Closed: 2.4.1962 (Goods).
Original Company: South Eastern Rly.

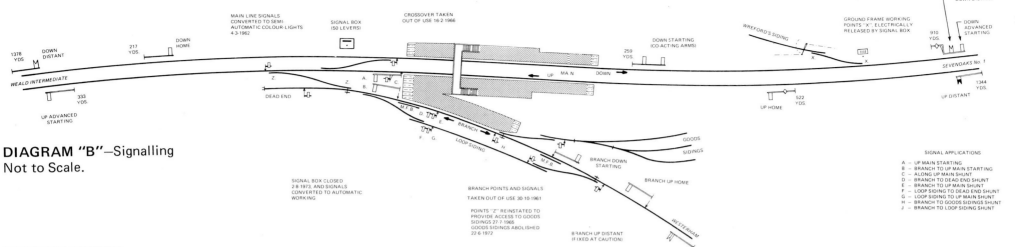

Labels in diagram (top):

SEVENOAKS No. 1 DOWN DISTANT

MAIN LINE SIGNALS CONVERTED TO SEMI-AUTOMATIC COLOUR-LIGHTS 4·3·1962

SIGNAL BOX (50 LEVERS)

CROSSOVER TAKEN OUT OF USE 16·2·1966

DOWN STARTING (CO-ACTING ARMS)

WREFORD'S SIDING

GROUND FRAME WORKING POINTS "X", ELECTRICALLY RELEASED BY SIGNAL BOX

910 YDS.

DOWN ADVANCED STARTING

1378 YDS.

DOWN DISTANT

217 YDS.

DOWN HOME

259 YDS.

WEALD INTERMEDIATE

UP   MA IN   DOWN

SEVENOAKS No. 1

1344 YDS.

333 YDS.

UP ADVANCED STARTING

DEAD END

Z.   Z.   A.   C.
B.

M.F.B.   D
E

BRANCH

F.   G.   LOOP SIDING   H

M.F.B.

UP HOME

522 YDS.

UP DISTANT

BRANCH DOWN STARTING

GOODS SIDINGS

BRANCH UP HOME

WESTERHAM

DIAGRAM "B"—Signalling
Not to Scale.

SIGNAL BOX CLOSED 2·8·1973, AND SIGNALS CONVERTED TO AUTOMATIC WORKING

BRANCH POINTS AND SIGNALS TAKEN OUT OF USE 30·10·1961

POINTS "Z" REINSTATED TO PROVIDE ACCESS TO GOODS SIDINGS 27·7·1965 GOODS SIDINGS ABOLISHED 22·6·1972

BRANCH UP DISTANT (FIXED AT CAUTION)

SIGNAL APPLICATIONS

A – UP MAIN STARTING
B – BRANCH TO UP MAIN STARTING
C – ALONG UP MAIN SHUNT
D – BRANCH TO DEAD END SHUNT
E – BRANCH TO UP MAIN SHUNT
F – LOOP SIDING TO DEAD END SHUNT
G – LOOP SIDING TO UP MAIN SHUNT
H – BRANCH TO GOODS SIDINGS SHUNT
J – BRANCH TO LOOP SIDING SHUNT

DUNTON GREEN

In its early years this was an insignificant wayside station known as "Dunton Green and Riverhead", the present shortened title being adopted on 1st July, 1873. It achieved junction status with the opening of the Westerham branch on 7th July, 1881, but the original weatherboarded buildings were retained with suitable extensions.

Originally a tall, narrow signal box stood at the end of the Up platform between the branch and main line, but the SE & CR replaced it with one of more standard appearance in the early 1900s. This was located on the Down side, and had the disadvantage of requiring the signalman to cross the main lines repeatedly with the single line tablet. To solve the problem an aerial cableway from the signal box to the branch platform was installed to convey the tablet, and this novel feature was only discontinued in 1934 prior to electrification. It was considered to be a potential hazard, as in the event of the cable breaking and falling upon the conductor rails a short circuit would be created. The cableway was replaced by auxiliary tablet instruments on the branch platform.

Electrification of the main lines in 1935 greatly improved the train service, but although plans were prepared, this benefit was never extended to the branch. The latter remained an island of steam working in a sea of EMUs (and therefore something of an operational nuisance) right up to closure on 30th October, 1961. Withdrawal of goods facilities the following year was the cue for much rationalisation of the track layout, some of which turned out to be premature, as the sidings were later reinstated to handle aggregate traffic in connection with the local programme of road construction (see diagram "B" for dates and details).

Wreford's private siding connected at one time with the internal rail system of The Brick and Tile Company, who operated an Aveling and Porter 2-2-0 locomotive. It was eventually cut back to serve a cold storage depot, and closed in 1957.

As with many stations in the Home Counties, passenger traffic, though reasonably heavy, is mainly of a "commuter" nature and concentrated into two daily peaks. As an economy measure the station was partially unstaffed in 1971, the morning and evening peaks being covered by one man on a split turn of duty. Vandalism soon made it necessary to board up the windows, and this, plus the liberal covering of graffiti, quickly

Looking towards Sevenoaks c. 1890, showing the old signal box on the end of the Up platform. The Westerham branch platform is on the right.   *photo: Lens of Sutton*

gave the buildings a derelict aspect. At the time of writing (1979) British Rail are embarking on a "tidy-up" operation which will eradicate most of the original "South Eastern" structure and leave little more than a small office and a couple of platform shelters.

OPERATING NOTE: When necessary, Wreford's Siding could be served by a shunting trip from Dunton Green station, engine and wagons returning on the Down line.

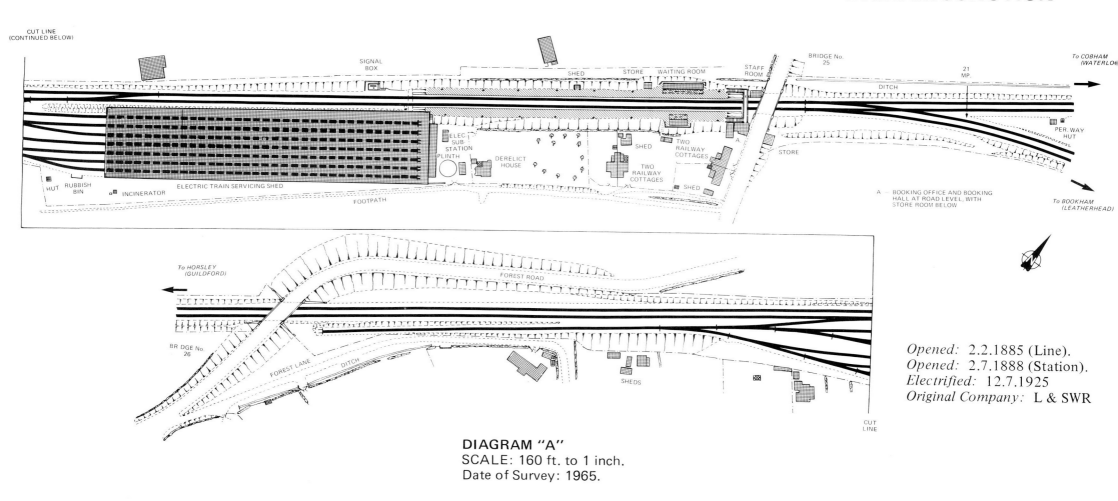

DIAGRAM "A"
SCALE: 160 ft. to 1 inch.
Date of Survey: 1965.

Opened: 2.2.1885 (Line).
Opened: 2.7.1888 (Station).
Electrified: 12.7.1925
Original Company: L & SWR

A — BOOKING OFFICE AND BOOKING
HALL AT ROAD LEVEL, WITH
STORE ROOM BELOW

EFFINGHAM JUNCTION

Originally intended for use purely as an interchange point for passengers changing between the main and Leatherhead lines, this station was situated some distance from the nearest town and passenger accommodation was far from lavish. No goods facilities were provided, the traffic being dealt with at Horsley.

The booking office and luggage lift at road level may not be original, but the waiting rooms on the platforms are assumed to be so. The original signal box (see diagram "B") was wedged between the footbridge and the road over-bridge, and has been drawn away from the line for the sake of clarity. It remains in use to this day as a staff room, and is shown as such on the scale plan.

A carriage shed was built in readiness for electrification, a new signal box being provided at the Guildford end of the station, and the old one closed.

Despite its apparent lack of interest, this station is worthy of inclusion as a good example of an outer-suburban junction, unusual in that it had neither terminal platforms or goods facilities. Terminating trains are quickly shunted to the carriage sidings and retrieved again as soon as the connecting through services have departed.

DIAGRAM "B"—Signalling
For old box, 1888, with
alterations completed 1897.

54

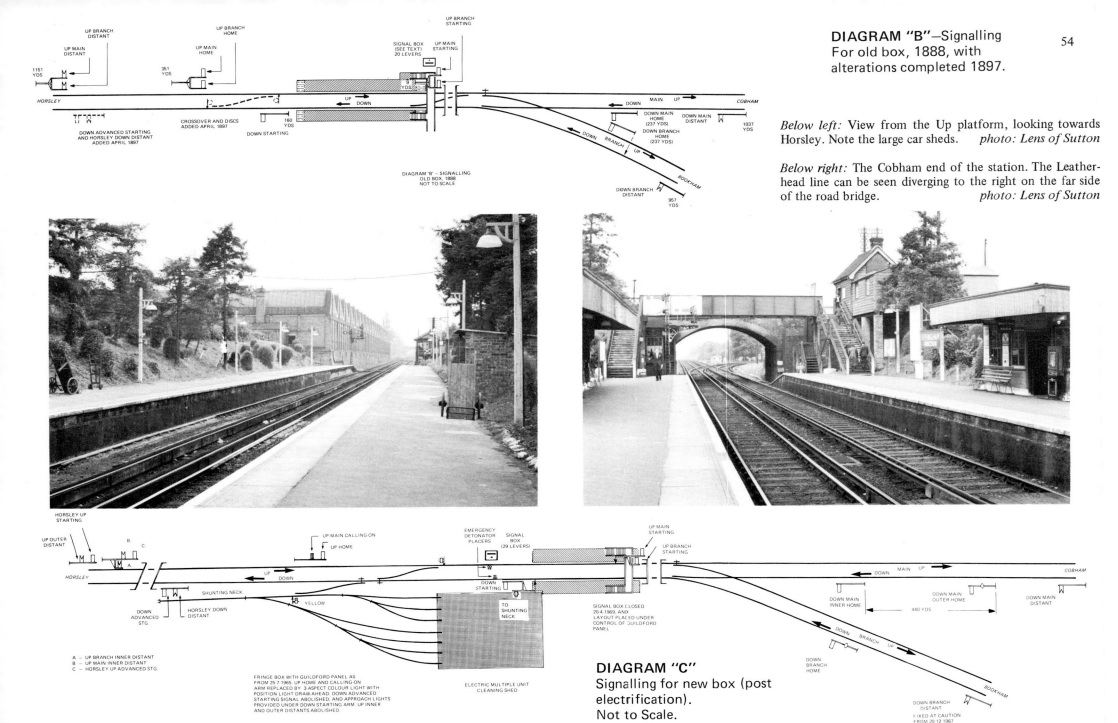

DIAGRAM "B"—Signalling
For old box, 1888, with
alterations completed 1897.

UP BRANCH
STARTING

UP BRANCH
DISTANT

UP BRANCH HOME

UP MAIN DISTANT

UP MAIN HOME

SIGNAL BOX
(SEE TEXT)
20 LEVERS

UP MAIN
STARTING

1151
YDS

351
YDS

9
YDS

HORSLEY

UP

DOWN

MAIN

UP

COBHAM

DOWN

DOWN ADVANCED STARTING
AND HORSLEY DOWN DISTANT
ADDED APRIL 1897

CROSSOVER AND DISCS
ADDED APRIL 1897

160
YDS

DOWN STARTING

DOWN MAIN
HOME (237 YDS)

DOWN MAIN DISTANT

1037
YDS

DOWN BRANCH
HOME (237 YDS)

DIAGRAM 'B' – SIGNALLING
OLD BOX, 1888
NOT TO SCALE

DOWN
BRANCH
UP

BOOKHAM

DOWN BRANCH
DISTANT

957
YDS

Below left: View from the Up platform, looking towards
Horsley. Note the large car sheds.   *photo: Lens of Sutton*

Below right: The Cobham end of the station. The Leatherhead line can be seen diverging to the right on the far side
of the road bridge.   *photo: Lens of Sutton*

DIAGRAM "C"
Signalling for new box (post
electrification).
Not to Scale.

HORSLEY UP
STARTING

UP OUTER
DISTANT

B.

C.

A

UP MAIN CALLING-ON

UP HOME

EMERGENCY
DETONATOR
PLACERS

SIGNAL
BOX
(29 LEVERS)

UP MAIN
STARTING

UP BRANCH
STARTING

HORSLEY

UP

DOWN

DOWN
STARTING

DOWN

MAIN

UP

COBHAM

DOWN
ADVANCED STG.

SHUNTING NECK

HORSLEY DOWN
DISTANT

YELLOW

TO SHUNTING
NECK

SIGNAL BOX CLOSED
20-4-1969, AND
LAYOUT PLACED UNDER
CONTROL OF GUILDFORD
PANEL

DOWN MAIN
INNER HOME

DOWN MAIN
OUTER HOME

440 YDS

DOWN MAIN
DISTANT

A — UP BRANCH INNER DISTANT
B — UP MAIN INNER DISTANT
C — HORSLEY UP ADVANCED STG.

FRINGE BOX WITH GUILDFORD PANEL AS
FROM 25-7-1965. UP HOME AND CALLING-ON
ARM REPLACED BY 3-ASPECT COLOUR LIGHT WITH
POSITION LIGHT DRAW AHEAD. DOWN ADVANCED
STARTING SIGNAL ABOLISHED, AND APPROACH LIGHTS
PROVIDED UNDER DOWN STARTING ARM. UP INNER
AND OUTER DISTANTS ABOLISHED.

ELECTRIC MULTIPLE UNIT
CLEANING SHED

DOWN
BRANCH
UP

DOWN
BRANCH
HOME

BOOKHAM

DOWN BRANCH
DISTANT
FIXED AT CAUTION
FROM 20-12-1967

EPSOM

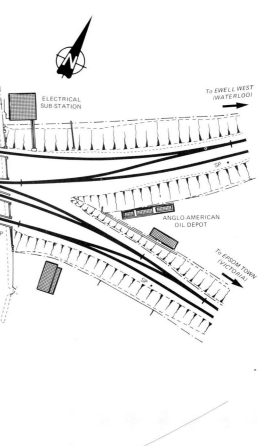

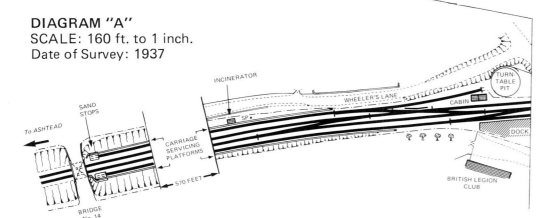

To EWELL WEST
(WATERLOO)

ELECTRICAL
SUB-STATION

GARDEN

SM's
HOUSE   SHED

LP   LP   LP   LP

SIGNAL
BOX

1   2

LIFT
SP   ELECTRIFICATION
HUT

SP

3   4

LIFT
SP

WRIGHT'S
TEA ROOMS

SP

LP   LP   LP

SUBWAY

LOADING DOCK

COAL
BIN   GATES   LAMP
ROOM

ANGLO-AMERICAN
OIL DEPOT

BRIDGE
No. 13   WEST STREET

WATERLOO ROAD

BOOKSTALL

BOOKING
OFFICE ETC.   PARCEL
OFFICE   LOADING
BAY   SHOP

SHOP

To EPSOM TOWN
(VICTORIA)

SP

GIRL GUIDES'
HUT

1. UP SIDE LAVATORY BLOCK
2. UP SIDE OFFICES
3. DOWN SIDE LAVATORY BLOCK
4. DOWN SIDE OFFICES

DIAGRAM "A"
SCALE: 160 ft. to 1 inch.
Date of Survey: 1937

INCINERATOR

TURN
TABLE
PIT

SAND
STOPS

WHEELER'S LANE

CABIN

To ASHTEAD

SP

DOCK

CARRIAGE
SERVICING
PLATFORMS

570 FEET

BRITISH LEGION
CLUB

BRIDGE
No. 14

Epsom station and its elevated signal box, looking towards London. The two loading dock roads are right foreground. Except for the colour light signal just visible in the distance, this view has changed little since Southern Railway days.   *photo: G.J. Bowring*

Opened: 3.3.1929
Original Company: Southern Railway
(see text).

LAYOUT AND SIGNAL ALTERATIONS

MAY 1960 — DOWN WATERLOO DISTANT MADE COLOUR LIGHT
26.4.1964 — COLOUR-LIGHT SIGNALLING TO LEATHERHEAD
(EPSOM COMMON) INTRODUCED. SIGNALS "X"
ABOLISHED AND "Y" MADE COLOUR LIGHT
27.2.1966 — COLOUR LIGHT SIGNALLING ON WATERLOO LINE
AND IN STATION AREA BROUGHT INTO USE
22.9.1968 — PORTION OF UP SIDING BETWEEN 17 POINTS
AND BUFFER STOPS TAKEN OUT. YELLOW ARM
SHUNT SIGNAL REPLACED BY RED DISC.
4.3.1969 — No. 45 POINTS TAKEN OUT OF USE
11.5.1969 — COLOUR-LIGHT SIGNALLING ON VICTORIA LINE
INTRODUCED
28.10.1969 — No. 2 DOCK SIDING PUT OUT OF USE. SLIP
POINTS 31 AND DISC 33 ABOLISHED
4.5.1977 — CROSSOVER 15 AND DISC 14 OUT OF USE
22.5.1977 — SLIP POINTS 17 AND 19 RELAID AS FACING CROSSOVER
AND TRAILING CONNECTION IN UP LINE. 16 AND 17
MOVED FURTHER FROM SIGNAL BOX

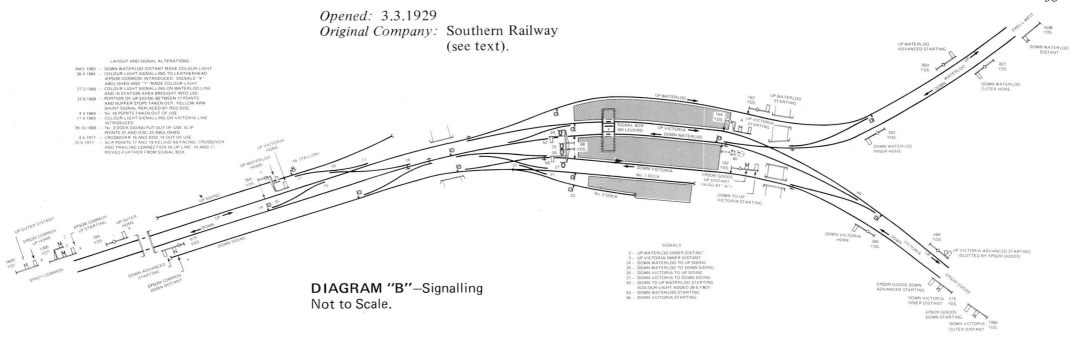

DIAGRAM "B"—Signalling
Not to Scale.

SIGNALS

2 — UP WATERLOO INNER DISTANT
3 — UP VICTORIA INNER DISTANT
24 — DOWN WATERLOO TO UP SIDING
25 — DOWN WATERLOO TO DOWN SIDING
26 — DOWN VICTORIA TO UP SIDING
27 — DOWN VICTORIA TO DOWN SIDING
50 — DOWN TO UP WATERLOO STARTING
(COLOUR LIGHT ADDED 28.5.1967)
52 — DOWN WATERLOO STARTING
56 — DOWN VICTORIA STARTING

EPSOM

The site was originally occupied by an L & SWR station, but only its replacement can be dealt with in this volume. The old station was considerably different in layout, making it impossible to incorporate any of its features into the plans now published.

It is purely a passenger station, freight traffic for Epsom being handled at the former LB & SCR station (Epsom Town). The two loading docks were built to accommodate parcel vans. Spacious platforms with long canopies are provided, the whole layout being designed to facilitate the speedy cross-platform exchange of passengers and their luggage. The frontage at road level is of concrete construction, and typical of much SR building of the period.

A new overhead signal box was provided with the building of the station, and the signalling was purely mechanical (see Diagram "B"). The layout was very versatile, but some of the connections were little used and have been taken out in recent years. The lines serving the station had recently been electrified when the station was opened, so the carriage sidings west of the platforms (used for berthing electric multiple units) were already in existence.

Thus Epsom has altered very little since opening—apart from the inevitable spread of colour-light signalling. This was installed between 1964 and 1969, although at the time of writing (1979) it is still controlled from the mechanical frame in the signal box. It survives as an excellent example of a Southern Railway suburban junction station.

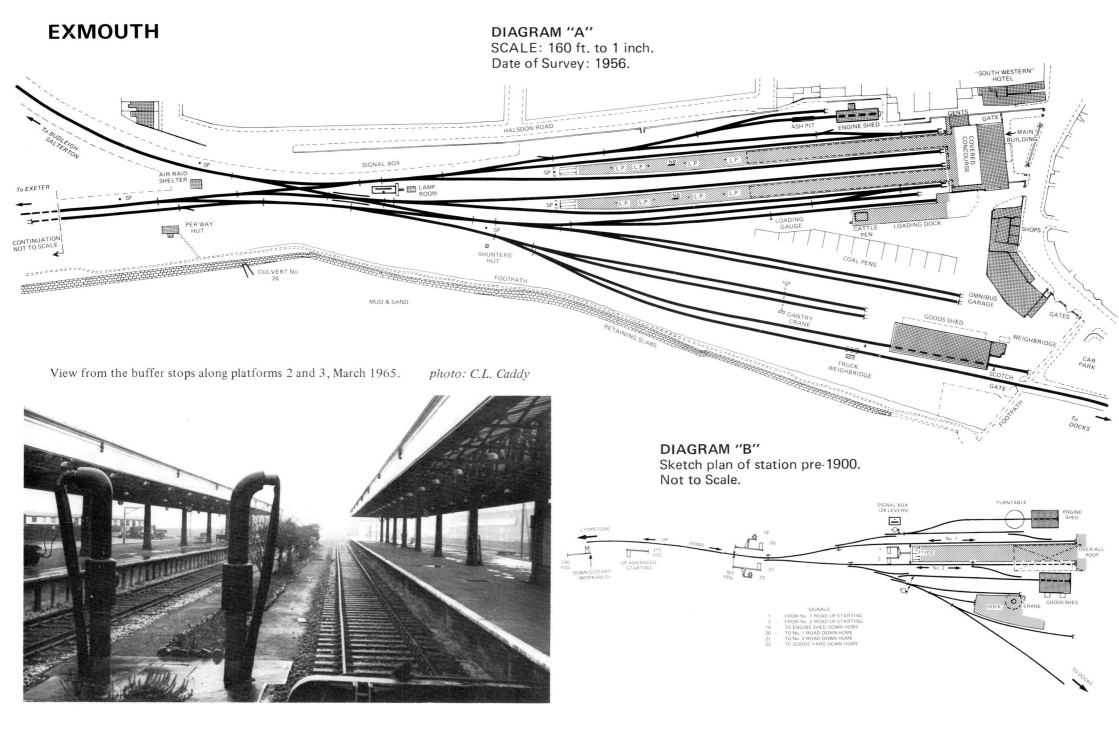

EXMOUTH

DIAGRAM "A"
SCALE: 160 ft. to 1 inch.
Date of Survey: 1956.

"SOUTH WESTERN" HOTEL

To BUDLEIGH SALTERTON

To EXETER

CONTINUATION NOT TO SCALE

AIR RAID SHELTER

SP

PER WAY HUT

CULVERT No. 26

MUD & SAND

RETAINING SLABS

FOOTPATH

HALSDON ROAD

SIGNAL BOX

LAMP ROOM

SHUNTERS' HUT

SP

SP

LP LP NB LP LP

LP LP NB LP LP

ASH PIT ENGINE SHED

GENTS GATE

COVERED CONCOURSE

MAIN BUILDING

LOADING GAUGE

CATTLE PEN LOADING DOCK

SHOPS

COAL PENS

GANTRY CRANE

TRUCK WEIGHBRIDGE

OMNIBUS GARAGE

GATES

GOODS SHED

WEIGHBRIDGE

CAR PARK

SCOTCH

GATE

FOOTPATH

To DOCKS

View from the buffer stops along platforms 2 and 3, March 1965.   *photo: C.L. Caddy*

DIAGRAM "B"
Sketch plan of station pre-1900.
Not to Scale.

SIGNAL BOX (24 LEVERS)

TURNTABLE

ENGINE SHED

LYMPSTONE

UP

DOWN

560 YDS

DOWN DISTANT (WORKABLE)

UP ADVANCED STARTING

313 YDS

19

20

153 YDS

21

22

No. 1

11 YDS

1

2

No. 2

OVER ALL ROOF

DOCK CRANE

GOODS SHED

SIGNALS

1   FROM No. 1 ROAD UP STARTING
2   FROM No. 2 ROAD UP STARTING
19   TO ENGINE SHED DOWN HOME
20   TO No. 1 ROAD DOWN HOME
21   TO No. 2 ROAD DOWN HOME
22   TO GOODS YARD DOWN HOME

TO DOCKS

EXMOUTH

As can be seen from diagram "B", the original station was a typical branch line terminus consisting of a fairly short island platform, part of which was covered by an overall roof. It was doubtless adequate for the traffic of the time, but became somewhat cramped with the opening of extension from Budleigh Salterton on 1st June, 1903. Plans for reconstruction were prepared by the L & SWR but it fell to the newly-formed Southern Railway to carry out this task during 1924/25. The rebuilding was on a grand scale, and included remodelling of the goods yard and a massive new goods shed. Diagrams "A" and "C" show the final results. In readiness for the improved layout the 70-lever signal box replaced the older one on 20th July, 1924.

With its glazed concourse, four platforms, bookstall and impressive office block surmounted by a clock, the new Exmouth station possessed something of a "commuter" air akin to that of outer-suburban termini in the Home Counties. Indeed, the line thence to Exeter was the only true commuter line in the West of England, a half-hourly service being operated through most of the day with additionals at peak times. This, plus the Budleigh Salterton trains and a considerable amount of freight shunting, made the signalman up to a well-earned "Class 2"!

In common with all former Southern lines west of Salisbury, Exmouth found itself under Western Region control on 1st January, 1963, and as this change of management coincided with the first enthusiasms of the Beeching plan the future seemed doubtful. Western diesel units first made an appearance on 12th June, 1963, and on 4th November that year the engine shed was closed, engines and men being transferred to Exmouth Junction (Exeter).

Opened: 1.5.1861
Opened: 1.6.1903 (Budleigh Branch).
Closed: 6.3.1967 (Budleigh Branch).
Closed: 4.12.1967 (Goods).
Original Company: Exeter & Exmouth Railway (amalgamated with L & SWR 1865).

It was not long before the entire passenger service over both lines was entrusted to DMUs, the only steam engines visiting Exmouth being on freight workings. Goods services over the Budleigh line ceased early in 1964, but facilities at Exmouth survived for another three years. 1967 was a black year, for besides the loss of goods traffic in December the Budleigh line closed completely on 6th March and the long siding to the docks on 2nd December. Thereafter it became possible to concentrate traffic on No. 4 platform, and on 10th March, 1968 the signal box closed and all points were secured out of use, the line below Topsham being worked under "One Train" regulations. Redundant track was removed during the following year.

For some time the station was a depressing place, passengers coming and going amidst the decaying fabric and deserted platforms of an establishment far exceeding present-day needs. However, what amounts to a new station, consisting of a single platform and brick-built office and booking hall, was opened on 2nd May, 1976. It is located on the site of the old No. 2 platform and, somewhat oddly, the public entrance is situated about halfway down the old platform, part of which survives in a derelict condition at the time of writing (1979). The commodious office block of 1925 still stands, although now used for non-railway purposes, and the goods shed has found a new lease of life as a skateboard and sports centre.

OPERATING NOTE: The line to Exmouth Docks could be worked in daylight only, speed being restricted to 4 m.p.h. throughout. A member of the station staff acted as pilotman, and walked in front of the train carrying a red flag. Wagons were propelled to the docks and drawn back to Exmouth station yard.

Signalman's view of Exmouth station in 1959, with train for Exeter departing.
photo: R.C. Riley

DIAGRAM "C"
Signalling for rebuilt station, from 1925.
Not to Scale.

FORDINGBRIDGE

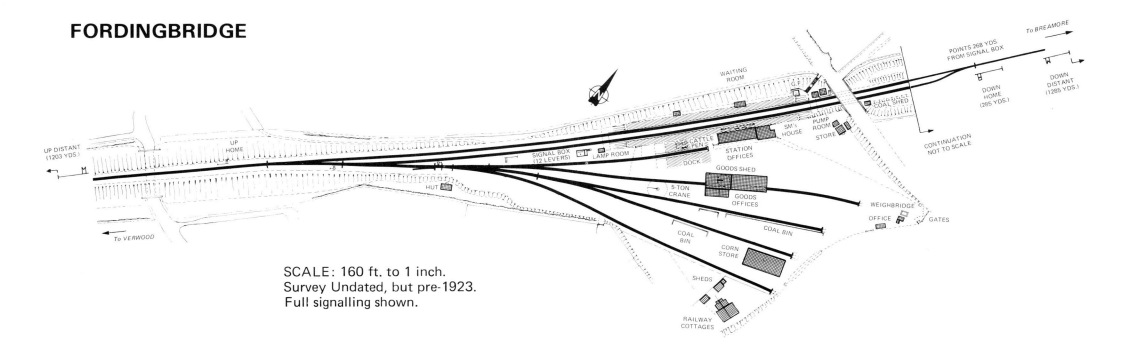

To BREAMORE

POINTS 268 YDS.
FROM SIGNAL BOX

WAITING ROOM

DOWN HOME (285 YDS.)

DOWN DISTANT (1285 YDS.)

COAL SHED

CONTINUATION NOT TO SCALE

UP DISTANT (1203 YDS.)

UP HOME

PUMP ROOM

STORE

SIGNAL BOX (12 LEVERS)

LAMP ROOM

CATTLE PENS

SM's HOUSE

STATION OFFICES

DOCK

GOODS SHED

HUT

5-TON CRANE

GOODS OFFICES

WEIGHBRIDGE

OFFICE

GATES

To VERWOOD

COAL BIN

COAL BIN

CORN STORE

SHEDS

RAILWAY COTTAGES

SCALE: 160 ft. to 1 inch.
Survey Undated, but pre-1923.
Full signalling shown.

FORDINGBRIDGE

Opened: 20.12.1866
Closed: 4.5.1964 (Completely).
Original Company: Salisbury & Dorset Junction Railway, absorbed by
L & SWR 1883.

Looking towards Verwood at the turn of the century. The large goods shed, which shows
clear signs of a fairly recent extension, can be seen behind the main station building.
photo: Lens of Sutton

This was the most important station on the cross-country link between Salisbury (Alderbury Junction) and West Moors, although it was not very conveniently sited as the centre of Fordingbridge was nearly a mile away. However, the station served a wide area of scattered population, and this was reflected in the size of the goods yard.

The main building (which incorporated offices and a house for the Station Master) was a solid brick structure, large but very plain in style. The goods shed was also of brick, and was extended considerably by the 1890s. The signal box was an example of the early "South Western" type (c. 1870) with external cross-framing, but this feature was later obscured with asbestos panels as shown in the photograph below. It originally contained ten levers, two more being added when the ground frame at the Breamore end of the Up platform was abolished and the points at that end of the loop coupled directly to the box.

The goods sidings covered a large area, but the track layout was simple enough and consisted of a fan of five sidings. No shunting neck was provided. Traffic was mainly coal, livestock and general agricultural merchandise.

The train service was thin by the standards of Southern England, and consisted mainly of six daily locals in each direction between Salisbury and Bournemouth West. Its most interesting feature was the 03.17 newspaper from Salisbury to Weymouth—a division of the West of England service. As none of the signal boxes (except Verwood) were provided with switching facilities, this meant that most of the staff on the line reported for duty at a very early hour, and as it was obviously desirable to cover the daily traffic with two turns of duty instead of three, the service finished quite early in the evening. It was therefore never possible for residents of Fordingbridge to use the train when going to evening entertainments in Poole or Bournemouth. During July and August there were additional through trains between Salisbury and Swanage and Salisbury and Weymouth, and some use was made of the line for long-distance expresses to Bournemouth at Summer weekends, but generally few people were carried, and the line was being considered for closure even before the Beeching plan was published.

Close-up study of the main buildings on the Down platform. The windows above the canopy belong to part of the Station Master's house.   *photo: Lens of Sutton*

The 12-lever signal box as it looked in later years, the original woodwork having been covered with asbestos panels by the Southern Railway.   *photo: B.L. Jackson*

GILLINGHAM (DORSET)

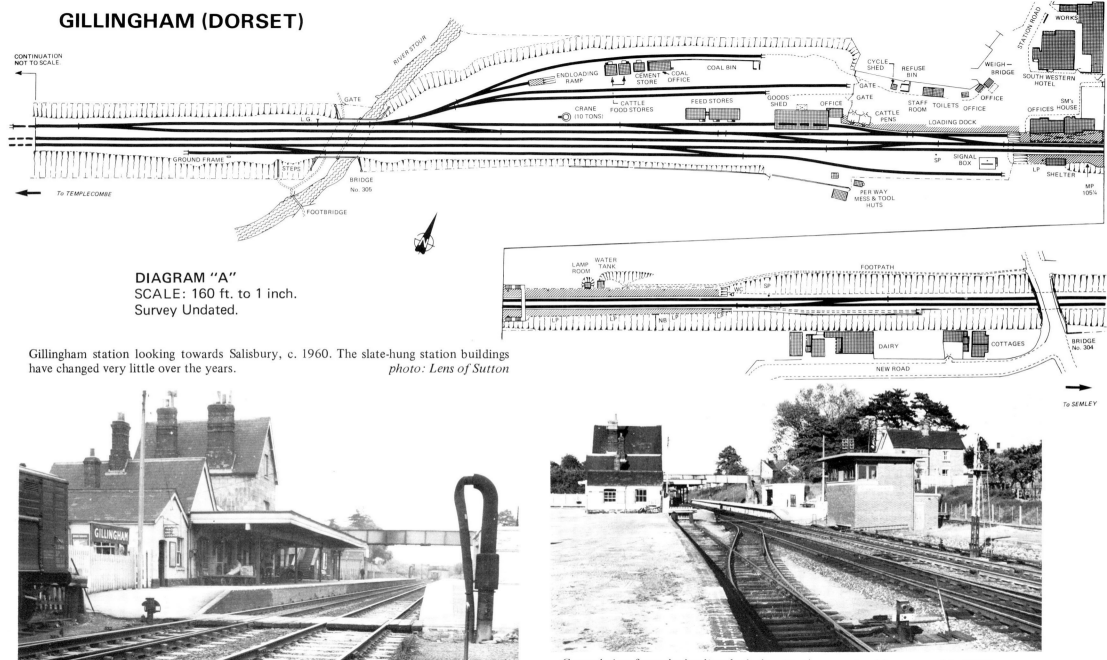

CONTINUATION NOT TO SCALE.

RIVER STOUR

ENDLOADING RAMP

CEMENT STORE

COAL OFFICE

COAL BIN

CYCLE SHED

REFUSE BIN

STATION ROAD

WORKS

WEIGH-BRIDGE

SOUTH WESTERN HOTEL

GATE

GATE

GATE

STAFF ROOM

TOILETS

OFFICE

OFFICE

SM's OFFICES

SM's HOUSE

L.G.

CRANE (10 TONS)

CATTLE FOOD STORES

FEED STORES

GOODS SHED

OFFICE

CATTLE PENS

LOADING DOCK

GROUND FRAME

STEPS

BRIDGE No. 305

FOOTBRIDGE

SP

SIGNAL BOX

LP

SHELTER

MP 105¼

To TEMPLECOMBE

PER WAY MESS & TOOL HUTS

DIAGRAM "A"
SCALE: 160 ft. to 1 inch.
Survey Undated.

LAMP ROOM

WATER TANK

FOOTPATH

WC

SP

LP

LP

NB

LP

LP

DAIRY

COTTAGES

NEW ROAD

BRIDGE No. 304

To SEMLEY

Gillingham station looking towards Salisbury, c. 1960. The slate-hung station buildings have changed very little over the years.

photo: Lens of Sutton

General view from the loading dock showing the new signal box opened in 1957.

photo: B.L. Jackson

61

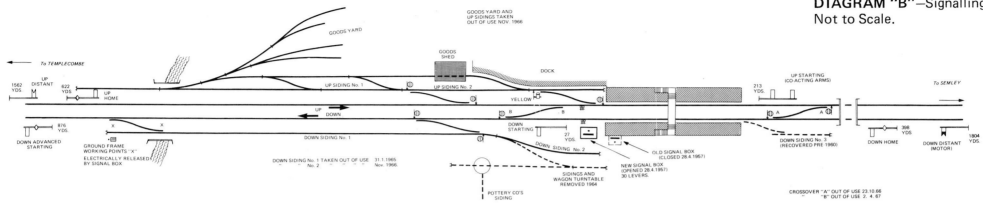

DIAGRAM "B"—Signalling
Not to Scale.

Opened: 2.5.1859
Closed: 5.4.1965 (Goods).
Original Company: Salisbury & Yeovil Railway, purchased by L & SWR 1878.

REVISED LAYOUT (SINGLING OF
LINE) BROUGHT INTO USE 2.4.67
NEW LAYOUT NOT SHOWN

GILLINGHAM (DORSET)

For the first year Gillingham formed the terminus of the line from Salisbury, but the section westward to Sherborne opened on 7th May, 1860 and Yeovil was reached on the 1st June. Trains ran through to Exeter from 19th July the same year.

As the Salisbury and Yeovil Railway was originally envisaged Gillingham was the junction for a branch to Shaftesbury. This never materialised, but it did later become a junction of sorts, the L & SWR operating a road motor service from the station yard to Mere and Zeals.

There have been few structural alterations since opening. The main buildings on the Up side (incorporating a Station Master's house) are to the design of Sir William Tite and very similar to others on the line, but they appear somewhat different by virtue of the tile-hung walls. The original footbridge had brick approach steps and an iron span, but this was replaced by a concrete one (second-hand from Dinton) when the singling scheme was being carried out in 1967. An 1870s pattern signal box stood on the Down platform until 1957 (see diagram "B"), when it was replaced by a large brick structure of BR design.

As diagram "A" shows, the goods yard was spacious, and handled a heavy general freight traffic until the Beeching era. The track layout has been subject to several minor alterations, but remained basically the same until the line was singled. The short Down Siding at the Semley end of the platform (shown dotted on the scale plan) was never connected to the new signal box. For many years there was a small engine shed on the

site of Down Siding No. 2 (see diagram "B")—probably a relic from the earliest days when Gillingham was a terminus—but this was out of use before the First World War and has long been demolished.

The line passed into Western Region control in January 1963, and was gradually run down as a through route between London and the West. Local trains were withdrawn on 7th March, 1966, the service being recast to provide semi-fast trains between Exeter and Waterloo at roughly two-hourly intervals. This paved the way for singling, and the first stage—Wilton to Templecombe—was brought into use on 2nd April, 1967. Gillingham signal box was retained to control the crossing loop.

In November 1968 "Shellstar" fertilizers (now UKF) opened a large distribution depot on the site of the goods shed, and a siding was provided on the Up side to serve it. The traffic is conveyed by a weekly block train of air-braked bogie pallet vans from Ince and Elton.

Passenger traffic—mainly long distance—is well maintained, the station being railhead for a large catchment area which includes the town of Shaftesbury.

OPERATING NOTE: GILLINGHAM POTTERY COMPANY'S SIDING (see diagram "B").

Wagons for this Company were placed in the siding by the Railway Company's shunting horses, to enable traffic to be loaded or unloaded over the boundary fence. Wagons for the works were placed on the turntable by the Railway Company, and taken from that point by employees of the Pottery Company. Engines were prohibited from passing over the turntable.

HAMPTON COURT

DIAGRAM "A"
SCALE: 160 ft. to 1 inch.
Date of Survey: 1949

Opened: 1.2.1849
Electrified: 18.6.1916
Closed: 3.5.1965 (Goods).
Original Company: L & SWR

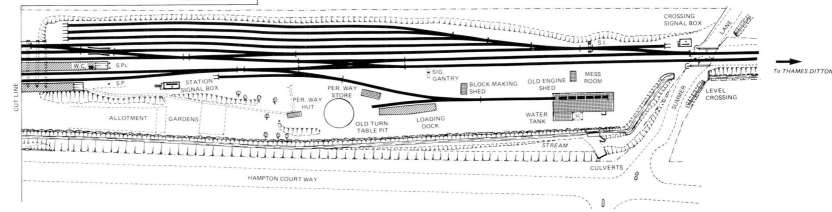

HAMPTON COURT

This suburban terminus stands at the end of a branch 1.75 miles in length which leaves the main line at Hampton Court Junction, immediately west of Surbiton. Its early history is uncertain, but until the close of the nineteenth century the station was still quite archaic. The Down line led into an arrival platform which was partially double-sided, the departure platform being alongside. Until rebuilding it was an "open" station, tickets being examined at a separate ticket platform on the approach side of the station and occupying a site between the signal gantry and mess room shown on the scale plan. Siding capacity was very limited, and there was no engine shed until July 1895. The station buildings were constructed in a Jacobean style while the contemporary goods shed almost resembled a tythe barn.

In 1899 the station was enlarged and the track layout greatly extended, a new 45-lever station signal box being installed to replace the original 12-lever box. Diagram "B" shows the new layout as first installed. The viaduct was widened, a third platform was provided, and the signalling was laid out to allow all three platforms to be used by both arrivals and departures.

Steam engines became a rarity at a very early date, the branch being included in the first L & SWR electrification scheme, but they continued to appear on excursions carrying

visitors to nearby Hampton Court Palace, and even today loco-hauled trains conveying this traffic are not unusual. The engine shed probably went out of regular use with the introduction of electric trains in 1916, but otherwise the only changes were the provision of two additional berthing sidings on the Up side and removal of the scissors crossovers between platforms 2 and 3. A mishap destroyed the Crossing Signal Box in November 1947, a temporary box being provided on the Thames Ditton side of the gates. This lasted for ten years, being eventually removed when the new signal box controlling the entire layout was opened on 28th April, 1957.

Inevitably there has been some running down of the station over the years. The canopy on No. 3 platform once extended to a point opposite that on the island platform as indicated on Diagram "A", but it was shortened as long ago as the 1920s. The remaining canopy received the same treatment during the 1960s, so that today the platforms are largely uncovered. Withdrawal of goods services in 1965 allowed the layout to be somewhat simplified (see diagram "C"), and on 1st March 1970 signalling was placed under the control of a new panel box at Surbiton. However, the signal box at Hampton Court remained in use as a gate box until full lifting barriers, controlled from Surbiton with the aid of closed-circuit television, were brought into use on 23rd September, 1979.

63

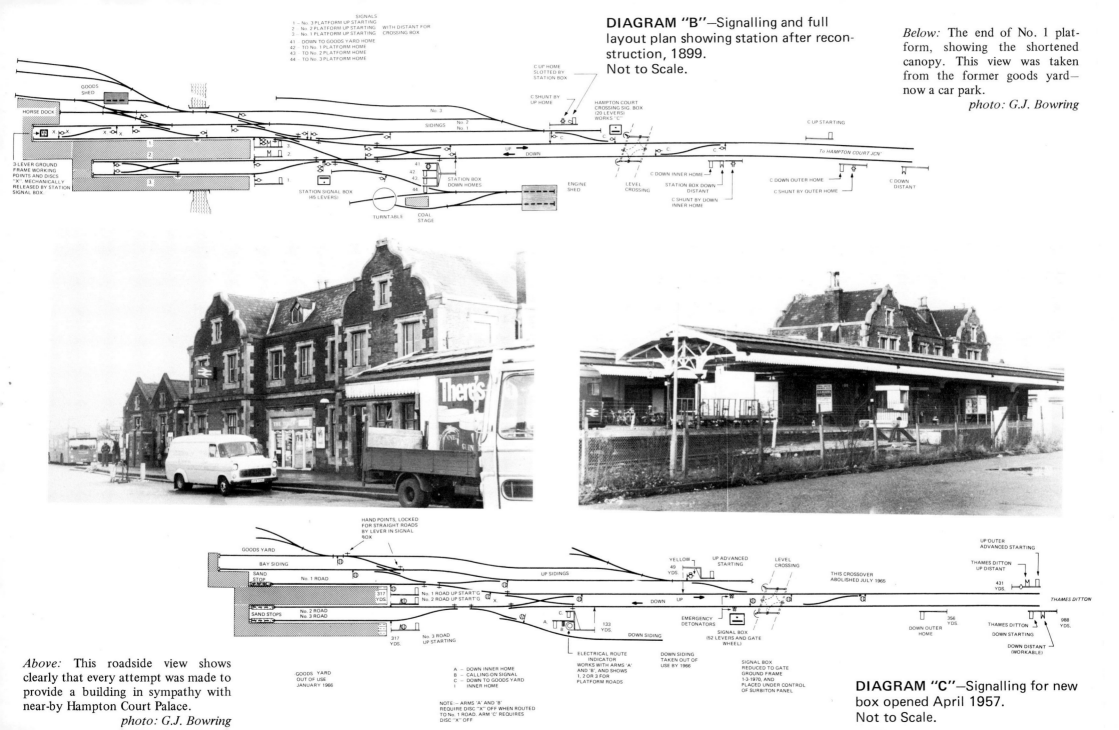

DIAGRAM "B"—Signalling and full layout plan showing station after reconstruction, 1899. Not to Scale.

Below: The end of No. 1 platform, showing the shortened canopy. This view was taken from the former goods yard—now a car park.

photo: G.J. Bowring

Above: This roadside view shows clearly that every attempt was made to provide a building in sympathy with near-by Hampton Court Palace.

photo: G.J. Bowring

DIAGRAM "C"—Signalling for new box opened April 1957. Not to Scale.

HAMWORTHY JUNCTION

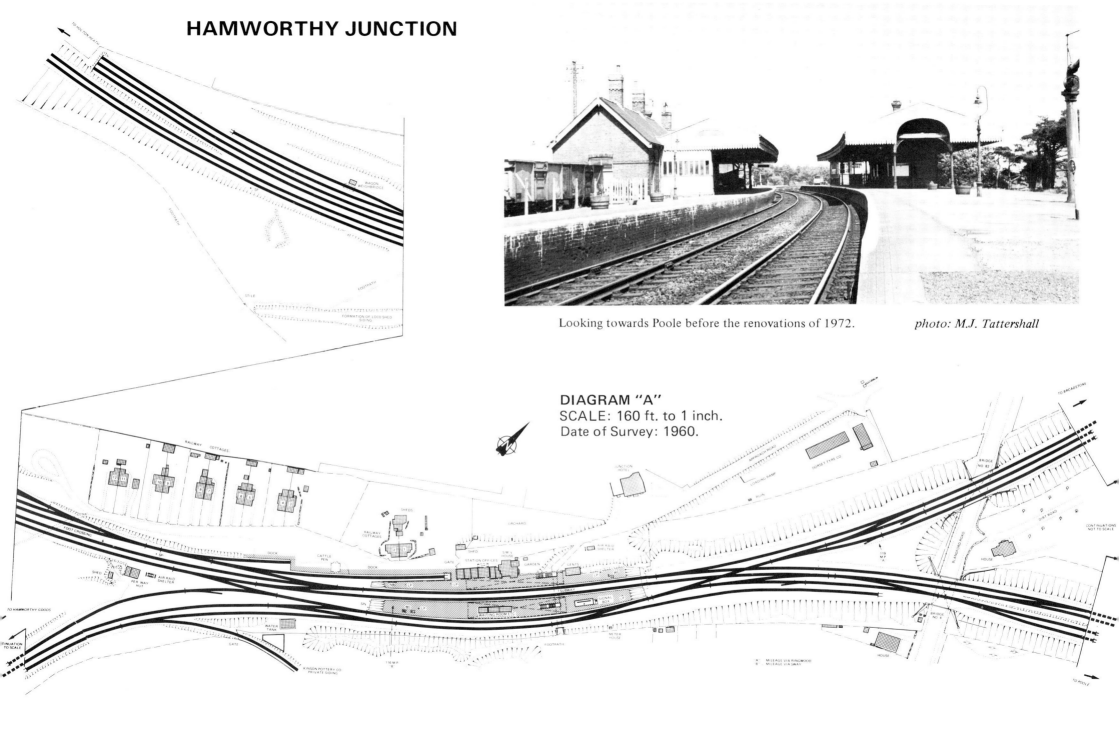

Looking towards Poole before the renovations of 1972.

photo: M.J. Tattershall

DIAGRAM "A"
SCALE: 160 ft. to 1 inch.
Date of Survey: 1960.

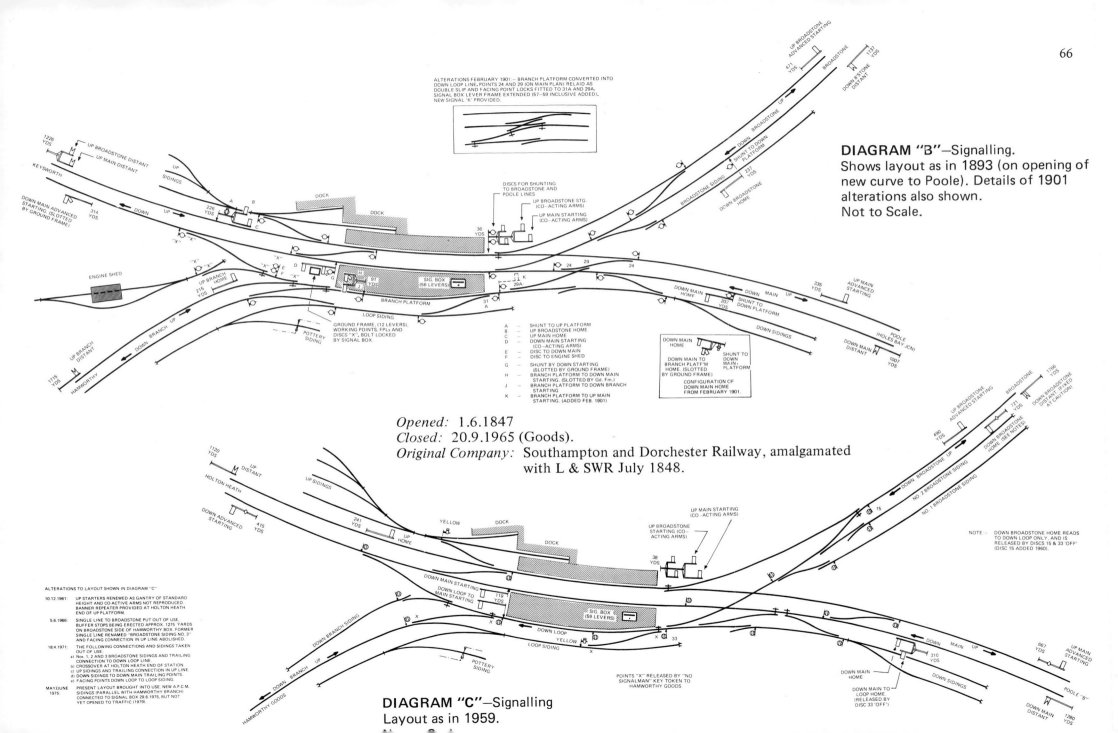

ALTERATIONS FEBRUARY 1901:— BRANCH PLATFORM CONVERTED INTO DOWN LOOP LINE. POINTS 24 AND 29 (ON MAIN PLAN) RELAID AS DOUBLE SLIP AND FACING POINT LOCKS FITTED TO 31A AND 29A. SIGNAL BOX LEVER FRAME EXTENDED (57—59 INCLUSIVE ADDED). NEW SIGNAL "K" PROVIDED.

DIAGRAM "B"—Signalling.
Shows layout as in 1893 (on opening of new curve to Poole). Details of 1901 alterations also shown.
Not to Scale.

A — SHUNT TO UP PLATFORM
B — UP BROADSTONE HOME
C — UP MAIN HOME
D — DOWN MAIN STARTING (CO—ACTING ARMS)
E — DISC TO DOWN MAIN
F — DISC TO ENGINE SHED
G — SHUNT BY DOWN STARTING (SLOTTED BY GROUND FRAME)
H — BRANCH PLATFORM TO DOWN MAIN STARTING. (SLOTTED BY Gd. Frm.)
J — BRANCH PLATFORM TO DOWN BRANCH STARTING
K — BRANCH PLATFORM TO UP MAIN STARTING. (ADDED FEB. 1901)

DOWN MAIN HOME
DOWN MAIN TO BRANCH PLATF'M HOME. (SLOTTED BY GROUND FRAME)
SHUNT TO DOWN MAIN PLATFORM
CONFIGURATION OF DOWN MAIN HOME FROM FEBRUARY 1901.

GROUND FRAME, (12 LEVERS), WORKING POINTS, FPLs AND DISCS "X", BOLT LOCKED BY SIGNAL BOX.

DISCS FOR SHUNTING TO BROADSTONE AND POOLE LINES

Opened: 1.6.1847
Closed: 20.9.1965 (Goods).
Original Company: Southampton and Dorchester Railway, amalgamated with L & SWR July 1848.

NOTE:— DOWN BROADSTONE HOME READS TO DOWN LOOP ONLY, AND IS RELEASED BY DISCS 15 & 33 'OFF'. (DISC 15 ADDED 1960).

ALTERATIONS TO LAYOUT SHOWN IN DIAGRAM "C".

10.12.1961: UP STARTERS RENEWED AS GANTRY OF STANDARD HEIGHT AND CO-ACTIVE ARMS NOT REPRODUCED. BANNER REPEATER PROVIDED AT HOLTON HEATH END OF UP PLATFORM.

5.6.1966: SINGLE LINE TO BROADSTONE PUT OUT OF USE, BUFFER STOPS BEING ERECTED APPROX. 1275 YARDS ON BROADSTONE SIDE OF HAMWORTHY BOX. FORMER SINGLE LINE RENAMED "BROADSTONE SIDING NO. 3" AND FACING CONNECTION IN UP LINE ABOLISHED.

18.4.1971: THE FOLLOWING CONNECTIONS AND SIDINGS TAKEN OUT OF USE:
a) Nos. 1, 2 AND 3 BROADSTONE SIDINGS AND TRAILING CONNECTION TO DOWN LOOP LINE.
b) CROSSOVER AT HOLTON HEATH END OF STATION.
c) UP SIDINGS AND TRAILING CONNECTION IN UP LINE.
d) DOWN SIDINGS AND DOWN MAIN TRAILING POINTS.
e) FACING POINTS DOWN LOOP TO LOOP SIDING.

MAY/JUNE 1975: PRESENT LAYOUT BROUGHT INTO USE. NEW A.P.C.M. SIDINGS (PARALLEL WITH HAMWORTHY BRANCH) CONNECTED TO SIGNAL BOX 29.6.1975, BUT NOT YET OPENED TO TRAFFIC (1979).

POINTS "X" RELEASED BY "NO SIGNALMAN" KEY TOKEN TO HAMWORTHY GOODS.

DIAGRAM "C"—Signalling
Layout as in 1959.

HAMWORTHY JUNCTION

Opened as "Poole Junction", the original station served purely as an interchange point for the Poole (later "Hamworthy") branch. It was renamed on 2nd December, 1872, when the new line was opened between Broadstone and a more centrally-situated station in Poole. This new line robbed both station and branch of much importance, but the construction of the Holes Bay Curve (providing a direct link between Bournemouth/Poole and Dorchester) caused the station to be completely rebuilt in 1892/93, the existing signal box on the island platform being installed at that time. The curve was opened to goods traffic on 18th May, 1893, passengers following on 1st June the same year. Diagram "B" shows the layout and signalling of the period.

Once Poole had secured a proper main line station in the heart of the town the Hamworthy branch became a white elephant, and the passenger service was withdrawn on 1st July, 1896. In 1901 the former Branch Platform line was converted into a Down Loop, the necessary signalling alterations being shown on diagram "B", and further changes took place on 25th November, 1905 when the branch was reduced to single track and down-graded to a goods line. "One Engine in Steam" working was introduced, the signal box at the branch terminus being closed. Passenger trains reappeared briefly on the Hamworthy branch during the First World War, a service for shipyard workers running to a new platform at Lake, but to avoid more costly signalling alterations to cater for such temporary traffic the points leading from the single line were fitted with facing point locks operated by ground levers. Freight traffic over the branch greatly increased in the '30s, and on 4th July, 1938 the method of working was altered to "No Signalman" key token.

Despite the grandiose suffix "Junction", the station sank into obscurity after 1896. Only the slowest trains called, and there was virtually no interchange traffic with the Broadstone line. It functioned mainly as a berthing point for spare carriages and for wagons awaiting acceptance at Hamworthy.

The engine shed once had an allocation of two locomotives; the Hamworthy shunter and a "B4" for working Poole Quay. It was closed on 3rd May, 1954, and thereafter motive power was supplied by Bournemouth depot. The former engine shed siding was then slewed onto the formation of the old Up Branch line to provide additional accommodation for carriage storage, this work being carried out in December 1956.

In recent years there have been so many alterations to the layout that it is impossible to mention them all. The original main line to Broadstone was singled on 11th December, 1932, and on 2nd November, 1947 the junction itself was relaid in such a manner that trains leaving the Broadstone line had to pass through the Down Loop, diagram "C" showing this arrangement. In an attempt to bring the reader reasonably up to date, later changes are given in tabular form.

Although the sidings were generally well filled with wagons freight traffic actually handled at the station was light; in latter years it was mainly coal. Housing development has now taken place near the railway, some of it on the site of the old Up Sidings, and passenger business has revived. The diesel service implemented on 10th July, 1967 provided for alternate trains to call at the station, thus providing a two-hourly interval service in each direction, but this was increased to hourly with the new timetable published in May 1979. Freight traffic over the Hamworthy branch remains heavy by present-day standards, and includes steel, imported motor cars and "Freightliners". Less happy has been the fate of the Broadstone line, which closed completely on 4th May, 1964. The track was later removed, but it was another eight years before the "Junction" was dropped from the station name on 1st May, 1972! That year the main buildings were given a "face lift" and the large canopy on the Down platform, together with all buildings on that side, was demolished and replaced by 'bus-shelter style waiting facilities.

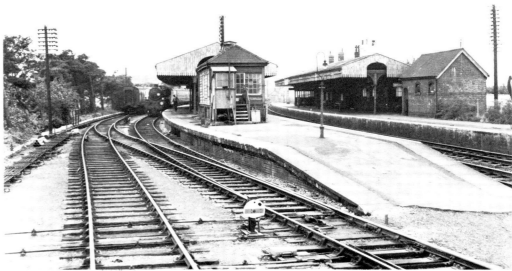

A once-familiar scene at Hamworthy Junction—carriage shunting on the Down Loop line.
photo: R.C. Riley

Looking towards Holton Heath from the end of the Up platform.　　*photo: R.C. Riley*

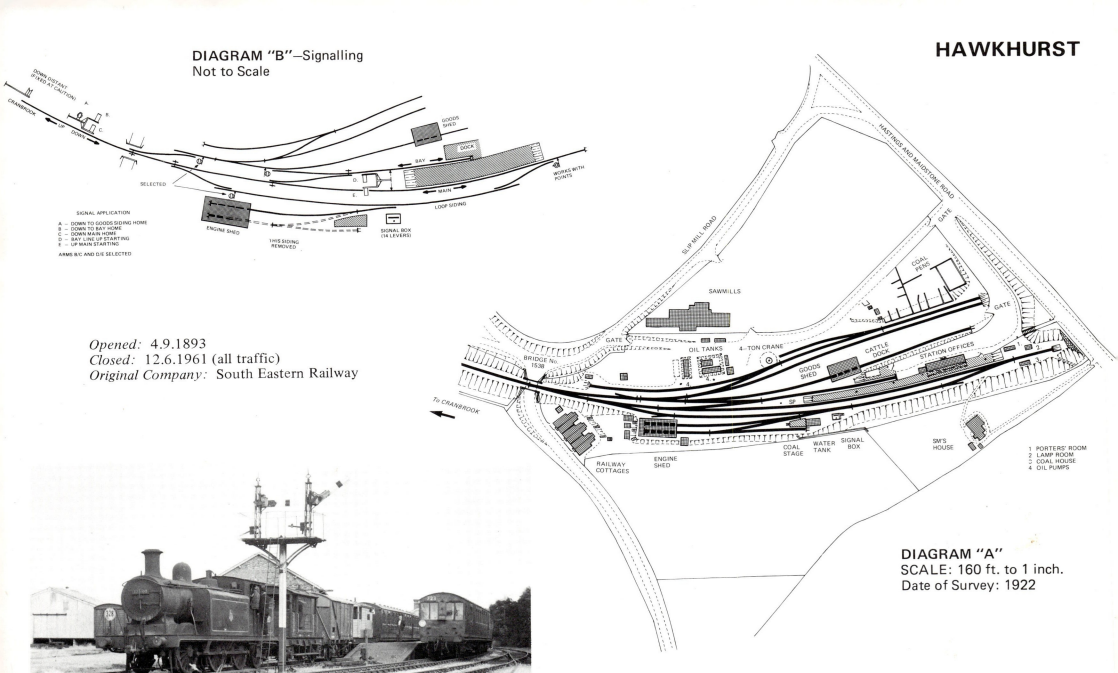

HAWKHURST

DIAGRAM "B"—Signalling
Not to Scale

DOWN DISTANT
(FIXED AT CAUTION)

A

CRANBROOK

B.

UP   DOWN

C.

GOODS
SHED

DOCK

BAY

WORKS WITH
POINTS

MAIN

SELECTED

D.

E.

LOOP SIDING

SIGNAL APPLICATION

A — DOWN TO GOODS SIDING HOME
B — DOWN TO BAY HOME
C — DOWN MAIN HOME
D — BAY LINE UP STARTING
E — UP MAIN STARTING

ARMS B/C AND D/E SELECTED

ENGINE SHED

THIS SIDING
REMOVED

SIGNAL BOX
(14 LEVERS)

Opened: 4.9.1893
Closed: 12.6.1961 (all traffic)
Original Company: South Eastern Railway

HASTINGS AND MAIDSTONE ROAD

SLIP MILL ROAD

GATE

GATE

COAL
PENS

SAWMILLS

GATE

GATE

OIL TANKS

4-TON CRANE

CATTLE
DOCK

STATION OFFICES

BRIDGE No.
1538

GOODS
SHED

SP

To CRANBROOK

SM'S
HOUSE

RAILWAY
COTTAGES

ENGINE
SHED

COAL
STAGE

WATER
TANK

SIGNAL
BOX

1 PORTERS' ROOM
2 LAMP ROOM
3 COAL HOUSE
4 OIL PUMPS

DIAGRAM "A"
SCALE: 160 ft. to 1 inch.
Date of Survey: 1922

Busy scene at Hawkhurst. The "push-and-pull" train for Paddock Wood is leaving the main platform as the goods is made up in the bay. The very overgrown track in the extreme right-hand corner leads to the engine shed.
photo: J.H. Aston

The main platform at Hawkhurst as viewed from the buffer stops in May 1961. The ground signal in the foreground dates from SE & CR days. *photo: J. Scrace*

HAWKHURST

Hawhurst was reached by an extension of the Paddock Wood and Cranbrook Railway, a local company that had been in financial difficulties in 1882 and was subsequently swallowed up by the South Eastern. The engineer for construction of the line was the famous Colonel H. F. Stephens, and it carried his stamp in steep gradients and stations built cheaply of wood and corrugated iron. Hopes were entertained that the branch might one day be extended to Rye, the terminus at Hawkhurst being laid out as a through station to facilitate this, but no further work was undertaken.

Most stations on the branch were inconveniently sited, Hawkhurst being no exception, and passenger traffic became light in latter years, but they came to life with the annual influx of hop pickers, many "specials" being run during the three-week season. Because the engine release spur at Hawkhurst was very short and only suitable for tank engines, a "pull-off" loco had to be provided whenever such trains were worked through by main line engines. Most of the traffic was lost by 1959, the normal weekday service of seven-to-ten "push-and-pull" trains being sufficient thereafter.

The engine shed was out of use by 1931, after which the engine for the first Up passenger train came down with an early morning goods. At that time there were two goods trips per day, but in 1956 sundries traffic was concentrated on Etchingham, and consequently the goods service was reduced to one trip daily worked by the Paddock Wood diesel shunter, the main traffic being coal.

The branch handled through trains from Charing Cross in connection with end-of-term traffic at Benenden School. Scholars used Cranbrook Station, but their luggage was loaded into parcel vans at Hawkhurst and despatched by the daily goods. Latterly a large number of pot-plants for Messrs. F. W. Woolworth were also forwarded, the vans being attached at the rear of the last Up train each evening, which departed from Hawkhurst formed "push-and-pull" set-engine-vans.

The station site is currently (1979) occupied by the Kent Turnery Co. and although the main building has disappeared, the signal box, platforms and several other structures survive in recognisable condition.

Looking towards the buffer stops.

photo: R.C. Riley

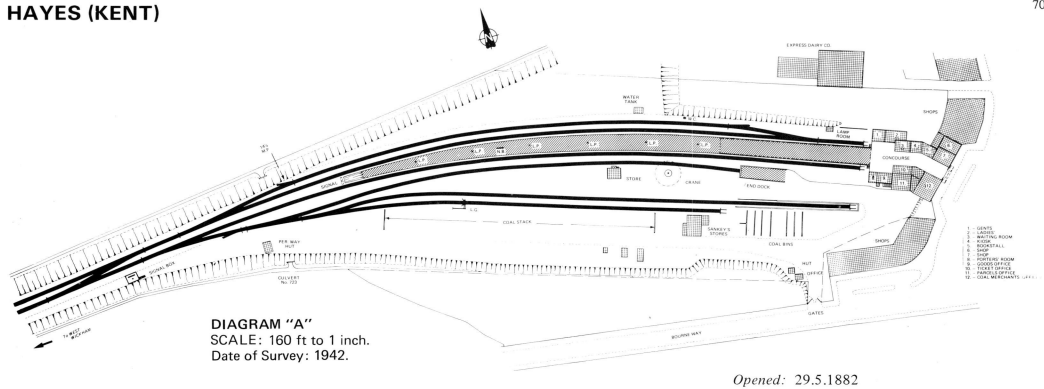

DIAGRAM "A"
SCALE: 160 ft to 1 inch.
Date of Survey: 1942.

Opened: 29.5.1882
Electrified: 28.2.1926
Closed: 19.4.1965 (Goods)
Original Company: South Eastern Railway

HAYES (KENT)

This branch from the Mid-Kent line was double track from the outset although quite rural in character. The station was provided with a wide platform and single-storey wooden building similar in style to the other two on the branch. Resignalling was carried out in 1899, this work including an additional connection to the goods yard (see diagram "B"). Unusually for a terminal, there has never been an engine shed, but there was a turntable at the end of the main platform line for many years.

After the turn of the century the traffic on the line began to change from that of a country branch with a shuttle service to Elmers End to that of an outer-suburban "commuter" line with through trains to Charing Cross. By the 1920s there was enough potential traffic for the Southern to include it in one of their early electrification schemes, but few other alterations were carried out until 1935 when the station was rebuilt. This

work involved considerable lengthening of the platforms and consequent alterations to the track layout, a new signal box being provided. Diagram "C" and the scale plan show the station in this form. The new building is functional and typically "Southern", having a large covered concourse flanked by various offices. The frontage was bombed in 1941, and was not rebuilt until 1956.

Goods traffic was never of much importance and consisted mainly of coal for local merchants. Facilities were withdrawn in 1965, and the sidings were later removed (see diagram "C" for dates). Part of the goods yard site (nearest the station offices) then became a car park, the remainder being let to a local firm. In 1975 the signal box was abolished, the area coming under the control of London Bridge Panel.

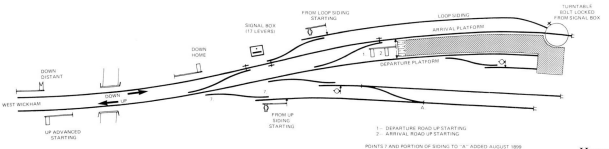

DIAGRAM "B"—Signalling for old layout, 1900.
Not to Scale.

Hayes station as the Southern rebuilt it. This picture was taken around 1960 from a similar position to that adopted by the photographer in the older view, thus making the changes all the more obvious.
photo: Lens of Sutton

Train in main platform c. 1910. The turntable was at the far end of the platform behind the train.
photo: Lens of Sutton

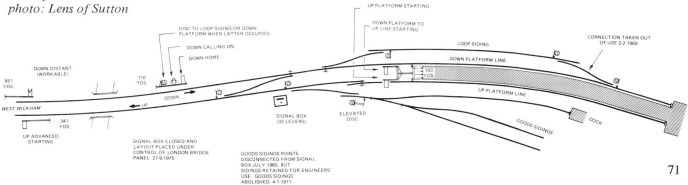

DIAGRAM "C"—Signalling for remodelled layout, 1947.
Not to Scale.

71

HAYLING ISLAND

SCALE: 160 ft. to 1 inch.
Survey Undated

Opened: 17.7.1867
Closed: 4.11.1963
Original Company: Hayling Island Railway,
amalgamated with
LB & SCR 1872

Former LB & SCR "Terrier" No. 32650 prepares to depart from the main platform with a train for Havant. Note the loco coaling stage between the two sidings on the left.
photo: J.H. Aston

Summer Saturday at Hayling Island. A "Terrier" runs round its train whilst (in the background) a train for Havant leaves the bay.
photo: R.C. Riley

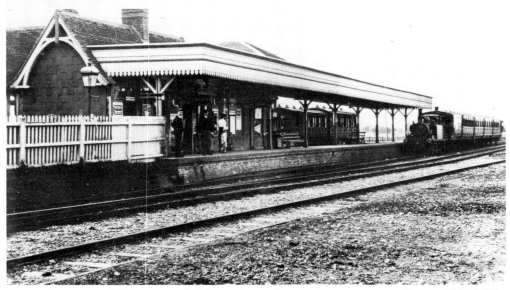

Looking towards Havant, probably not long after the improvements of around 1900. The newer woodwork of the canopy extension can plainly be seen.
photo: Lens of Sutton

Right: Ex-LB & SCR "Terrier" No. 32662 on arrival with a train from Havant.   *photo: R.C. Riley*

HAYLING ISLAND

The station was originally called "South Hayling", and received the name "Hayling Island" on 1st June, 1892. The O.S. map of 1898 shows early accommodation to have been very simple: only the main platform existed, and the yard consisted of two sidings and a run-round loop. A third siding terminated in a small engine shed just north of the platform.

The single and two-storey platform buildings were both original, although the single-storey ticket office was enlarged at the rear in the late 1890s. The canopy alongside the building was provided around the same time.

Major alterations took place between 1897 and 1900, the engine shed being demolished and the track which served it extended to form a bay platform. The canopy was also doubled in length, and a coal stage was erected in the position indicated on the scale plan. The large goods shed also dates from this period, as does the end loading dock, but the third siding east of the goods shed seems to have been added later.

The station escaped any noticeable change during Southern Railway rule apart from the replacement of some signals with standard "rail-built" types. The Bay Starting signal survived as an LB & SCR lower quadrant until closure. The canopy in front of the station was removed in the 1950s, and after the line was closed most of the buildings were demolished. However, at the time of writing (1979) the goods shed remains intact.

Closure of this line was an unfortunate business brought about, not by lack of traffic, but by the condition of the line's chief engineering feature—the long wooden bridge linking Hayling to the mainland. This structure had always been something of a nuisance as it imposed a weight restriction so severe that the only locomotives permitted were the ex-LB & SCR "Terrier" tanks. These had a weight of only 28 tons 5 cwt. This in turn limited the number of vehicles that could be conveyed, so no matter how heavy the holiday traffic, the maximum load of any one train was four coaches and a van for perambulators. There were no intermediate crossing loops, and some smart working was required to operate the half-hourly interval service at Summer weekends. One odd feature was that branch engines could not be serviced in one go; the water supply was at Havant and the coal at Hayling!

Below: The miniscule signal box at Hayling Island, with empty stock being shunted into the bay.   *photo: C.L. Caddy*

HERNE BAY

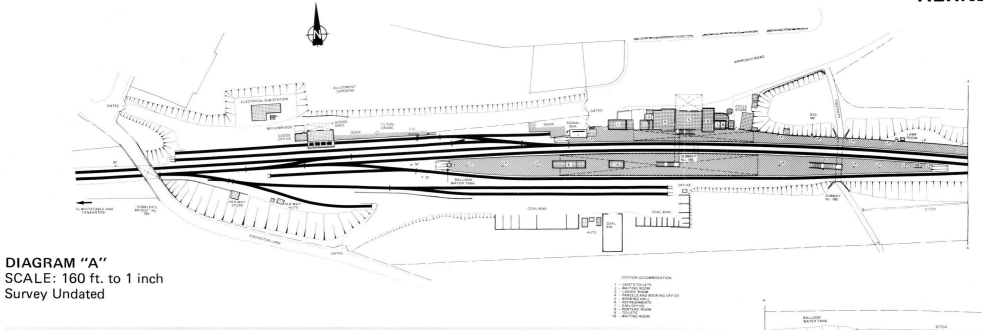

DIAGRAM "A"
SCALE: 160 ft. to 1 inch
Survey Undated

STATION ACCOMMODATION

1 – GENT'S TOILETS
2 – WAITING ROOM
3 – LADIES' ROOM
4 – PARCELS AND BOOKING OFFICE
5 – BOOKING HALL
6 – REFRESHMENTS
7 – S.M's OFFICE
8 – PORTERS' ROOM
9 – TOILETS
10 – WAITING ROOM

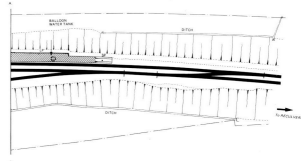

Opened: 13.7.1861
Electrified: 15.6.1959
Closed: 7.10.1968 (Goods)
Original Company: Herne Bay and Faversham
Railway, purchased by
LC & DR 1871

Looking east in pre-electrification days.
photo: H.C. Casserley

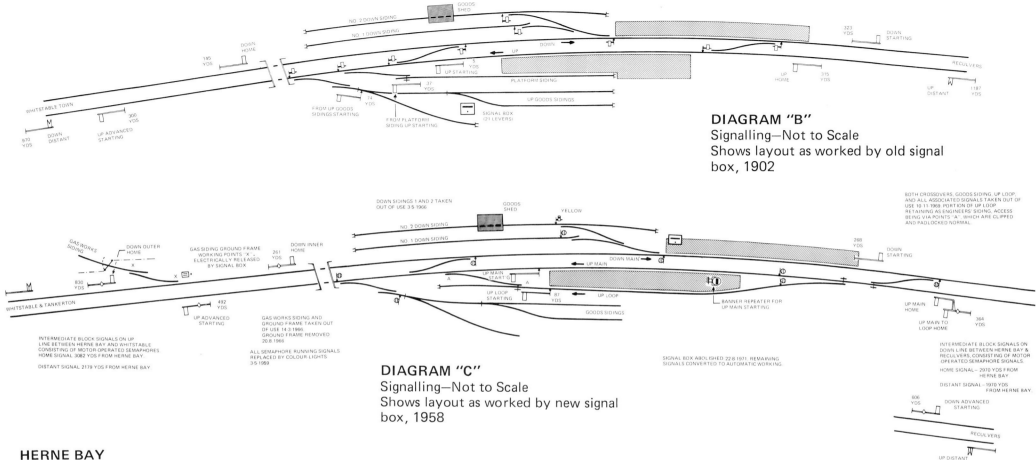

DIAGRAM "B"
Signalling—Not to Scale
Shows layout as worked by old signal box, 1902

DIAGRAM "C"
Signalling—Not to Scale
Shows layout as worked by new signal box, 1958

HERNE BAY

For a little over two years this station (called "Herne Bay and Hampton-on-Sea" until March 1951) was the terminus of a line from Faversham, the extension to Ramsgate opening on 5th October, 1863. The property of a local Company, it was leased and worked by the "Chatham" from the outset, and acquired by that Company in 1871.

The main buildings on the Down platform are all that remain of the original station, the Up side having been reconstructed by the SR as part of their general improvements to the Thanet lines in 1926. Both platforms were lengthened at the eastern end and the old dead-end bay converted into an Up Loop, the newly-formed island receiving a new canopy and buildings. A new signal box was also provided to control this extended layout (compare diagrams "B" and "C").

Original goods facilities were rather limited and consisted of two sidings on the Down side (only one of which had access for loading or unloading), a goods shed and two loading docks. Coal sidings on the Up side were added in 1902, and a private siding into the gas works followed in 1914. The only alteration in connection with electrification was the replacement of the semaphore running signals with colour-lights, and dates of this and subsequent alterations are given on diagram "C". General goods traffic ceased from 16th October, 1965, but coal continued to be handled in the Up yard until 1968. Since then the layout has been reduced to the barest minimum and the signal box has closed, the remaining colour-light signals being converted to automatic operation.

HOLSWORTHY

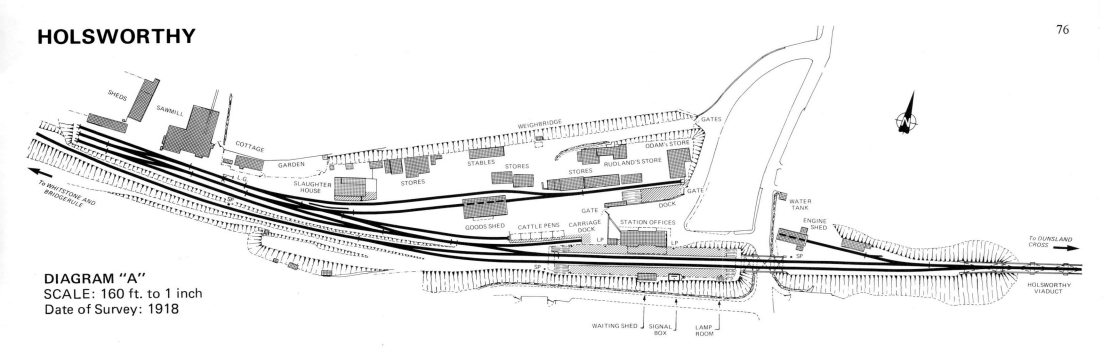

DIAGRAM "A"
SCALE: 160 ft. to 1 inch
Date of Survey: 1918

Looking towards Dunsland Cross about 1905. The engine shed is just visible between the rear of the train and the station building.   *photo: Lens of Sutton*

The Down platform waiting shed and signal box c. 1960.   *photo: Lens of Sutton*

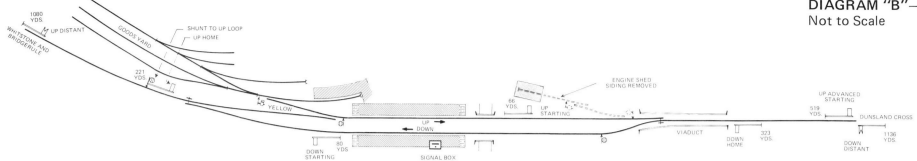

1080 YDS.
WHITSTONE AND BRIDGERULE
UP DISTANT
SHUNT TO UP LOOP
UP HOME
GOODS YARD
221 YDS.
YELLOW
ENGINE SHED SIDING REMOVED
66 YDS.
UP STARTING
UP ADVANCED STARTING
519 YDS.
DUNSLAND CROSS
UP
DOWN
VIADUCT
DOWN HOME
323 YDS.
DOWN DISTANT
1136 YDS.
80 YDS.
DOWN STARTING
SIGNAL BOX (20 LEVERS)

Opened: 20.1.1879
Closed: 7.9.1964 (Goods)
Closed: 3.10.1966 (Passengers)
Original Company: L & SWR

HOLSWORTHY

Powers for a line to Bude were obtained as early as 1865, but they lapsed, and when the scheme was finally revived it was decided to proceed only as far as Holsworthy. The original station of 1879 was therefore a terminus, but the L & SWR operated a smart horse-bus service to Bude in connection with the trains.

Little is known about arrangements at the original station, as no plans or photographs appear to have survived, but the Board of Trade report states that a turntable was provided and that traffic was controlled by Train Staff and Ticket, the signal box at Holsworthy containing ten levers. The station was approached across Holsworthy Viaduct—a structure of nine 50 ft spans and the first work of that size to be built entirely of concrete.

When the line was extended to Bude (opened 11th August, 1898) the station was rebuilt in the form illustrated here and a new 20-lever signal box installed. The engine shed and turntable survived for a time, although now little used as the main depot for engines had been transferred to Bude. The turntable was abolished on 1st January, 1911, and is therefore missing on diagram "A", but the shed itself lasted into the 1920s.

For many years the line enjoyed through carriages to Waterloo, but these were withdrawn following transfer to the Western Region in January 1963, and for the last few months the service was operated entirely by diesel multiple units running as "locals" between Okehampton and Bude.

The goods yard was large and unusually complicated for a branch line station. Short trains could be run round without fouling the main lines, and the only item that was not provided was a yard crane—although there was one capable of lifting two tons in the goods shed.

Holsworthy station buildings seen from the road. Photographed in 1963.

photo: J.S. Nicholas

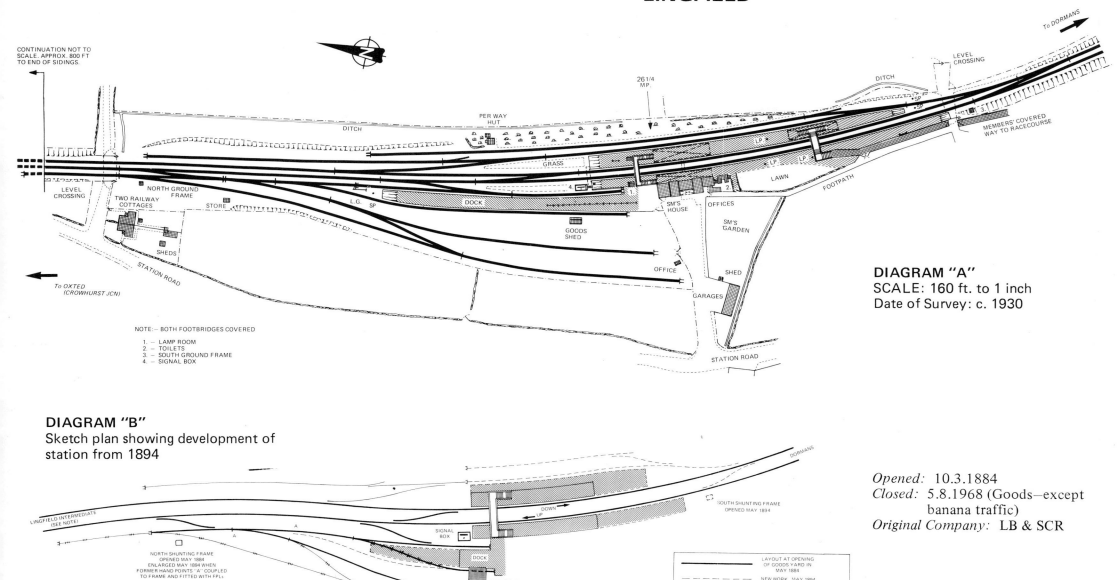

CONTINUATION NOT TO SCALE. APPROX. 800 FT TO END OF SIDINGS.

To DORMANS

LEVEL CROSSING

DITCH

26 1/4 M.P.

PER WAY HUT

DITCH

LEVEL CROSSING

SP
SP

MEMBERS' COVERED WAY TO RACECOURSE

3.

GRASS

LP

TWO RAILWAY COTTAGES

NORTH GROUND FRAME

STORE

4.

L.G. SP

DOCK

LP

LP

LP

1.

SM'S HOUSE

OFFICES

2.

LAWN

FOOTPATH

LEVEL CROSSING

STATION ROAD

SHEDS

GOODS SHED

SM'S GARDEN

OFFICE

SHED

GARAGES

To OXTED (CROWHURST JCN)

STATION ROAD

NOTE:— BOTH FOOTBRIDGES COVERED

1. — LAMP ROOM
2. — TOILETS
3. — SOUTH GROUND FRAME
4. — SIGNAL BOX

DIAGRAM "A"
SCALE: 160 ft. to 1 inch
Date of Survey: c. 1930

DIAGRAM "B"
Sketch plan showing development of station from 1894

DORMANS

LINGFIELD INTERMEDIATE (SEE NOTE)

A

A

DOWN
UP

SOUTH SHUNTING FRAME OPENED MAY 1894

SIGNAL BOX

DOCK

NORTH SHUNTING FRAME OPENED MAY 1884 ENLARGED MAY 1894 WHEN FORMER HAND POINTS "A" COUPLED TO FRAME AND FITTED WITH FPLs

GOODS SHED (SEE TEXT)

NOTE:— LINGFIELD INTERMEDIATE BOX OPENED SEPT. 1899. BLOCK SECTION PREVIOUSLY TO CROWHURST JCN. NORTH

LAYOUT AT OPENING OF GOODS YARD IN MAY 1884

NEW WORK MAY 1894

XXXXX TAKEN OUT MAY 1894

ADDITIONAL SIDING AND CONNECTION NOVEMBER 1894

EXTENSIONS LATER THAN 1894

Opened: 10.3.1884
Closed: 5.8.1968 (Goods—except banana traffic)
Original Company: LB & SCR

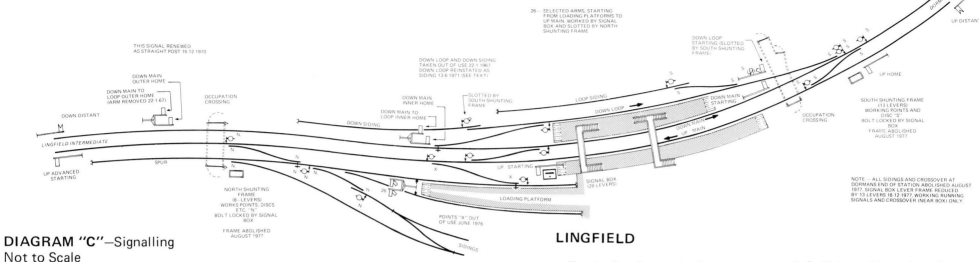

26 — SELECTED ARMS, STARTING FROM LOADING PLATFORMS TO UP MAIN. WORKED BY SIGNAL BOX AND SLOTTED BY NORTH SHUNTING FRAME

DOWN ADVANCED STARTING

DORMANS

UP DISTANT

DOWN LOOP STARTING (SLOTTED BY SOUTH SHUNTING FRAME)

UP HOME

THIS SIGNAL RENEWED AS STRAIGHT POST 15.12.1970

DOWN MAIN OUTER HOME

DOWN MAIN TO LOOP OUTER HOME (ARM REMOVED 22.1.67)

OCCUPATION CROSSING

DOWN LOOP AND DOWN SIDING TAKEN OUT OF USE 22.1.1967 DOWN LOOP REINSTATED AS SIDING 13.6.1971 (SEE TEXT)

DOWN MAIN INNER HOME

—SLOTTED BY SOUTH SHUNTING FRAME

LOOP SIDING

DOWN LOOP

DOWN MAIN STARTING

SOUTH SHUNTING FRAME (13 LEVERS) WORKING POINTS AND DISC "S" BOLT LOCKED BY SIGNAL BOX FRAME ABOLISHED AUGUST 1977

DOWN DISTANT

DOWN SIDING

DOWN MAIN TO LOOP INNER HOME

DOWN MAIN UP MAIN

OCCUPATION CROSSING

LINGFIELD INTERMEDIATE

UP STARTING

UP HOME

UP ADVANCED STARTING

SPUR

NORTH SHUNTING FRAME (8 — LEVERS) WORKS POINTS, DISCS ETC. "N" BOLT LOCKED BY SIGNAL BOX

FRAME ABOLISHED AUGUST 1977

26

LOADING PLATFORM

SIGNAL BOX (29 LEVERS)

NOTE — ALL SIDINGS AND CROSSOVER AT DORMANS END OF STATION ABOLISHED AUGUST 1977. SIGNAL BOX LEVER FRAME REDUCED BY 13 LEVERS 18.12.1977, WORKING RUNNING SIGNALS AND CROSSOVER (NEAR BOX) ONLY.

POINTS "X" OUT OF USE JUNE 1976

SIDINGS

DIAGRAM "C"—Signalling
Not to Scale
Date of layout: 1913

LINGFIELD

For the first few weeks there were no goods facilities at this station, the two sidings on the Up side, loading dock, and goods shed being added in May 1884 (see diagram "B"). Development might well have stopped there, but Lingfield Racecourse was opened in 1890. The resulting occasional large crowds were handled with existing limited facilities for a time, but the station was considerably extended in 1894, the extent of the work being shown on diagram "B". The Down platform became an island, and the loading dock behind the signal box was extended to allow it to be used as a departure platform for race specials. For this reason the two sidings serving the dock were signalled as passenger lines. Other alterations of the time included demolition of the original goods shed and its replacement with a small lineside structure as shown on the scale plan, and a second covered footbridge at the South end of the platforms giving direct access to a covered way leading to the racecourse. Many of these improvements could have become redundant only four years later, the LB & SCR obtaining authority to construct a branch to the course in 1898, but this scheme failed to materialise.

The spacious goods sidings have handled some interesting traffic over the years. Horse boxes and cattle wagons were once numerous, and during the last war it was a stabling point for one of the emergency tank trains. In the late '50s a large banana ripening shed was erected, and this was served by block trains from Avonmouth Docks. This traffic ceased on 1st October, 1971, from which date the bananas were containerised and transported by road. Since then the track layout has been progressively reduced, (see diagram "C"), and the signal box is now in circuit only during the morning and evening peaks.

Race traffic has also declined, and today it is possible to handle most of what remains by strengthening ordinary services. In 1972 the station was modernised, the goods shed and Down platform canopy being demolished. More recent alterations have removed the roof from the second (race) footbridge and the section of covered way behind the Up platform, but the main buildings with adjoining Station Master's house still survive as a good example of an LB & SCR country station.

Up local train from East Grinstead leaving the station. The signal box is typically LB & SCR, and was erected by the well-known signalling contractors, Saxby & Farmer.

photo: R.C. Riley

Looking north from the race-course footbridge.

photo: the late R.H. Clark

LYME REGIS

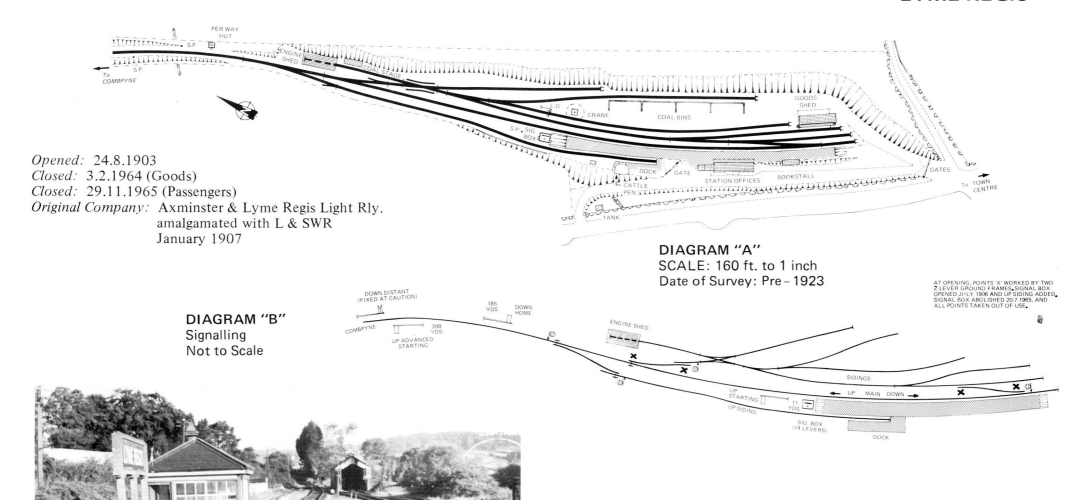

Opened: 24.8.1903
Closed: 3.2.1964 (Goods)
Closed: 29.11.1965 (Passengers)
Original Company: Axminster & Lyme Regis Light Rly.
amalgamated with L & SWR
January 1907

PER WAY HUT

S.P.

To COMBPYNE

S.P.

ENGINE SHED

COAL STAGE

S.P. SIG BOX

L G

CRANE

COAL BINS

GOODS SHED

DOCK

GATE

STATION OFFICES

BOOKSTALL

GATES

CATTLE PEN

To TOWN CENTRE

TANK

DIAGRAM "A"
SCALE: 160 ft. to 1 inch
Date of Survey: Pre – 1923

AT OPENING, POINTS 'X' WORKED BY TWO 2-LEVER GROUND FRAMES. SIGNAL BOX OPENED JULY 1906 AND UP SIDING ADDED. SIGNAL BOX ABOLISHED 20-7-1965, AND ALL POINTS TAKEN OUT OF USE.

DIAGRAM "B"
Signalling
Not to Scale

DOWN DISTANT
(FIXED AT CAUTION)

COMBPYNE

209 YDS.

UP ADVANCED STARTING

185 YDS

DOWN HOME

ENGINE SHED

SIDINGS

UP STARTING

UP SIDING

11 YDS

UP   MAIN   DOWN

SIG. BOX
(14 LEVERS)

DOCK

OPERATING NOTE: Passenger vehicles were prohibited from being loose-shunted into the platform line. All such movements were to be made with engine attached.

View from the platform end, looking towards Combpyne, shortly after the closure of the signal box in 1965. Note the engine shed in the background.

photo: Lens of Sutton   81

Looking towards the buffer stops.

photo: Lens of Sutton

View from the buffer stops in the mid-1950's.

photo: Lens of Sutton

LYME REGIS

Lyme Regis station was perched 250 ft above the town and some distance from its centre, features combining to make the branch very vulnerable to competition from road transport.

Originally owned by a local company, it bore all the hallmarks of cheap construction. Curves were sharp and frequent and gradients severe, the "Light Railway" status imposing an overall speed limit of 25 m.p.h., but even this stately progress was too much for some of the tighter bends and there were numerous greater restrictions.

The station itself was built of wood, as were all the associated structures including the original engine shed. The latter was destroyed by fire on 28th December, 1912, and subsequently rebuilt in sheet asbestos.

At first traffic was worked under "One Engine in Steam" regulations, the points at Lyme Regis being released by the key on the wooden train staff. Full signalling was added in 1906 (see diagram "B"), the siding behind the platform being installed at the same time. On 17th June, 1930 manpower economies were achieved by transferring the tablet instruments from the signal box to the parcel office, thus enabling the signalman to perform general station duties between trains.

Being an area without industry, goods traffic was never very heavy and consisted mainly of coal, bagged cement, and sundries for the local shops. Down goods trains were restricted to twelve wagons, but fifteen could be conveyed in the Up direction subject to a maximum load of 120 tons. This was the maximum weight for any class of train worked by one engine, but for double-headed workings this could be increased to 220 tons.

The service varied very little over the years, an average of eight or nine daily trains using the station. A single carriage sufficed during the Winter months, but two ran on most Summer trains with a third on those services conveying through Waterloo coaches. The summer timetable of 1963 was the last to advertise these through workings, and on 4th November that year diesel multiple units were introduced, the engine shed being closed. Following the withdrawal of goods facilities the signal box was abolished (see diagram "B") and all points and sidings taken out of use, the final method of working being the same as the first.

After closure the station stood in a derelict condition for several years, but the wooden building was eventually purchased by the Mid-Hants Railway who plan to re-erect it at Alresford to serve as a gift shop and office.

MIDHURST (LB & SCR)

Original station opened: 15.11.1866 (terminus of extension from Petworth)
Second station opened: 11.7.1881 (original terminus closed same day)
Connecting line to L & SWR upgraded for use by passengers: 12.7.1925
Closed: 7.2.1955 (Passengers)
Closed: 12.10.1964 (Goods)

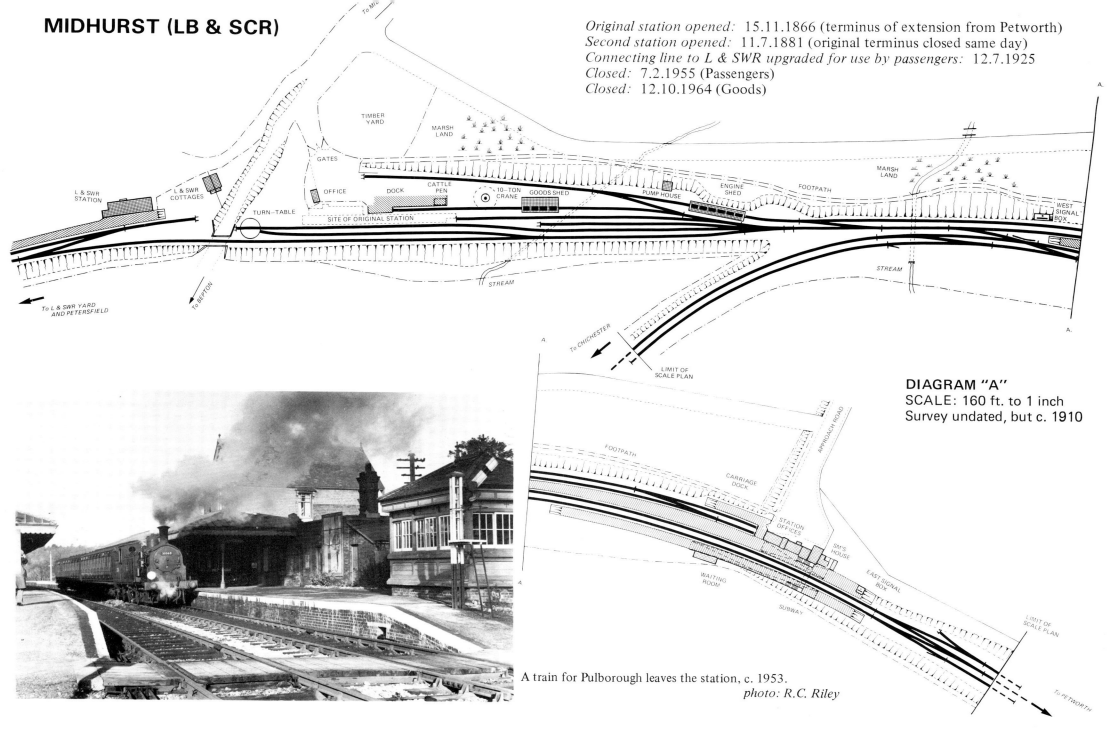

To Midhurst

TIMBER YARD

MARSH LAND

GATES

OFFICE

DOCK

CATTLE PEN

10-TON CRANE

GOODS SHED

PUMP HOUSE

ENGINE SHED

FOOTPATH

MARSH LAND

WEST SIGNAL BOX

L & SWR STATION

L & SWR COTTAGES

TURN-TABLE

SITE OF ORIGINAL STATION

A.

A.

To L & SWR YARD AND PETERSFIELD

To BEPTON

STREAM

STREAM

A.

A.

To CHICHESTER

LIMIT OF SCALE PLAN

A

A

FOOTPATH

CARRIAGE DOCK

APPROACH ROAD

STATION OFFICES

SM'S HOUSE

EAST SIGNAL BOX

WAITING ROOM

SUBWAY

LIMIT OF SCALE PLAN

To PETWORTH

DIAGRAM "A"
SCALE: 160 ft. to 1 inch
Survey undated, but c. 1910

A train for Pulborough leaves the station, c. 1953.
photo: R.C. Riley

Above left: View from above the tunnel at the Petworth end shortly after the station amalgamation of 1925. The excavations (which appear to be for chalk) and associated siding are not shown on the scale plan, and are probably later developments.

Above right: The junction, engine shed and goods yard in early SR days. The approaching train is coming off the Chichester line.

Left: The two through platforms at Midhurst c. 1952, looking towards Petersfield. The old East box (closed in 1925) can be seen on the extreme right.   *photos: Lens of Sutton*

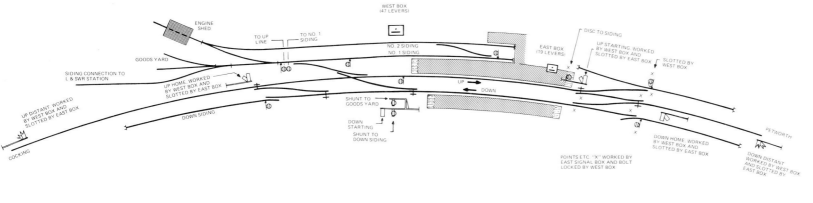

DIAGRAM "B"
Signalling—Not to Scale
Layout pre-1925

Diagram "B" labels:

- WEST BOX (47 LEVERS)
- ENGINE SHED
- TO UP LINE
- TO NO. 1 SIDING
- NO. 2 SIDING
- NO. 1 SIDING
- GOODS YARD
- SIDING CONNECTION TO L & SWR STATION
- DISC TO SIDING
- EAST BOX (19 LEVERS)
- UP STARTING WORKED BY WEST BOX AND SLOTTED BY EAST BOX
- SLOTTED BY WEST BOX
- UP HOME WORKED BY WEST BOX AND SLOTTED BY EAST BOX
- UP DISTANT WORKED BY WEST BOX AND SLOTTED BY EAST BOX
- UP
- DOWN
- SHUNT TO GOODS YARD
- DOWN STARTING
- SHUNT TO DOWN SIDING
- DOWN SIDING
- COCKING
- POINTS ETC. "X" WORKED BY EAST SIGNAL BOX AND BOLT LOCKED BY WEST BOX
- DOWN HOME WORKED BY WEST BOX AND SLOTTED BY EAST BOX
- PETWORTH
- DOWN DISTANT WORKED BY WEST BOX AND SLOTTED BY EAST BOX

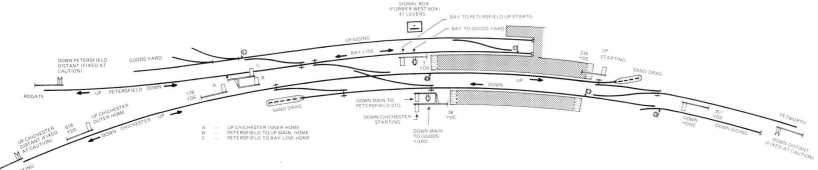

DIAGRAM "C"
Signalling—Not to Scale
Layout following amalgamation of stations, 1925

Diagram "C" labels:

- SIGNAL BOX (FORMER WEST BOX) 47 LEVERS
- BAY TO PETERSFIELD UP STARTG
- BAY TO GOODS YARD
- UP SIDING
- BAY LINE
- GOODS YARD
- 235 YDS
- UP STARTING
- SAND DRAG
- DOWN PETERSFIELD DISTANT (FIXED AT CAUTION)
- 3 YDS
- ROGATE
- UP PETERSFIELD DOWN
- 178 YDS
- A
- B
- C
- SAND DRAG
- DOWN MAIN TO PETERSFIELD STG
- DOWN CHICHESTER STARTING
- 38 YDS
- DOWN MAIN TO GOODS YARD
- DOWN
- UP
- DOWN HOME
- 357 YDS
- DOWN SIDING
- PETWORTH
- UP CHICHESTER INNER HOME
- UP CHICHESTER OUTER HOME
- 618 YDS
- DOWN CHICHESTER UP
- UP CHICHESTER DISTANT (FIXED AT CAUTION)
- COCKING
- DOWN DISTANT (FIXED AT CAUTION)
- A — UP CHICHESTER INNER HOME
- B — PETERSFIELD TO UP MAIN HOME
- C — PETERSFIELD TO BAY LINE HOME

MIDHURST (LB & SCR)

As might be expected for a junction between three branches, the story of Midhurst (LB & SCR) station is far from simple. Train services and other facilities were added (and later withdrawn) in stages, and only the briefest details can be given here.

The site of the original terminus is clearly indicated on diagram "A". At first there was no physical connection with the L & SWR station (which had opened as the terminus of the line from Petersfield in 1864), but the link line was brought into use on 17th December, 1866 to facilitate the transfer of goods. Passengers were left to find their own way between the stations, which was no great hardship until the LB & SCR station was resited in 1881. This trebled the distance and there were numerous public complaints, but the "Brighton" refused to permit passenger trains over the connection on the grounds that the bridge over the Bepton Road was too weak!

The reason for the resiting was the new line to Chichester, which opened on 11th July, 1881. The new station was laid out on a grand scale, the buildings being executed in the distinctive "Norman Shaw" style then in vogue. Facilities included a refreshment room 20 ft x 15 ft, ample canopies, and a subway connecting the platforms. Two signal boxes were provided, their design being sympathetic to that of the main buildings—even to the extent of the motifs above the windows!

After the Grouping it was an obvious move to rationalise the rather wasteful arrange-ments at Midhurst, and the Southern Railway concentrated all passenger services at this station. The troublesome Bepton Road bridge was at last strengthened and there was some reorganisation of the track layout and signalling (compare diagrams "B" and "C"). The East signal box was closed, although it found a new use as a Porters' Room. On 12th July, 1925 the former L & SWR station was closed to passengers, but it was retained as a goods yard. Within ten years the motor 'bus and private car were having a serious effect on very rural lines, and passenger trains between Midhurst and Chichester were withdrawn on 8th July, 1935. The service was then reorganised, some trains forming through workings between Pulborough and Petersfield.

The remaining goods traffic over the Chichester line ended abruptly. On 19th November, 1951 an embankment was washed away by flood water, and the meagre traffic failed to justify the cost of reinstatement. All passenger services were withdrawn on 7th February, 1955, the section from Midhurst to Petersfield closing completely. Freight, in the form of a daily trip from Horsham Yard, continued until 1964.

At the time of writing (1979) there is little left of either station, the chief relic being the large brick LB & SCR goods shed which is now in the hands of a private firm. The engine shed—a small wooden structure which closed shortly after the 1925 alterations—has vanished without trace, and most of the site has been redeveloped.

MILBORNE PORT

Right: Looking towards Templecombe c. 1960. Note the alterations to the signal box steps (compare with other photograph).   *photo: Lens of Sutton*

Opened: 7.5.1860
Closed: 6.11.1961 (Goods)
Closed: 7.3.1966 (Passengers)
Original Company: Salisbury & Yeovil Railway, purchased by L & SWR 1878.

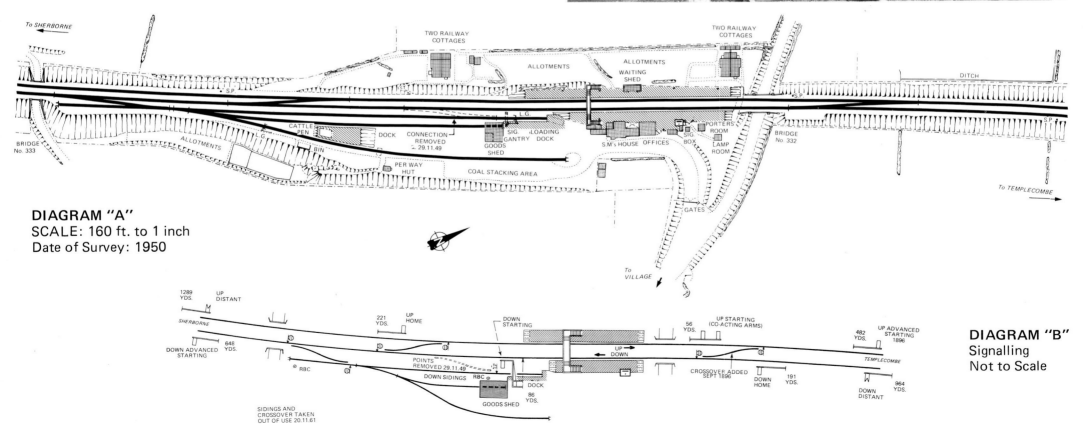

DIAGRAM "A"
SCALE: 160 ft. to 1 inch
Date of Survey: 1950

DIAGRAM "B"
Signalling
Not to Scale

MILBORNE PORT

This little station is included as an example of the smallest type to be found on the main line between Salisbury and Exeter. There were two others with almost identical layouts—Whimple and Sutton Bingham.

There was virtually no modernisation of the station throughout its 106 years of public service, and even at closure it gave a very good impression of what a country station on the L & SWR looked like in the nineteenth century. Once the Motor Age got into its stride, passenger business was slight, as the village of Milborne Port was over a mile away and situated on the main A30 road. Local people soon found it more convenient to use the 'bus for short journeys, whilst those travelling longer distances preferred to use Templecombe or Sherborne stations, where faster trains could be caught.

The signal box was opened in July 1875, and did duty for ninety years. The track layout was altered slightly over the years (see diagram "B" for details), and latterly there was very little left, but it was a useful block section on the approach to busy Templecombe. Transfer to the Western Region in January 1963 soon reduced the volume of passing traffic, and the box was finally abolished on 21st June, 1965.

With the withdrawal of freight in 1961 the station was reduced to the status of a halt. The booking office was closed, but the passengers could still purchase tickets at the signal box. The box steps had been altered around 1960, and a wooden porch provided, so these transactions could take place under cover from the weather. Following the closure of the box it was proposed to make it a true halt by withdrawing the staff altogether, but as total closure was then in the offing no action was taken, and the office had to be temporarily reopened.

Both platforms remain intact and the main building on the Down side has become a private house, but the waiting shelter on the Up platform and the footbridge were demolished shortly after closure. Whilst most of the Salisbury—Exeter line has been singled, there are still two tracks through the platforms at Milborne Port, and the section between Templecombe and Yeovil remains double.

Right: The main buildings at Milborne Port as seen from the window of an Up stopping train c. 1955. The signal box was then in its original form dating from 1875.   *photo: Lens of Sutton*

PADSTOW

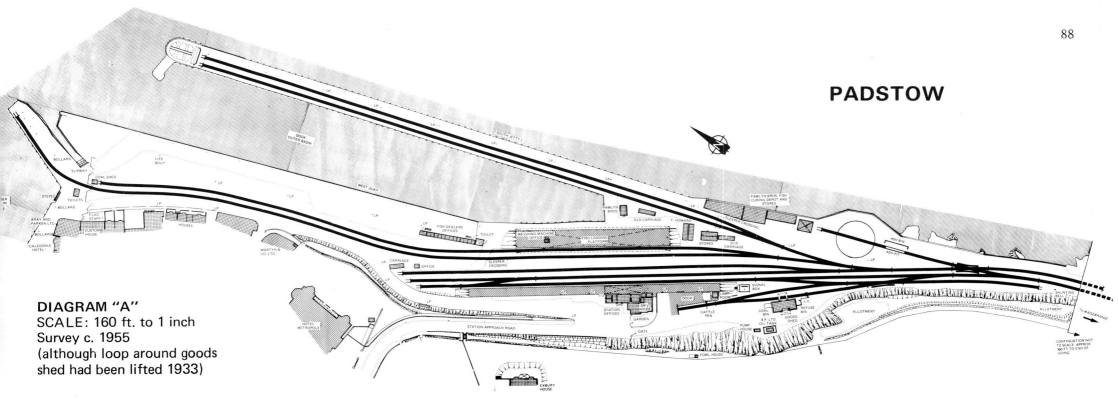

DIAGRAM "A"
SCALE: 160 ft. to 1 inch
Survey c. 1955
(although loop around goods
shed had been lifted 1933)

Looking towards the buffer stops in the early 1900's before the building of the South Jetty and provision of the carriage siding.
photo: Lens of Sutton

The stone signal box at Padstow in July 1961.
Photo: J. Scrace

Opened: 27.3.1899
Closed: 7.9.1964 (Goods)
Closed: 30.1.1967 (Passengers)
Original Company: L & SWR

NOTE: CARRIAGE SIDING, DOCK LINES AND SOUTH JETTY LINES REMOVED
BETWEEN JANUARY AND MARCH 1965. ENGINE SIDING & DOWN
SIDING ABOLISHED AT CLOSURE OF SIGNAL BOX, BUT UP SIDING
RETAINED AS RUN-ROUND.

SOUTH JETTY LINES

FISH PLATFORM

DOCK LINES

CARRIAGE SIDING

UP SIDING

ENGINE SIDING

NEW CONNECTION AND 2 LEVER GROUND FRAME
(RELEASED BY KEY ON WOODEN TRAIN STAFF)
BROUGHT INTO USE 9.1.1966

DOWN   MAIN   UP

4 YDS

UP STARTING

11

10   6 PULL

DOWN HOME

357 YDS

UP ADVANCED STARTING

WADEBRIDGE WEST

DOCK

DOWN SIDING

177 YDS

SIGNAL BOX
(18 LEVERS)
CLOSED 9.1.1966

PORTION OF SIDING
REMOVED 1933

GOODS SHED

6 PUSH

POINTS 10, F.P.L.11 AND DISC 6 PULL &
6 PUSH, TOGETHER WITH SIDING SERVING
GOODS SHED, TAKEN OUT OF USE 31.3.1965

DOWN DISTANT
(FIXED AT CAUTION)

1111 YDS

DIAGRAM "B"
Signalling
Not to Scale

PADSTOW

This station is one of the most popular amongst "South Western" modellers, which is surprising when the amount of space required for a 4 mm scale model of the layout is calculated. However, the interesting train workings always seem to justify squeezing it in!

As first opened the station consisted of the platform 100 yds in length, a run-round loop, the siding to the harbour with fish shed (as in the early photograph) and the little goods yard on the Down side of the line. This latter part of the layout was typical of stations on the North Cornwall line, as was the main platform building which incorporated a house for the Station Master and was solidly constructed of local stone. The canopy was decorated with saw-tooth valancing – a favourite device of the L & SWR! The signal box was another standard L & SW building, made slightly unusual by being constructed of stone instead of brick, and yet another stone building—the goods shed—had short canopies over the loading points on each side.

No turntable was provided initially, but on 4th April, 1900 the Board of Trade was informed that one had been installed. Around 1910 the carriage siding (next to the run-round loop) was added, and this was followed by the building of the South Jetty with its two long sidings and the long shunting neck on the Up side.

Hence by the Grouping the station had reached its peak, traffic being sufficient to persuade the Southern to rebuild the fish station in the early 1930s. To accommodate the "Bulleid Pacifics" after the Second World War the turntable was resited slightly and enlarged, the connections to the fish sidings being altered at the same time although by now the amount of rail-borne fish, which in the line's heyday often reached 1,000 wagonloads in a Spring season, was declining. The siding serving the fish station was finally severed about 1959, and the canopy on the rail side of the goods shed was taken down.

Transfer to the Western Region in January 1963 was the prelude to reductions in service. First to vanish was the goods traffic in 1964, followed by most of the through trains to Waterloo, and all through services ceased in September 1966. From 1st October that year the station could only be reached from Bodmin Road (on the former GWR main line through Cornwall), the old North Cornwall route between Wadebridge and Halwill Junction being closed to all traffic. It was hoped locally that this last link with the outside world would be saved, but the line was closed completely within a few months.

A "T9" shunts stock in the carriage siding.

photo: R.C. Riley

PORTON

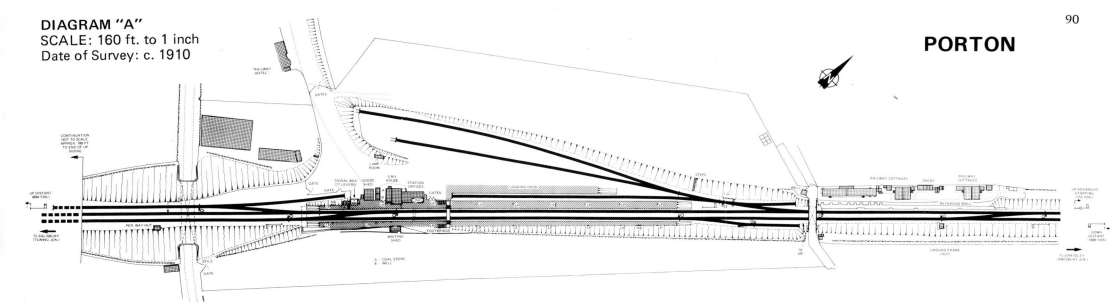

DIAGRAM "A"
SCALE: 160 ft. to 1 inch
Date of Survey: c. 1910

CONTINUATION
NOT TO SCALE
APPROX. 780 FT
TO END OF UP
SIDING

RAILWAY
HOTEL

GATES

LAMP
ROOM

GATE

GATE

GATE

SIGNAL BOX
(17 LEVERS)

GOODS
SHED

S.M's
HOUSE

STATION
OFFICES

GATES

STEPS

RAILWAY COTTAGES

SHEDS

RAILWAY
COTTAGES

UP DISTANT
(894 YDS.)

NB

LOADING DOCK

WELL

RETAINING WALL

UP ADVANCED
STARTING
(755 YDS.)

PER. WAY HUT

NB

LP

7B
MP

To SALISBURY
(TUNNEL JCN.)

WAITING
SHED

FOOTBRIDGE

A - COAL STORE
B - WELL

GROUND FRAME
(HUT)

DOWN
DISTANT
(1888 YDS.)

To GRATELEY
(AMESBURY JCN.)

STILE

GATE

DIAGRAM "B"
Shows layout of goods yard after opening of
Military Light Railway c. 1916
SCALE: 160 ft. to 1 inch

MILITARY LIGHT RAILWAY
(NARROW GAUGE)

STATION APPROACH ROAD

UP PLATFORM

LOADING DOCK

DOWN PLATFORM

TO PORTON DOWN
CAMP

Looking towards Grateley. The overbridge in the background once carried the light railway to Porton Down camp.

photo: Lens of Sutton

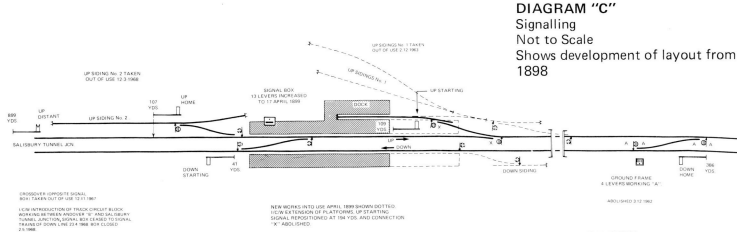

DIAGRAM "C"
Signalling
Not to Scale
Shows development of layout from
1898

UP SIDINGS No. 1 TAKEN
OUT OF USE 2.12.1963

UP SIDINGS No. 1

UP STARTING

UP SIDING No. 2 TAKEN
OUT OF USE 12-3-1968

SIGNAL BOX
13 LEVERS INCREASED
TO 17 APRIL 1899

DOCK

UP STARTING

UP ADVANCED
STARTING
(SLOTTED BY
GROUND FRAME)

899
YDS

UP
DISTANT

107
YDS

UP
HOME

UP SIDING No. 2

109
YDS

502
YDS

SALISBURY TUNNEL JCN.

UP

DOWN

X

A

A

A

A

GRATELEY

DOWN
STARTING

41
YDS

DOWN SIDING

GROUND FRAME
4 LEVERS WORKING "A".

DOWN
HOME

386
YDS

DOWN
DISTANT

1276
YDS

CROSSOVER (OPPOSITE SIGNAL
BOX) TAKEN OUT OF USE 12.11.1967

I/C/W INTRODUCTION OF TRACK CIRCUIT BLOCK
WORKING BETWEEN ANDOVER "B" AND SALISBURY
TUNNEL JUNCTION, SIGNAL BOX CEASED TO SIGNAL
TRAINS OF DOWN LINE 23.4.1968. BOX CLOSED
2.5.1968.

NEW WORKS INTO USE APRIL 1899 SHOWN DOTTED.
I/C/W EXTENSION OF PLATFORMS, UP STARTING
SIGNAL REPOSITIONED AT 194 YDS. AND CONNECTION
"X" ABOLISHED.

ABOLISHED 3.12.1962

Opened: 1.5.1857
Closed: 10.9.1962 (Goods)
Closed: 9.9.1968 (Passengers)
Original Company: L & SWR

PORTON

Porton's little L & SWR signal box (1875 type). The picture also shows the sliding doors
of the goods shed on the extreme right.
photo: C.L. Caddy

Porton started life as a humble wayside station serving a small village of that name, and it would certainly have developed very little had not the War Department purchased large tracts of land on Salisbury Plain for troop training purposes. Several camps were constructed in the area during the closing years of the nineteenth century, and as in those days an efficient Army required good rail facilities, much new work was put in hand to improve the rather basic equipment then provided at the local stations. Whole new lines were built (see the feature on Amesbury) and most places received additional or extended sidings. Porton's share of this work was carried out in April 1899, and involved a considerable lengthening of the platforms, an enlarged goods yard, and an additional siding on the Down side. Diagram "C" shows the extent of the improvements

During the First World War (c.1916) a new camp was established in a remote spot on Porton Down, together with a Trench Warfare Experimental Station for the Royal Engineers, and these were linked to the station by a 600 mm-gauge light railway which ran right into the yard (see diagram "B"). The existing brick-arch bridge, which had previously carried nothing more momentous than a rough farm track, was used to carry the light railway over the main line. Physical connection was of course ruled out by the difference in gauge, but the transfer of goods was expedited by the installation of a 2-ton runway crane spanning the two "Back" sidings and the narrow gauge lines. The camp railway was worked mainly with four-wheeled petrol engines, the only steam loco (an 0-6-0 tank) being sold to a Nottingham firm of contractors by 1924. It remained active until after the Second World War, but was then closed and the rails were later removed.

The station itself was always a rather bleak place, the site being very exposed and the accommodation available to passengers decidedly limited. The goods shed stood on the Up platform, and was of the type used for handling road box traffic rather than full wagon loads of sundries. Traffic naturally declined with the demise of the Military Railway and in BR days the sidings were gradually taken out. First to go was the short Down Siding, which had only been of use for detaching tail traffic from stopping trains, and later alterations are shown on diagram "C". After closure the station was demolished and today Porton is marked solely by an automatic colour-light signal on each line.

PULBOROUGH

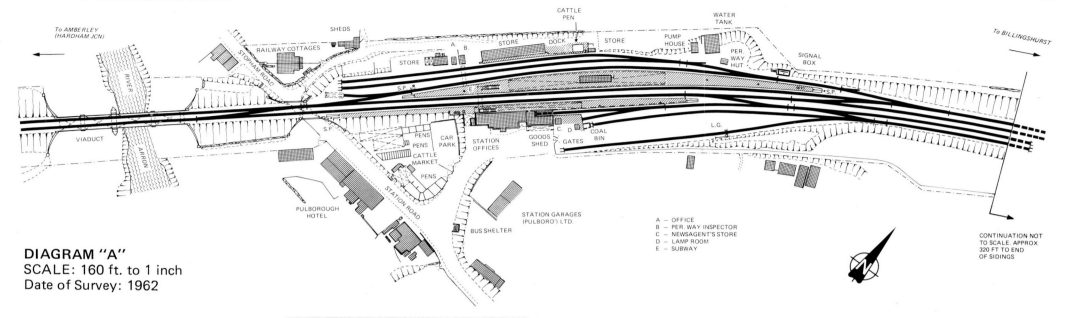

To AMBERLEY (HARDHAM JCN)

To BILLINGSHURST

RIVER ARRON

VIADUCT

STOPHAM ROAD

RAILWAY COTTAGES

SHEDS

STORE

S.P.

S.P.

PENS
PENS
PENS

CAR PARK

CATTLE MARKET

PENS

STATION ROAD

PULBOROUGH HOTEL

BUS SHELTER

STATION GARAGES (PULBORO') LTD.

STATION OFFICES

GOODS SHED

GATES

CATTLE PEN

STORE
DOCK

STORE

WATER TANK

PUMP HOUSE

PER. WAY HUT

SIGNAL BOX

S.P.

L.G.

COAL BIN

A
B

C. D.

E

A — OFFICE
B — PER. WAY INSPECTOR
C — NEWSAGENT'S STORE
D — LAMP ROOM
E — SUBWAY

CONTINUATION NOT TO SCALE. APPROX 320 FT TO END OF SIDINGS

DIAGRAM "A"
SCALE: 160 ft. to 1 inch
Date of Survey: 1962

Looking along the platform towards Amberley. The SR-style canopy extension on the Down side is obvious!
photo: Lens of Sutton

Pulborough station entrance in 1974. The central two-storey block is the original Mid-Sussex station of 1859.
photo: G.J. Bowring

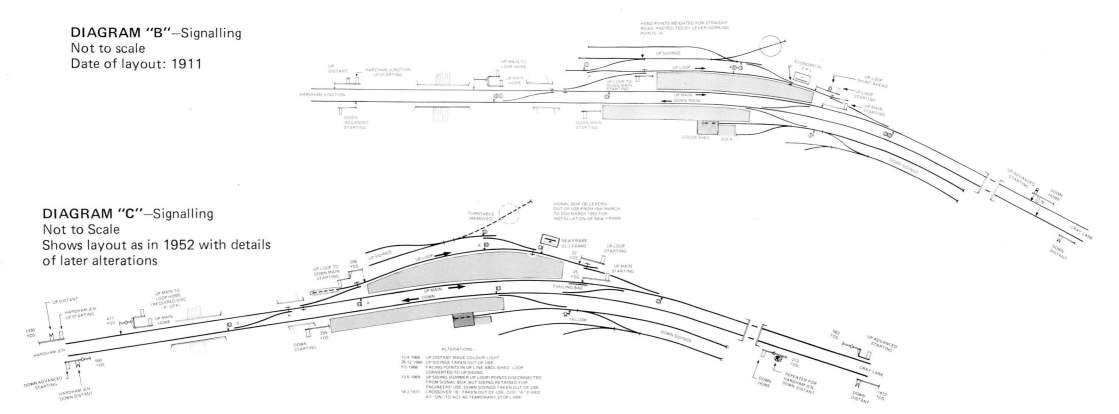

DIAGRAM "B"—Signalling
Not to scale
Date of layout: 1911

DIAGRAM "C"—Signalling
Not to Scale
Shows layout as in 1952 with details
of later alterations

ALTERATIONS —

12·4·1966   UP DISTANT MADE COLOUR LIGHT
28·12·1966 UP SIDINGS TAKEN OUT OF USE
5·5·1968   FACING POINTS IN UP LINE ABOLISHED. LOOP
            CONVERTED TO UP SIDING
13·5·1969   UP SIDING (FORMER UP LOOP) POINTS DISCONNECTED
            FROM SIGNAL BOX, BUT SIDING RETAINED FOR
            ENGINEERS' USE. DOWN SIDINGS TAKEN OUT OF USE.
14·2·1971   CROSSOVER "B" TAKEN OUT OF USE. DISC "A" FIXED
            AT "ON" TO ACT AS TEMPORARY STOP LAMP.

Opened: 10.10.1859 *Electrified:* 3.7.1938 *Closed:* 5.9.1966 (Goods)
Original Company: Mid-Sussex Railway, amalgamated with LB & SCR 1859.

PULBOROUGH

Somewhat unusually, this station started life on a branch line and later found itself on the main line to the West Sussex resorts. The original Mid-Sussex Railway linked Horsham with the little town of Petworth, (this line eventually reached Midhurst in October 1866), the double-track line down the Arun Valley between Hardham Junction and Arundel Junction not being opened until 3rd August, 1863. Pulborough achieved both junction and main line status on that date, the Petworth section becoming a branch with services connecting at Pulborough.

The main part of the two-storey buildings on the Down side is original. Solid and rectangular, it was handsomely treated by the Press of mid-nineteenth century Sussex, one reporter describing the station as being "of very superior character". Single-storey extensions were made later, and the canopies were rebuilt at various times—that on the Up platform in the early 1900s and that adjoining the goods shed was added in the 1930s. The goods shed itself is part of the original station, and its location right next to the main passenger entrance is unusual in general railway practice.

For many years there was no facing connection in the Up line. The loop behind the Up platform was therefore available only for branch departures, incoming branch trains arriving at the main platform then shunting into the loop for running round. This inconvenient arrangement came to an end in May 1911, when the diamond crossing in the Up line was removed and replaced by facing points and a crossover.

The signal box (still in use in 1979) dates from 1878 and is a typical LB & SCR structure of the pattern much favoured in the 1870s. It has been fitted with a new lever frame (see Diagram "C")—much of which is now spare—but externally it has altered little.

As diagram "B" shows, a turntable, 41 ft 9 in in diameter, was provided for the branch locomotive. It was still there in 1934, but was gone by 1947. Other loco facilities included a small coaling stage and three water columns—one at the end of each platform.

In readiness for electrification both platforms were lengthened at the South end, the loop facing points and crossover being repositioned accordingly. Recent alterations, details of which appear on Diagram "C", have reduced the track layout to the barest minimum, but at the time of writing (1979) all the principal buildings remain intact.

93

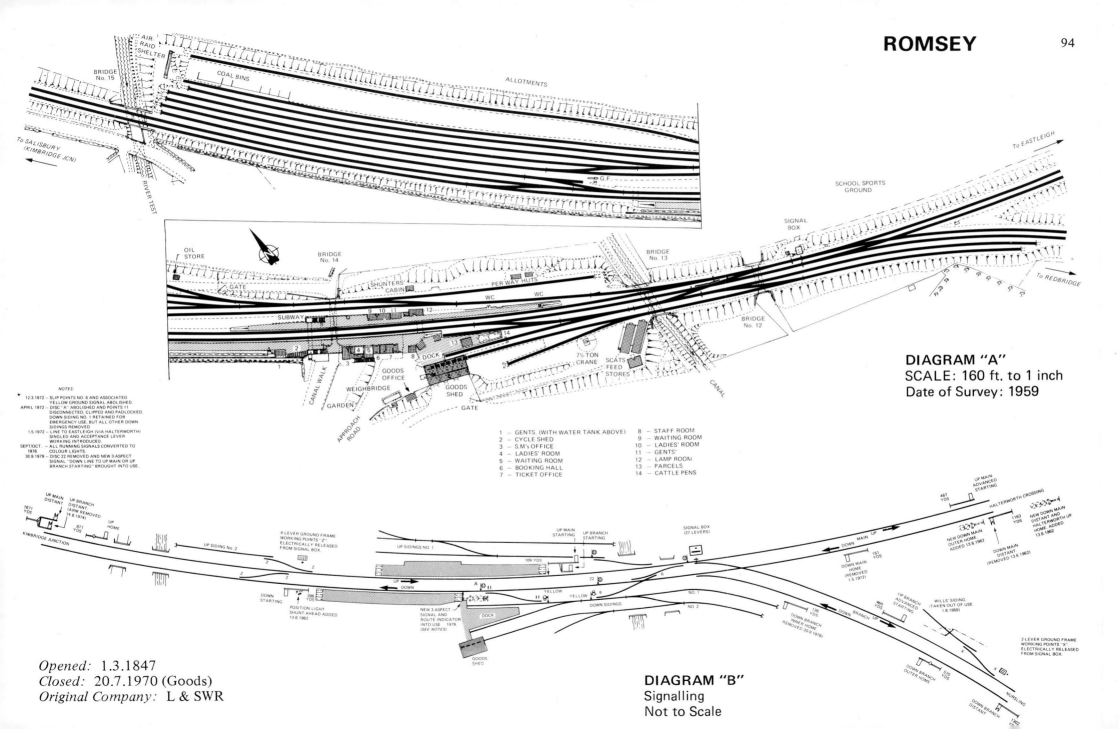

ALLOTMENTS

BRIDGE
No. 15

AIR
RAID
SHELTER

COAL BINS

To SALISBURY
(KIMBRIDGE JCN)

To EASTLEIGH

RIVER TEST

G.F.

SCHOOL SPORTS
GROUND

SIGNAL
BOX

OIL
STORE

BRIDGE
No. 14

BRIDGE
No. 13

To REDBRIDGE

GATE

SHUNTERS'
CABIN

PER WAY HUTS

BRIDGE
No. 12

SUBWAY

WC   WC

9 10 11   12

CANAL WALK

WEIGHBRIDGE

GARDEN

APPROACH ROAD

2
3   4 5
6 7   8 DOCK

GOODS
OFFICE

GOODS
SHED

13

14

GATE

7½ TON
CRANE

SCATS
FEED
STORES

CANAL

DIAGRAM "A"
SCALE: 160 ft. to 1 inch
Date of Survey: 1959

NOTES:
* 12.3.1972 – SLIP POINTS NO. 6 AND ASSOCIATED
  YELLOW GROUND SIGNAL ABOLISHED.
APRIL 1972 – DISC "A" ABOLISHED AND POINTS 11
  DISCONNECTED, CLIPPED AND PADLOCKED.
  DOWN SIDING NO. 1 RETAINED FOR
  EMERGENCY USE, BUT ALL OTHER DOWN
  SIDINGS REMOVED
1.5.1972 – LINE TO EASTLEIGH (VIA HALTERWORTH)
  SINGLED AND ACCEPTANCE LEVER
  WORKING INTRODUCED.
SEPT/OCT. – ALL RUNNING SIGNALS CONVERTED TO
1976   COLOUR LIGHTS.
30.9.1979 – DISC 22 REMOVED AND NEW 3-ASPECT
  SIGNAL "DOWN LINE TO UP MAIN OR UP
  BRANCH STARTING" BROUGHT INTO USE.

1 — GENTS. (WITH WATER TANK ABOVE)	8 — STAFF ROOM
2 — CYCLE SHED	9 — WAITING ROOM
3 — S.M.'s OFFICE	10 — LADIES' ROOM
4 — LADIES' ROOM	11 — GENTS'
5 — WAITING ROOM	12 — LAMP ROOM
6 — BOOKING HALL	13 — PARCELS
7 — TICKET OFFICE	14 — CATTLE PENS

UP MAIN
DISTANT

UP BRANCH
DISTANT.
(ARM REMOVED)
14.8.1974

UP MAIN
ADVANCED
STARTING

467
YDS

HALTERWORTH CROSSING

1671
YDS

UP
HOME

871
YDS

4-LEVER GROUND FRAME
WORKING POINTS "Z"
ELECTRICALLY RELEASED
FROM SIGNAL BOX

UP MAIN
STARTING

UP BRANCH
STARTING

SIGNAL BOX
(27 LEVERS)

1163
YDS

NEW DOWN MAIN
DISTANT AND
HALTERWORTH UP
HOME. ADDED
13.6.1962

KIMBRIDGE JUNCTION

UP SIDING No. 2

UP SIDINGS No. 1

109 YDS

MAIN   UP

DOWN   MAIN   UP

DOWN MAIN
HOME
(REMOVED
1.5.1972)

NEW DOWN MAIN
OUTER HOME
ADDED 13.6.1962

151
YDS

DOWN MAIN
DISTANT
(REMOVED 13.6.1962)

Z Z Z Z

Z Z

DOWN   DOWN

A

YELLOW

YELLOW

22

6

NO. 1

465
YDS

UP BRANCH
ADVANCED
STARTING

WILLS' SIDING
(TAKEN OUT OF USE
1.8.1959)

DOWN
STARTING

396
YDS

POSITION LIGHT
SHUNT AHEAD ADDED
13.6.1962

NEW 3-ASPECT
SIGNAL AND
ROUTE INDICATOR
INTO USE 1979.
(SEE NOTES)

DOCK

11   11

6

DOWN SIDINGS

NO. 2

136
YDS

DOWN BRANCH
INNER HOME
REMOVED 20.9.1976

DOWN
BRANCH
UP

GOODS
SHED

DOWN BRANCH
OUTER HOME

570
YDS

2-LEVER GROUND FRAME
WORKING POINTS "X"
ELECTRICALLY RELEASED
FROM SIGNAL BOX

NURSLING

DOWN BRANCH
DISTANT

1302
YDS

DIAGRAM "B"
Signalling
Not to Scale

Opened: 1.3.1847
Closed: 20.7.1970 (Goods)
Original Company: L & SWR

Romsey signal box in 1978, with 3-car "Hampshire" Unit approaching off the Redbridge line on a Portsmouth–Salisbury service.   *photo: B.L. Jackson*

Looking towards Eastleigh in 1970. Apart from a new coat of paint, the station has altered very little in the forty years since the older picture was taken.   *photo: B.L. Jackson*

ROMSEY

Romsey might well have functioned as a goods station only for a few weeks, as the line between Eastleigh and Salisbury was opened for freight traffic on 27th January, 1847. The main office buildings date from these earliest days, although there were later extensions—notably in 1884, when the canopy on the Down platform was lengthened on each side of the central section.

The line between Andover Junction and Redbridge opened on 6th March, 1865, and thereafter Romsey became something of an interchange station for goods, a modest marshalling yard developing behind the Up platform. The Andover section of this new line actually met the existing railway at Kimbridge Junction, about 3 miles north-west of Romsey, but there were never any transfer facilities at that location for either goods or passengers. Train services over any of the routes converging on Romsey were not particularly lavish in steam days, but were vastly improved with the introduction of diesel-electric multiple units in 1957.

Traffic began to decline with the withdrawal of the Andover service on 7th September, 1964, although for a few years a truncated version operated between Portsmouth and Romsey only (via Eastleigh). This ceased on 5th May, 1969 and the station then entered its quietest period, but since the Summer of 1979 there has been an increase in the number of inter-regional trains and many of the Portsmouth–Southampton locals have been extended to Romsey. To reduce shunt moves with empty units, the Down platform has now been signalled for the starting of trains in the Up direction (see diagram "B"). Many of the Up sidings have been taken out, but the nucleus of the little marshalling yard survives and is currently (1980) used by the Signal & Telegraph Department as a depot for materials in connection with the Southampton Resignalling Scheme.

Looking towards Eastleigh c. 1930, showing the crossover and Up siding No. 2 points in their old position. These were later moved to the position indicated on the scale plan.

photo: Lens of Sutton

The impressive frontage of Rye station as seen from approach road in 1974.

photo: J. Minnis

Looking along the Down platform towards Winchelsea.

photo: Oxford Publishing Co. collection

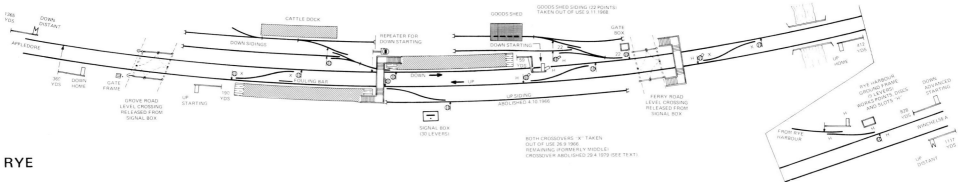

RYE

DIAGRAM "B"—Signalling
Not to Scale

Opened: 13.2.1851
Closed: 9.9.1963 (Goods)
Original Company: South Eastern Railway

RYE

This has always been the most important station on the line from Ashford to Hastings, and its handsome buildings deserve more than a brief description. The main offices were designed by William Tress, who did a fair amount of work for the SER including stations on the main Hastings line. At Rye he adopted a Classical style; with its projecting wings and arcaded facade it is indeed impressive when seen from the long approach road. The central portion, elevated above the main rectangle and flanked by chimneys, gives the building height and importance.

The goods shed also dates from the opening of the line, and although it lacks the architectural pretensions of the station buildings, it is a large and imposing structure. It has two through passages—one for rail and the other for road vehicles—thus enabling the transfer of freight to be carried out with full protection from the weather.

The remaining buildings deserve a mention. Level crossings at both ends of the station were adorned with cottages and gate boxes of characteristic SER design. The platforms were staggered, and no footbridge was provided until around 1900 when one was erected at Ferry Road Crossing. There was no footbridge between the platforms until BR days. The existing signal box dates from the resignalling of the station in 1893, and with its brick base and wooden superstructure with gable-ended roof, is another typically SER building. The ground frame controlling access to the Harbour branch dates from the same time, and the layout was much criticised by the Board of Trade when it was first installed. Apparently the crossover near the River Tillingham bridge (see diagram "B") was connected to the Harbour Ground Frame, which was also provided with running signals on the Up line. The inspecting officer stated that either the ground frame should be upgraded to a block post or the crossover should be worked from the main signal box. The latter option was taken, the alteration being carried out by December 1893.

For many years the train service was not very good, but a rail motor service between Hastings and Rye was inaugurated in 1907. Diesel electric multiple units took over the working in the early '60s, and at present there are sixteen daily trains in each direction. With the loss of goods traffic and a passenger service operated on a regular interval basis the need for a double track has vanished. Work started on singling on 29th April, 1979 when the last remaining crossover was disconnected from the box, and single line working (on the Tokenless Block system) was introduced on 30th September, 1979, the sections being Appledore—Rye—Ore.

The Harbour branch was opened in 1854. It was single track throughout and was never used by passenger trains. Latterly it carried very little traffic and was closed in 1962.

Hastings-bound train in the Down platform.   *photo: R.C. Riley*

The Up platform, looking towards Appledore. The cattle pens are on the extreme right.

photo: H.C. Casserley

SANDGATE

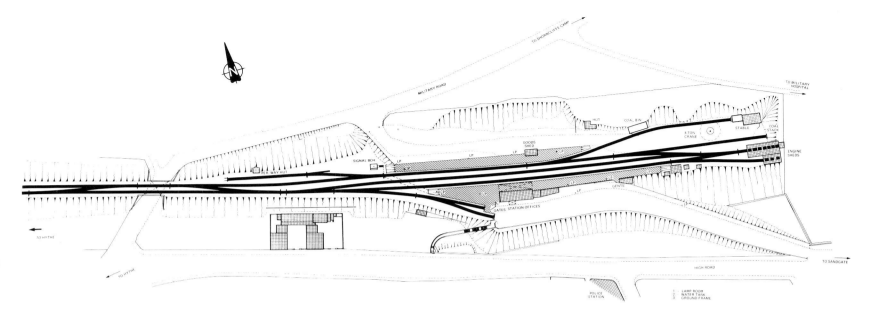

DIAGRAM "A"
SCALE: 160 ft. to 1 inch
Date of Survey: c. 1900

Opened: 9.10.1874
Closed: 1.4.1931
Original Company: South Eastern Railway

SANDGATE

This relatively unknown terminus was actually situated in Seabrook, the line stopping a mile short of Sandgate. The branch left the main line at Sandling Junction, and was built with double track to facilitate extension along the shore to Folkestone Harbour. The South Eastern was very keen on this scheme, as the 1 in 30 gradient of the existing Folkestone Harbour line was a great inconvenience to the working of heavy boat trains. However, local residents were not impressed by the idea of a railway along the foot of the cliffs and fought it to such effect that when the extension bill was eventually passed the route deviated slightly inland and involved a long tunnel. The Company considered this too expensive, and dropped the idea altogether.

Although the line almost became a route for boat expresses, facilities at Sandgate were definitely second-rate, possibly because the station was considered to be temporary. The main building was a simple timber structure of the type so common on the SER in the 'eighties. It stood on the Departure platform, no shelter being provided on the Arrival side, from which passengers leaving the station had to cross three tracks by a sleeper crossing. The Arrival platform doubled as the goods station, the goods shed standing thereon being a small wooden hut. Diagram "A" shows a two-road engine shed, but the photograph clearly shows it as a single-road affair. Later extension is possible, but unlikely in view of the sparse traffic on the branch.

For many years all arriving services had to run to the Arrival platform then shunt to the Departure line, but the layout was improved in July 1900 by the installation of a facing crossover (see diagram "B"). Trains could then run directly into the Departure side ready for the return journey, and the other platform probably saw little use thereafter.

Passenger traffic was always negligible, as both Hythe and Sandgate stations were badly sited and it was more convenient to use stations on the main line. Closure was complete between Hythe and Sandgate, the rails being removed. The site of the station was taken over by the East Kent Road Car Company for use as a 'bus depot, only the "Gents" being retained for the use of crews, but even this has now gone.

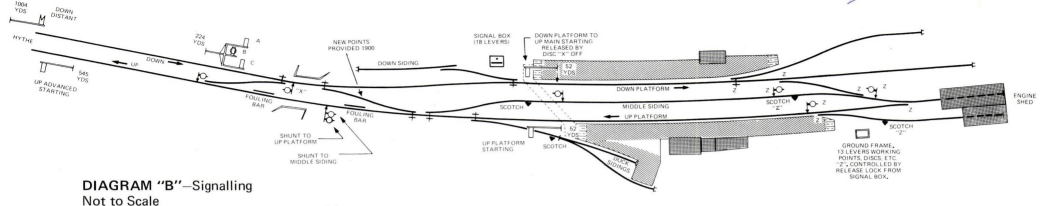

A — DOWN HOME
B — TO MIDDLE SIDING HOME
C — TO UP PLATFORM HOME

1004 YDS — DOWN DISTANT

HYTHE

224 YDS — A B C

545 YDS — UP ADVANCED STARTING

UP · DOWN · DOWN

FOULING BAR

"X"

FOULING BAR

SHUNT TO UP PLATFORM

SHUNT TO MIDDLE SIDING

NEW POINTS PROVIDED 1900

DOWN SIDING

SIGNAL BOX (18 LEVERS)

DOWN PLATFORM TO UP MAIN STARTING RELEASED BY DISC "X" OFF

52 YDS

DOWN PLATFORM →

SCOTCH

MIDDLE SIDING

← UP PLATFORM

52 YDS

UP PLATFORM STARTING

SCOTCH

DOCK SIDINGS

SCOTCH "Z"

Z Z Z Z

Z Z Z Z

ENGINE SHED

SCOTCH "Z"

GROUND FRAME.
13 LEVERS WORKING POINTS, DISCS, ETC.
"Z", CONTROLLED BY RELEASE LOCK FROM SIGNAL BOX.

DIAGRAM "B"—Signalling
Not to Scale
Date of Diagram: 1900

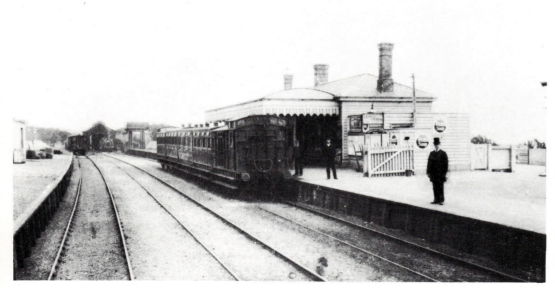

Sandgate station in 1891, looking towards the buffer stops. The carriages are standing in the Departure platform. The engine shed and water tank are visible in the distance.

photo: Lens of Sutton

Seabrook in Sandgate.

General view from the hill behind the station, looking towards Hythe in 1900. The small building on the platform nearest the camera was the goods shed.

photo: Lens of Sutton

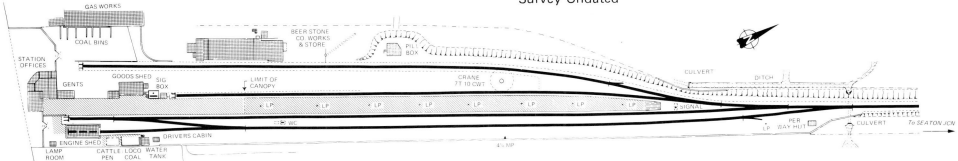

DIAGRAM "A"
SCALE: 160 ft. to 1 inch
Survey Undated

Looking north along the platform of the old station, with the original wooden engine shed on the right. This view was drastically altered with the rebuilding of 1936.

photo: Lens of Sutton

View towards the buffer stops of the rebuilt station, showing the replacement engine shed.

photo: Lens of Sutton

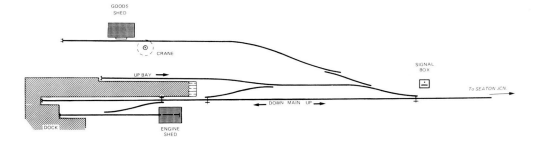

DIAGRAM "B"
Sketch plan showing original track
layout.
Not to Scale

DIAGRAM "C"
Signalling c. 1959
Not to Scale

Opened: 16.3.1868
Closed: 3.2.1964 (Goods)
Closed: 7.3.1966 (Passengers)
Original Company: Seaton and Beer Railway, amalgamated
with L & SWR 1.1.1888

SEATON

As diagram "B" shows, the original station at Seaton was very small, and more suited to the needs of an inland village than a seaside resort. The platforms were so short that the L & SWR, (who operated the service from the outset), insisted that they be extended to the modest length of 180 ft to accommodate excursion traffic, this being done in the spring of 1869 in readiness for the season's rush of visitors.

Heavy summer traffic always caused problems which even complete rebuilding by the SR failed to remove completely. Stabling facilities for coaching stock were decidedly limited, trains of empties being worked elsewhere for berthing whenever possible, but occasionally it was necessary to clear out the solitary goods siding on Friday nights so that it could be used for carriages. Freight traffic never amounted to much and was very light in latter years, although at one time a considerable tonnage of Beer stone was forwarded.

Between the wars 'bus competition and the growth of private transport began to make economies necessary, and on 11th January, 1930 the tablet instruments were taken from the signal box and transferred to a new ground frame, the box being manned only when the bay platform line was used. This odd arrangement allowed the signalman to be employed on general station duties between trains, and when the new signal box was opened on 28th June, 1936 its position on the platform perpetuated the arrangement. The station was completely rebuilt in 1936 to the form illustrated by diagrams "A" and "C", the Southern Railway providing a full-length platform to cater for long distance excursions.

As recently as August 1959 passenger traffic was quite heavy, 3,500 tickets being issued and 12,000 collected at Seaton during the month. Many of these were patrons of Warner's Holiday Camp which adjoined the station, for unlike the other resorts of East Devon which strive even now to remain "select", Seaton was happy to cater for a more working-class clientele. Despite this, the Beeching report recommended closure, and when the Western Region assumed control on 1st January, 1963 the scene was set for running down the branch. Diesel units were introduced on 4th November, 1963, the

Typical SR architecture of the '30s; the frontage of Seaton station.

photo: C.L. Caddy

engine shed being closed the same day, and the withdrawal of goods services followed four months later. These measures made even greater simplicity of working possible, and on 2nd May, 1965 the signal box was closed and all points clipped and padlocked, trains using the main platform line only. For the remaining life of the branch, traffic was controlled by wooden train staff.

Following complete closure in 1966, Modern Electric Tramways Ltd. constructed a 2 ft 9 in-gauge line over much of the branch, the first section opening on 28th August, 1970. The station site is now occupied by their terminal, car sheds and car park.

SHERBORNE

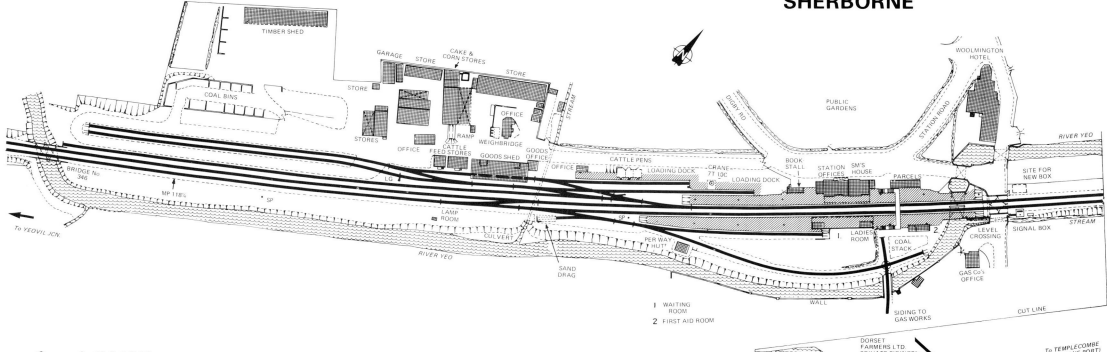

TIMBER SHED

CAKE & CORN STORES

GARAGE STORE STORE

STORE

WOOLMINGTON HOTEL

COAL BINS

STORES OFFICE

CATTLE FEED STORES

RAMP WEIGHBRIDGE

GOODS OFFICE

OFFICE

STREAM

DIGBY RD

PUBLIC GARDENS

STATION ROAD

RIVER YEO

BRIDGE No. 346

MP 118¼

SP

LG

GOODS SHED

OFFICE

CATTLE PENS

LOADING DOCK

CRANE 7T 10C

LOADING DOCK

BOOK STALL

STATION OFFICES

SM'S HOUSE

PARCELS

SITE FOR NEW BOX

STREAM

To YEOVIL JCN.

LAMP ROOM

CULVERT

RIVER YEO

PER WAY HUTT

SP

SAND DRAG

WAITING ROOM

FIRST AID ROOM

LADIES ROOM

COAL STACK

1

2

SIDING TO GAS WORKS

WALL

GAS Co's OFFICE

LEVEL CROSSING

SIGNAL BOX

STREAM

CUT LINE

Opened: 7.5.1860
Closed: 18.4.1966 (Goods)
Original Company: Salisbury & Yeovil Railway, purchased
by L & SWR 1878

DIAGRAM "A"
SCALE: 160 ft. to 1 inch
Date of Survey: 1956

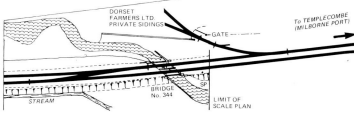

DORSET FARMERS LTD. PRIVATE SIDINGS

GATE

To TEMPLECOMBE (MILBORNE PORT)

STREAM

BRIDGE No. 344

SP

LIMIT OF SCALE PLAN

DIAGRAM "B"
Signalling
Not to Scale

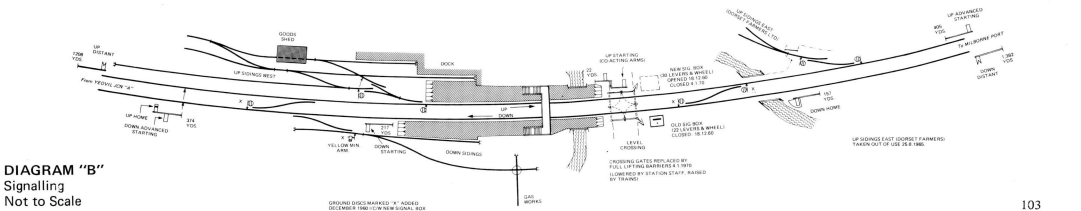

GOODS SHED

UP SIDINGS EAST (DORSET FARMERS LTD.)

UP ADVANCED STARTING

1208 YDS.

UP DISTANT

405 YDS.

To Milborne Port

1,382 YDS.

DOWN DISTANT

From YEOVIL JCN "A"

UP SIDINGS WEST

DOCK

UP STARTING (CO ACTING ARMS)

22 YDS.

NEW SIG. BOX (30 LEVERS & WHEEL) OPENED 18.12.60 CLOSED 4.1.70

UP HOME

DOWN ADVANCED STARTING

374 YDS.

X

X

UP

DOWN

X

X

157 YDS.

DOWN HOME

YELLOW MIN. ARM.

217 YDS.

DOWN STARTING

DOWN SIDINGS

OLD SIG BOX (22 LEVERS & WHEEL) CLOSED: 18.12.60

LEVEL CROSSING

UP SIDINGS EAST (DORSET FARMERS) TAKEN OUT OF USE 25.8.1965.

GAS WORKS

CROSSING GATES REPLACED BY FULL LIFTING BARRIERS 4.1.1970 (LOWERED BY STATION STAFF, RAISED BY TRAINS)

GROUND DISCS MARKED "X" ADDED DECEMBER 1960 I/C/W NEW SIGNAL BOX

ALL POINTS (INCLUDING BOTH CROSSOVERS) TAKEN OUT OF USE 5.2.1967.

LINE SINGLED SHERBORNE – YEOVIL JC 7.5.1967

DOUBLE LINE TO YEOVIL JCN. RE-INSTATED 2.10.1967

103

SHERBORNE

Sherborne was one of the principal stations between Salisbury and Exeter, and in fact it still possesses an air of importance despite the line's loss of status and the general economies of recent years. For a short time after opening it served as the terminus, the line westward to Yeovil being opened for traffic on 1st June, 1860.

The main buildings (which include a house for the Station Master), the large goods shed, and several other structures are attractively executed in rock-faced Ham Hill Stone, and blend in well with the ancient buildings of this picturesque Abbey town. The station was considerably modernised in 1962, the delapidated wooden waiting room on the Down side being replaced by a modern structure of brick and glass, but work on the main offices was confined mainly to interior refitting and the original character of the station is thus preserved.

Until the singling of the line in 1967 the track layout changed very little, the original layout being similar to that illustrated by the two diagrams. In August 1890 a siding was added for the Sherborne Coal & Timber Company, and this later became the property of Dorset Farmers Ltd. and survived until 1965. The Up Advanced Starting signal was added at the same time. In December 1960 the old signal box—then eighty-five years old and rather shaky—was replaced by a large brick box of BR design on the opposite side of the line, although the only signalling alterations brought about by this were a few additional ground discs to accord with standard Southern Region practice.

All lines west of Salisbury were transferred to the Western Region from 1st January, 1963, and the new management soon announced plans to concentrate West of England traffic on the Paddington route. In 1964 there was a scheme to close Yeovil Junction station and develop Sherborne as the railhead, but as the result of strong local opposition this was not pursued. Decline was then the order of the day, a first step being taken on 5th April, 1965 when the goods shed was closed and sundries traffic concentrated at Yeovil Hendford. Wagon load traffic continued for another year, but as a prelude to singling all sidings were taken out of use in February 1967 (see diagram "B"). The train service was also drastically reduced, local trains being withdrawn from 7th March, 1966. This left only a two-hourly service of semi-fast Waterloo—Exeter trains, all of which called at Sherborne, and this pattern is maintained at the time of writing (1979). The section between Sherborne and Chard Junction was singled in May 1967, but this arrangement caused so much delay that double line as far as Yeovil Junction was restored a few months later (see diagram for dates). The signal box survived until 1970, when the crossing gates were replaced by lifting barriers, but the modern building still serves a useful purpose as a Permanent Way office and staff room.

OPERATING NOTES: Movements to Dorset Farmers Ltd. siding had always to be supervised by a competent shunter. Engines prohibited from passing beyond the boundary gate, and a sufficient number of wagons were to be attached next to the engine to obviate the necessity of this.

Passenger bogie stock prohibited from passing through goods shed.

Looking towards Milborne Port in 1962, showing the rebuilt Down side buildings.

photo: R.T.H. Platt

SHORNCLIFFE

DIAGRAM 'A'
SCALE: 160 ft. to 1 inch
Date of Survey: c. 1940

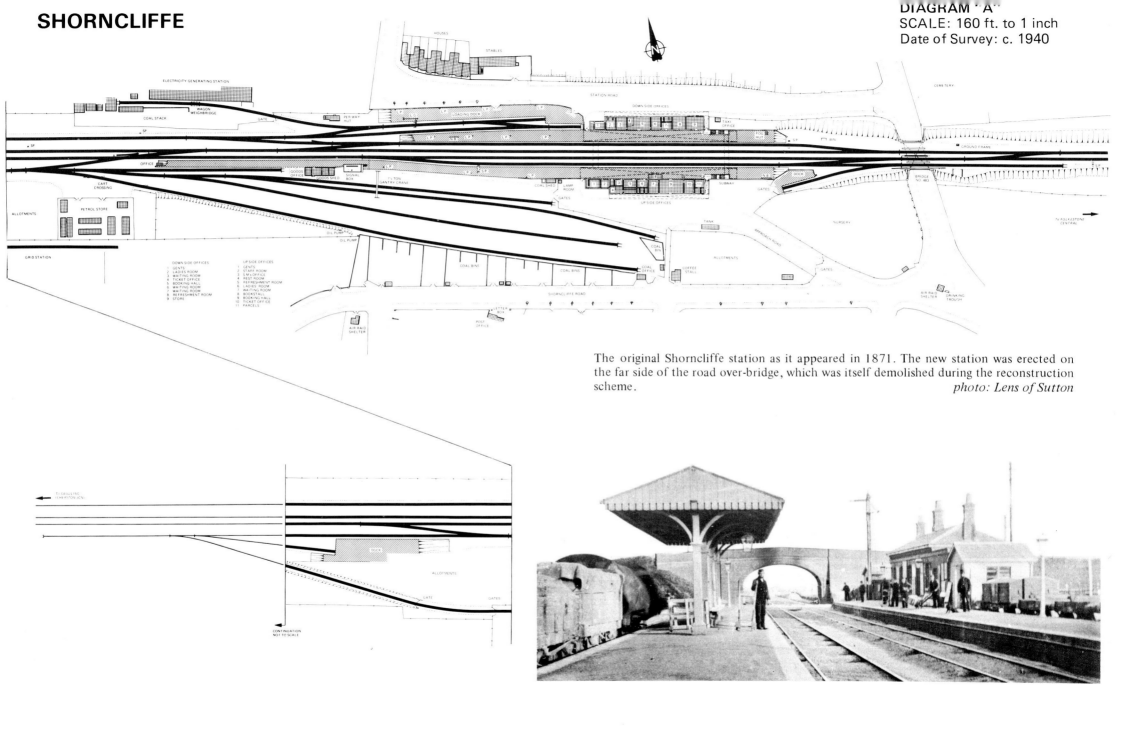

The original Shorncliffe station as it appeared in 1871. The new station was erected on the far side of the road over-bridge, which was itself demolished during the reconstruction scheme.

photo: Lens of Sutton

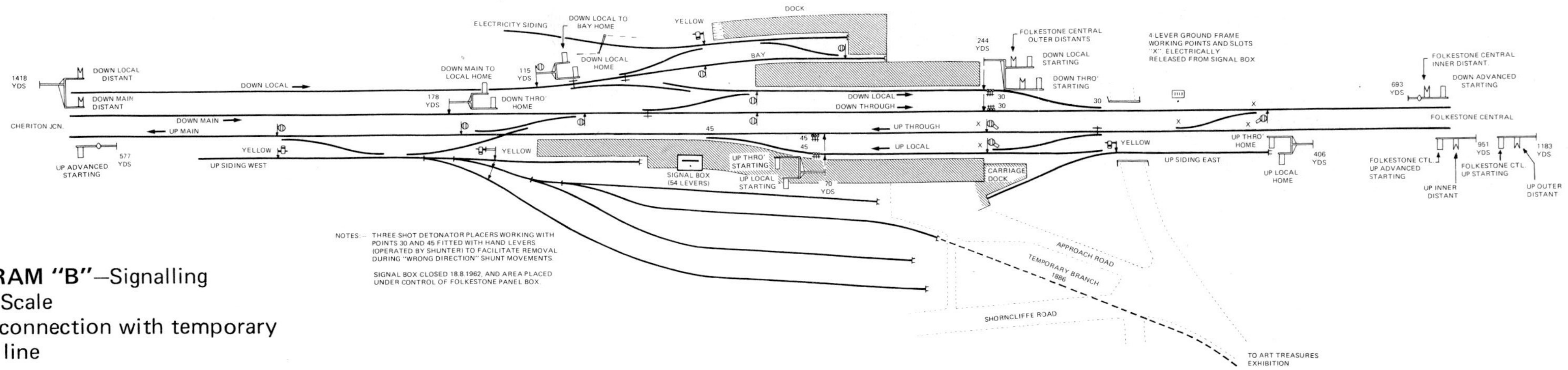
DOCK
YELLOW
ELECTRICITY SIDING
DOWN LOCAL TO BAY HOME
BAY
DOWN LOCAL HOME
DOWN MAIN TO LOCAL HOME
115 YDS
178 YDS
DOWN THRO' HOME
1418 YDS
DOWN LOCAL DISTANT
DOWN MAIN DISTANT
DOWN LOCAL
DOWN MAIN
UP MAIN
CHERITON JCN.
UP ADVANCED STARTING
577 YDS
YELLOW
UP SIDING WEST
YELLOW
45
SIGNAL BOX (54 LEVERS)
UP THRO' STARTING
UP LOCAL STARTING
70 YDS
CARRIAGE DOCK
244 YDS
FOLKESTONE CENTRAL OUTER DISTANTS
DOWN LOCAL STARTING
DOWN THRO' STARTING
DOWN LOCAL
DOWN THROUGH
UP THROUGH
UP LOCAL
4 LEVER GROUND FRAME WORKING POINTS AND SLOTS "X" ELECTRICALLY RELEASED FROM SIGNAL BOX
UP SIDING EAST
YELLOW
UP THRO' HOME
UP LOCAL HOME
406 YDS
FOLKESTONE CENTRAL INNER DISTANT
DOWN ADVANCED STARTING
693 YDS
FOLKESTONE CENTRAL
FOLKESTONE CTL. UP ADVANCED STARTING
951 YDS
1183 YDS
FOLKESTONE CTL. UP STARTING
UP INNER DISTANT
UP OUTER DISTANT
APPROACH ROAD
TEMPORARY BRANCH 1886
SHORNCLIFFE ROAD
TO ART TREASURES EXHIBITION
NOTES:— THREE SHOT DETONATOR PLACERS WORKING WITH POINTS 30 AND 45 FITTED WITH HAND LEVERS (OPERATED BY SHUNTER) TO FACILITATE REMOVAL DURING "WRONG DIRECTION" SHUNT MOVEMENTS.
SIGNAL BOX CLOSED 18.8.1962, AND AREA PLACED UNDER CONTROL OF FOLKESTONE PANEL BOX.

DIAGRAM "B"—Signalling
Not to Scale
Shows connection with temporary branch line

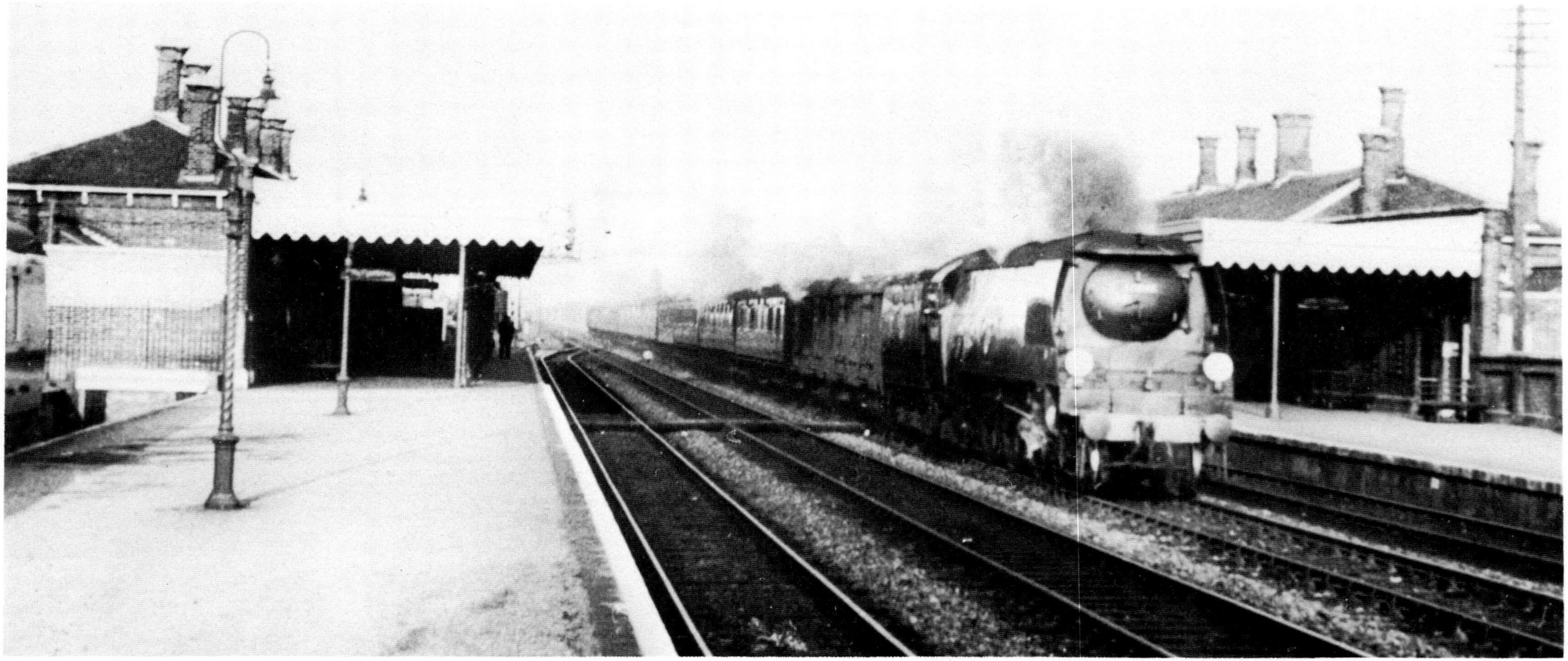

An Up express passing through the spacious rebuilt station. Compare this view with the older photograph! *photo: H.C. Casserley*

SHORNCLIFFE

The original station was sited about 150 yds west of the one illustrated by these plans, and as the old photograph shows, it was a humble wooden edifice servicing the needs of a neighbouring Army camp. Its later expansion into a spacious and well-appointed station was the direct result of bitter rivalry between the SER and LC & DR, and demonstrates the lengths to which one Company was prepared to go in attempting to out-smart the other.

In 1865 both Companies had signed an agreement to share receipts derived from Continental traffic, the takings of the Folkestone stations being included in the pooling arrangements. The South Eastern therefore rebuilt their Shorncliffe station on a lavish scale with the sole intention of drawing Folkestone passengers to it, then by claiming that it was "not Folkestone", withholding any share the "Chatham" should have received under the terms of the agreement. The LC & DR engaged the SER in litigation, the latter Company eventually being forced to pay a large sum of money, but the large station was later put to some use with the opening of the Elham Valley Line, of which more anon.

Shorncliffe's first taste of junction status came in 1886, when a temporary branch, some 1,500 yds in length, was built to serve an Arts Treasures Exhibition. This line connected with the Up sidings, and its course is shown on Diagram "B". Although primarily intended for the conveyance of materials, the Board of Trade passed it for use by passenger trains in June 1886. Once the exhibition was over the line was, of course, removed.

The Elham Valley line was opened between Shorncliffe and Barham on 4th July, 1887, an independent Down line being provided between the junction at Cheriton and the station. This was later known as the "Down Local", and remained in use after removal of the branch. Up trains had to run over the main line, crossing onto the branch by a facing connection at Cheriton Junction. Although this line was laid out with double track, and was extended to Canterbury on 1st July, 1889, it was never a financial success. Services ceased between Lyminge and Canterbury on 2nd December, 1940, and after a period of suspension, the entire line was closed in October 1947.

The track layout was extensively rationalised in 1960 during preparatory work for electrification. As this involved the provision of four running roads from Folkestone right through to Cheriton Junction, the Up platform had to be straightened to conform to the new layout.

Despite the removal of the signal box and sidings and the closure of the refreshment rooms and some of the offices in recent years, most of the buildings remain intact to serve as a monument to the cut-and-thrust of Victorian railway politics.

OPERATING NOTES: Board of Trade approved instructions for working over the Arts Treasures Exhibition Branch—1886.

All movements to be under the control of the Station Master or Chief Station Inspector, who must accompany every train and take with him a Train Staff as authority to occupy the single line. Only one train to be upon the line at a time.

Changes of Name

Opened as "Shorncliffe Camp" and renamed "Shorncliffe & Sandgate" on 1.12.1863. Reverted to original name 1.10.1874, and this title was transferred to the new station. "Camp" dropped from title 2.7.1926. Station renamed "Folkestone West" 10.9.1962.

Opened: 1.11.1863 (1st station)
Opened: 1.2.1881 (2nd station)
Electrified: 12.6.1961
Closed: 22.4.1968 (Goods)
Original Company: South Eastern Railway

SIDMOUTH JUNCTION

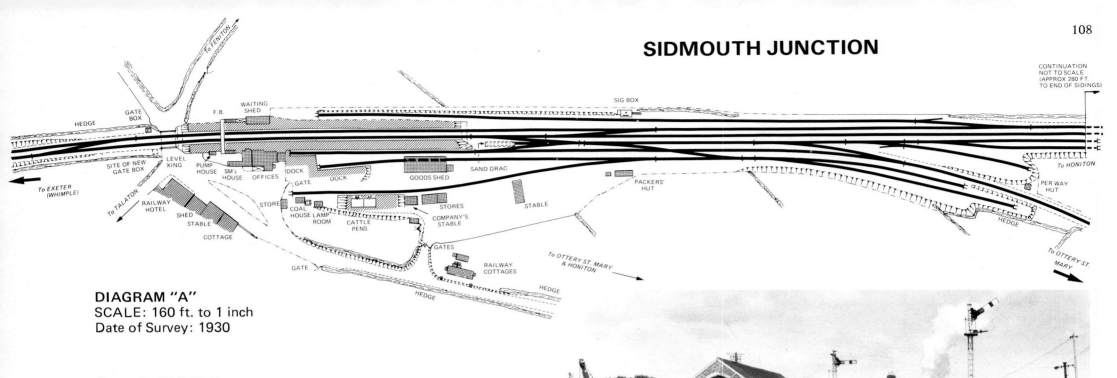

To FENITON

CONTINUATION
NOT TO SCALE
(APPROX 280 FT.
TO END OF SIDINGS)

SIG BOX

WAITING
SHED

F.B.

GATE
BOX

HEDGE

SITE OF NEW
GATE BOX

LEVEL
XING

PUMP
HOUSE

SM's
HOUSE

OFFICES

DOCK

GATE

DOCK

GOODS SHED

SAND DRAG

PACKERS'
HUT

PER WAY
HUT

To HONITON

To EXETER
(WHIMPLE)

To TALATON

RAILWAY
HOTEL

SHED
STABLE

COTTAGE

STORE

COAL
HOUSE LAMP
ROOM

CATTLE
PENS

COMPANY'S
STABLE

STORES

STABLE

HEDGE

GATE

GATES

RAILWAY
COTTAGES

To OTTERY ST. MARY
& HONITON

To OTTERY ST.
MARY

HEDGE

HEDGE

DIAGRAM "A"
SCALE: 160 ft. to 1 inch
Date of Survey: 1930

Opened: 19.7.1860
Closed: 6.9.1965 (Goods)
Closed: 6.3.1967 (Passengers)
Re-opened: 3.5.1971 (as "Feniton")

Right: Up Waterloo train leaves the station whilst
the Sidmouth connection waits in the bay.
photo: R.C. Riley

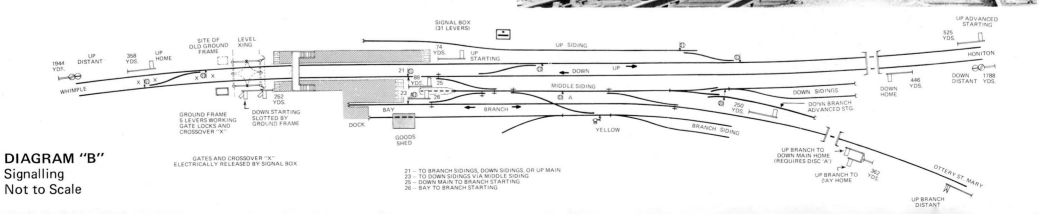

DIAGRAM "B"
Signalling
Not to Scale

SIGNAL BOX
(31 LEVERS)

UP ADVANCED
STARTING

525
YDS.

SITE OF
OLD GROUND
FRAME

LEVEL
XING

74
YDS.

UP
STARTING

UP SIDING

HONITON

1944
YDS.

UP
DISTANT

358
YDS.

UP
HOME

21
88
YDS.

25

DOWN

UP

446
YDS.

DOWN
DISTANT

1788
YDS.

WHIMPLE

X   X

X

X

252
YDS.

23

26

MIDDLE SIDING

A

DOWN SIDINGS

DOWN HOME

GROUND FRAME
5 LEVERS WORKING
GATE LOCKS AND
CROSSOVER "X"

DOWN STARTING
SLOTTED BY
GROUND FRAME

DOCK

BAY

BRANCH

250
YDS.

DOWN BRANCH
ADVANCED STG.

GOODS
SHED

YELLOW

BRANCH SIDING

UP BRANCH TO
DOWN MAIN HOME
(REQUIRES DISC 'A')

GATES AND CROSSOVER "X"
ELECTRICALLY RELEASED BY SIGNAL BOX

21 — TO BRANCH SIDINGS, DOWN SIDINGS, OR UP MAIN
23 — TO DOWN SIDINGS VIA MIDDLE SIDING
25 — DOWN MAIN TO BRANCH STARTING
26 — BAY TO BRANCH STARTING

UP BRANCH TO
BAY HOME

362
YDS.

OTTERY ST. MARY

UP BRANCH
DISTANT

Looking towards Whimple in 1964. The Western Region had been in possession for over a year, but had made little impression on the scene except for the diesel multiple unit forming the Sidmouth branch train.
photo: C.L. Caddy

General view of the eastern approach to Sidmouth Junction station, showing a branch train standing in the bay. The lofty signal box was fitted with a wire pulley for delivering the tablet for the single line to train crews.
photo: Lens of Sutton

SIDMOUTH JUNCTION

When first opened this station was of very little importance and was situated literally in the middle of nowhere—a fact reflected by the difficulty the L & SWR experienced in selecting a suitable name! Originally called "Feniton", it became "Ottery Road" on 1st July, 1861, retaining this name until February 1868 when it was given the misleading title "Ottery St. Mary". The town of that name was a good five miles away by indifferent lanes, and public complaints must have been loud for after two months it reverted to "Ottery Road". This name was quite suitable and would probably have lasted but for the opening of the Sidmouth Railway on 6th July, 1874, for which event it was renamed "Sidmouth Junction".

The station then became one of the most important on the line, although the original office and other buildings were retained, the platforms being lengthened and the canopy on the Down platform extended. At first the only connection between branch and main lines was an indirect one for the exchange of goods, but this arrangement was soon altered.

Traffic originating at the station was never very heavy, and became negligible once Ottery St. Mary received its own station on the branch. The crowds thronging the platforms were merely changing between the two lines, and most of the wagons in the yard were likewise transfers, but ironically passenger business improved when the motor car became popular. Some people living at places served by the branch then preferred to drive to Sidmouth Junction to start their rail journeys rather than change trains.

For many years there were daily through coaches between Waterloo and Sidmouth/Exmouth—and whole trains at Summer weekends—but the junction layout was hardly convenient and these movements were quite complicated. Down trains gained the branch via the Middle Siding, whilst Up ones required the crossover at the east end of the station to be clipped. These through workings did not last long after transfer to the Western Region in January 1963 (see "Budleigh Salterton").

Although local services on the main line were withdrawn on 7th March, 1966 Sidmouth Junction survived for another year, closure taking place when the branch services ceased. On 21st May, 1967 all points and sidings were taken out of use and the signal box closed, but the gate ground frame remained to control the crossing. The section from Honiton to Pinhoe was singled on 11th June, 1967.

Just before the closure of the station a large housing estate was being developed at Feniton on a site very close to the station, and after a prolonged struggle on the part of residents a train service was restored in 1971. The former Down platform was used, although it was shortened to accommodate just three coaches. The station buildings were demolished and a 'bus shelter-type waiting room was erected, tickets being issued from the gate box by the crossing keeper. This arrangement remains at the time of writing, although on 23rd June, 1974 the gate box was abolished, lifting barriers controlled from a new office on the platform being provided.

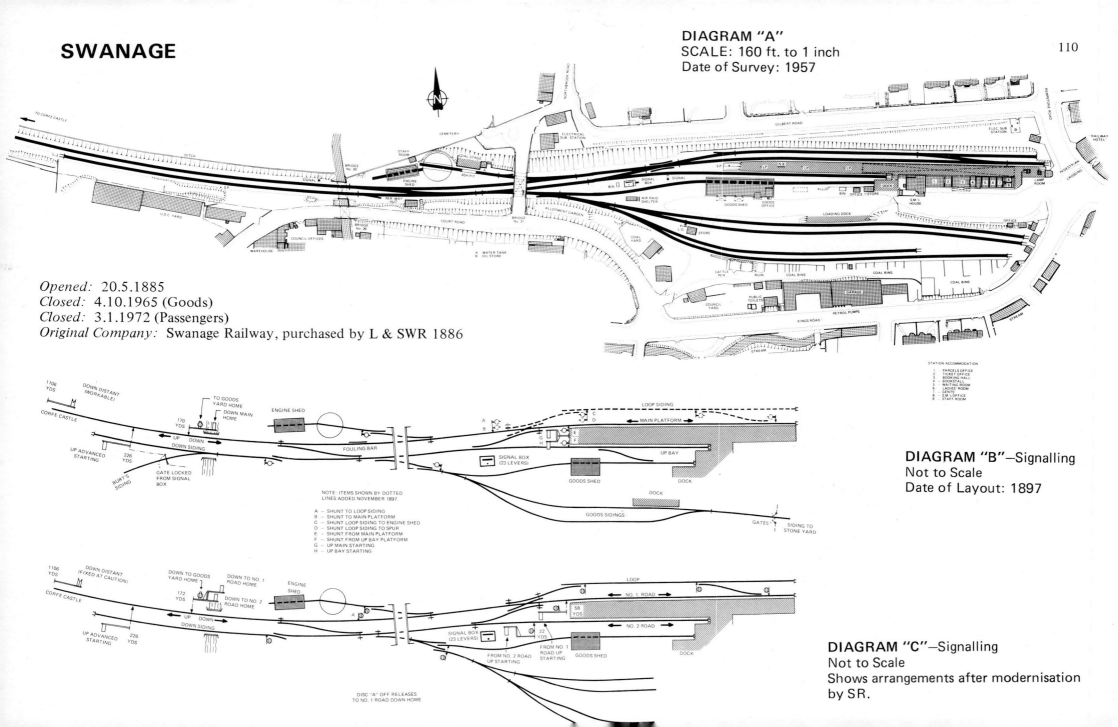

SWANAGE

DIAGRAM "A"
SCALE: 160 ft. to 1 inch
Date of Survey: 1957

110

Opened: 20.5.1885
Closed: 4.10.1965 (Goods)
Closed: 3.1.1972 (Passengers)
Original Company: Swanage Railway, purchased by L & SWR 1886

DIAGRAM "B"—Signalling
Not to Scale
Date of Layout: 1897

DIAGRAM "C"—Signalling
Not to Scale
Shows arrangements after modernisation by SR.

A – SHUNT TO LOOP SIDING
B – SHUNT TO MAIN PLATFORM
C – SHUNT LOOP SIDING TO ENGINE SHED
D – SHUNT LOOP SIDING TO SPUR
E – SHUNT FROM MAIN PLATFORM
F – SHUNT FROM UP BAY PLATFORM
G – UP MAIN STARTING
H – UP BAY STARTING

NOTE: ITEMS SHOWN BY DOTTED LINES ADDED NOVEMBER 1897.

STATION ACCOMMODATION
1. PARCELS OFFICE
2. TICKET OFFICE
3. BOOKING HALL
4. BOOKSTALL
5. WAITING ROOM
6. LADIES' ROOM
7. GENTS'
8. S.M.'s OFFICE
9. STAFF ROOM

SWANAGE

This Dorset terminus has been frequently featured in the railway press, but it is so well suited to modelling that it must be included in any book on Southern stations.

Although the Swanage Railway was only a small local Company, their stations had none of the air of poverty often encountered on such lines. Purbeck Stone was used for the offices and adjoining Station Master's house, and both the engine shed and the goods shed were of the same material. However, the original track layout was not as generous as the buildings. Trains could only arrive at the main platform and the stock had to be propelled out of the station to be run round between the crossovers, before being shunted back into the platform ready for the departure. This was remedied in November 1897, when a loop was provided (see diagram "B"). Also shown on diagram "B" is the full extent of the original goods yard; the two additional sidings were laid in around 1900. At that time "Kings Road" only existed as a footpath, and a siding to a stone yard crossed it and ran behind the buildings in Station Road. This siding terminated within about 200 yds of the pier tramway, and in view of its proximity it is rather surprising that no attempt was made to link the harbour to the railway system.

The Victorians began to develop Swanage as a resort, but it was between the Wars that it finally ceased to be a quarrying/fishing settlement and gave itself up to catering for visitors. In recognition of the expanding passenger business, the Southern carried out extensive modernisation about 1938. The booking hall was finished in glazed tiles and the old cast iron gas lamp standards gave way to more mundane concrete fittings, but although the buildings were also considerably extended at the same time this work was carried out to the same style of architecture and in the same materials, thus preserving the overall neat appearance. In December 1945 the signalling was altered so that trains could arrive at either platform, the points between the Bay Line and the Loading Dock (near the goods shed) being taken out to create a lever for working the additional facing-point locks. The truck weighbridge was also abolished. Diagrams "A" and "C" show the station in this modernised form.

The large goods yard once dealt with considerable stone traffic, but latterly goods traffic was light and only justified two trains per week—on Tuesdays and Thursdays. The sidings were still well used, however, for the berthing of coaching stock, there being no proper carriage sidings.

In the respects the branch was by far the busiest in Dorset, there being seventeen trains each way per day—three conveying through Waterloo carriages—and this number was often swollen by excursions.

Although the Beeching report did not recommend Swanage for closure, economies started to be made in the late 'sixties. Following the withdrawal of freight and the change from steam traction to diesel-electric multiple units, all sidings were taken out of use and the signal box closed on 6th June, 1967. The line below Corfe Castle was then worked under "One Train" regulations, all trains running to the main platform (No. 1 Road) at Swanage. Through carriages to Waterloo ceased on 3rd October, 1969.

Most of the station buildings (except the signal box) still stand in good condition, and a preservation society is currently hoping to relay track in the platforms and operate a service for visitors. The goods yard and forecourt have become a depot for 'buses and motor coaches.

In conclusion it is worth noting that "Burt's Siding" on diagram "B" served a stone yard. This site was later taken over by the local authority, and is shown as "U.D.C. Yard" on the scale plan.

2-6-2 tank No. 41224 on the turntable at Swanage in 1963. *photo: C.L. Caddy*

Swanage in the '60s. The reconstructed canopy can be seen behind the train, and the ornamental gas lamps have given way to Southern concrete standards. *photo: C.L. Caddy*

View from the road bridge showing the signal box and goods shed. The small building behind the carriages in the yard (next to the loading gauge) was the old wagon weighbridge, taken out of use in 1938.

photo: B.L. Jackson

Swanage in the '30s, showing the original canopy and gas lamps before the station was modernised. The engine is one of Drummond's "M7" class—regular performers on the line for many years.

photo: Lens of Sutton

Looking through the road bridge towards Corfe Castle. The "M7" is propelling its push-and-pull set out of the station. The engine shed can be seen on the right.

photo: J.H. Aston

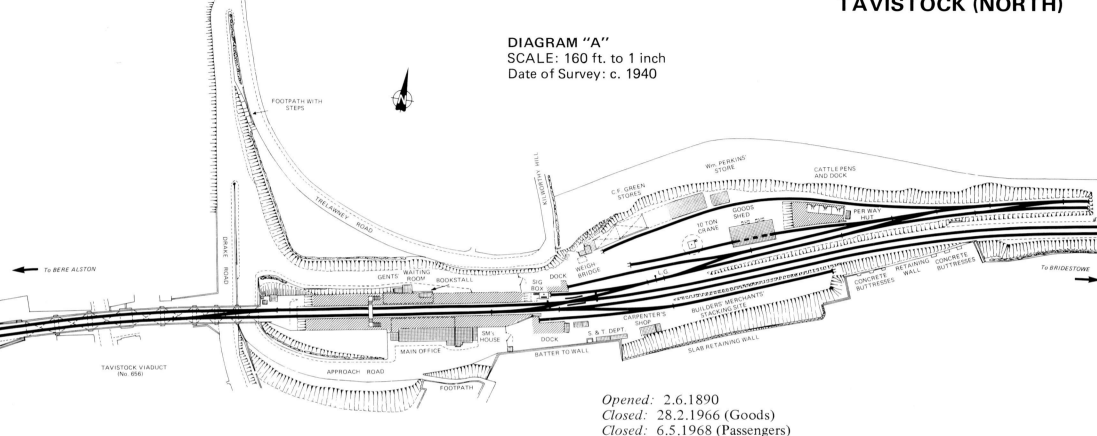

TAVISTOCK (NORTH)

DIAGRAM "A"
SCALE: 160 ft. to 1 inch
Date of Survey: c. 1940

To BERE ALSTON

FOOTPATH WITH STEPS

TRELAWNEY ROAD

KILWORTHY HILL

Wm. PERKINS' STORE

C.F. GREEN STORES

CATTLE PENS AND DOCK

PER WAY HUT

GOODS SHED

10 TON CRANE

DRAKE ROAD

GENTS'
WAITING ROOM
BOOKSTALL

WEIGH-BRIDGE

DOCK

SIG BOX

L.G.

CONCRETE RETAINING WALL CONCRETE BUTTRESSES

To BRIDESTOWE

CONCRETE BUTTRESSES

BUILDERS' MERCHANTS' STACKING SITE

CARPENTER'S SHOP

SM's HOUSE

DOCK

S & T DEPT.

SLAB RETAINING WALL

MAIN OFFICE

BATTER TO WALL

APPROACH ROAD

FOOTPATH

TAVISTOCK VIADUCT (No. 656)

Opened: 2.6.1890
Closed: 28.2.1966 (Goods)
Closed: 6.5.1968 (Passengers)
Original Company: Plymouth, Devonport and South Western Junction Rly. amalgamated with Southern Railway 1923.

DIAGRAM "B"
Signalling
Not to Scale

UP STARTING (CO-ACTING)

DISC TO UP SDGS.

UP SIDINGS

UP ADVANCED STARTING

13 YDS.

SIG. BOX 21 LEVERS

389 YDS.

To BRENTOR

1151 YDS.

UP DISTANT

314 YDS.

UP HOME.

UP

DOWN

1267 YDS.

DOWN DISTANT

From BERE ALSTON

VIADUCT

151 YDS.

DOWN STARTING

74 YDS.

DOWN HOME

DOWN SIDING

328 YDS.

DOWN ADVANCED STARTING

113

Below: In Western Region days. No. D831 *Monarch* enters the station with the 10.25 Brighton to Plymouth on 3rd October, 1964.   *photo: C.L. Caddy*

TAVISTOCK (NORTH)

As main line stations go, Tavistock North is a comparative new-comer. L & SWR trains reached Plymouth on 17th May, 1876 by sharing the GWR's single line south of Lydford, but this arrangement was far from satisfactory and caused much delay.

Competition was keen for West of England traffic, particularly the ocean liner business from Plymouth docks, and in a bid to free itself of GWR domination, the L & SWR supported the local company in its scheme to construct a double-track link between Lydford and the existing terminus at Devonport. The terrain was difficult for railway building, viaducts, tunnels and heavy earthworks being necessary. As can be seen from diagram "A" the Tavistock station site was blasted out of the steep hillside, and reaching it from the town centre involved quite a climb! The difficulty of the site resulted in a rather cramped and awkward goods yard layout, excessive earthmoving being needed to provide a more convenient arrangement.

From the outset the line was leased and worked by the L & SWR, although the independent Company remained in existence until the Grouping. Normal weekday services consisted of about five Waterloo expresses in each direction, a through Brighton–Plymouth train, and a few "locals", some of which terminated at Tavistock or Brentor. This pattern survived until September 1966, when the through Waterloo service was withdrawn. The Brighton train lasted until 6th March, 1967, but thereafter there was nothing except an infrequent stopping service of diesel multiple units.

The suffix "North" was added after Nationalisation to distinguish it from the former GWR establishment, which became "South". The station passed into Western Region control for the first time in 1950, but operationally it was still tied to Waterloo, and the Southern re-gained it in 1958. Further regional boundary changes took place in January 1963 and the line once again became Western Region territory, and this time there was no going back.

The station buildings were solidly constructed of local stone, and there were few alterations to either the station itself or the signalling throughout its working life. Despite the loss of goods traffic in 1966 there was no attempt to rationalise the layout, the sidings remaining rusty and unused until the demolition trains arrived.

TIPTON ST. JOHN'S

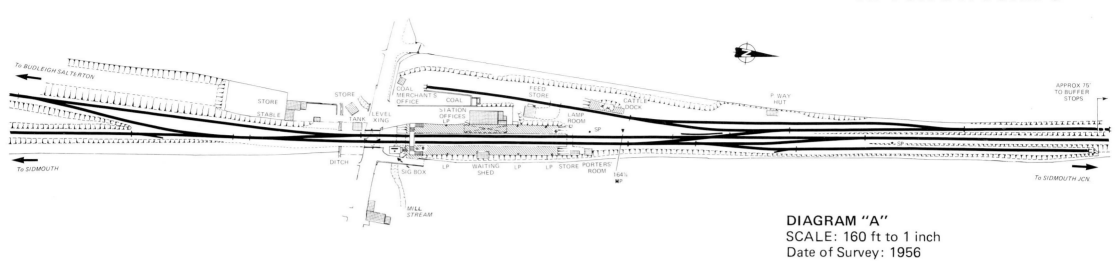

DIAGRAM "A"
SCALE: 160 ft to 1 inch
Date of Survey: 1956

Opened: 6.7.1874
Closed: 27.1.1964 (Goods)
Closed: 6.3.1967 (Passengers)
Original Company: Sidmouth Railway & Harbour Co.

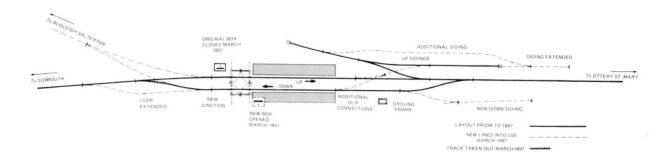

DIAGRAM "B"
New works of 1897
Not to Scale

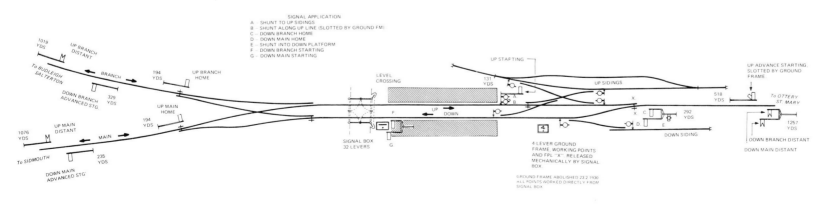

SIGNAL APPLICATION

A – SHUNT TO UP SIDINGS
B – SHUNT ALONG UP LINE (SLOTTED BY GROUND FM)
C – DOWN BRANCH HOME
D – DOWN MAIN HOME
E – SHUNT INTO DOWN PLATFORM
F – DOWN BRANCH STARTING
G – DOWN MAIN STARTING

DIAGRAM "C"
Signalling—1898
Not to Scale

115

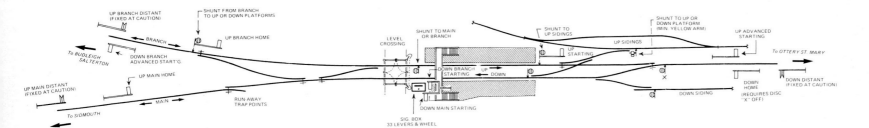

DIAGRAM "D"
Layout & Signalling following alterations to junction layout, 1953
Not to Scale

TIPTON ST JOHN'S

Opened as "Tipton", the station was renamed in February 1881. It served a small village, and at that time was the least important station on the Sidmouth line, one solitary siding being sufficient for goods traffic. Much new work was necessary when the Budleigh Salterton Railway selected it as the junction for their branch (diagram "B" shows the extent of the alterations) the new signal box and additional sidings being inspected by the Board of Trade on 17th April, 1897. The inspector was less than happy about passengers changing trains having to cross the line by a sleeper crossing, and recommended that a footbridge be provided, this being done by February 1898.

The Budleigh Salterton branch opened on 15th May, 1897 and was extended through to Exmouth on 1st June, 1903.

For a branch line station the traffic working was complicated, the signal box being a well-deserved "Class 3" at a time when many principal main line boxes rated no higher. The pattern for connecting trains was as follows: Two Up trains would approach Tipton St. John's within a few minutes of each other, one of them going forward to Sidmouth Junction and the other terminating. The terminating train would be admitted first and having disgorged its passengers, would be drawn ahead to the Up Sidings, where a useful loop enabled running-round to take place without fouling the main lines. Up and Down through trains would then pass in the platforms, after which the train in the Up Sidings was drawn into the Down Platform to form a connecting service for whichever line had not been served by the preceding through train. These hectic bouts of activity were repeated several times in the course of a shift.

Leaving Tipton the line to Sidmouth climbed at 1 in 45 for two miles, and this imposed severe restrictions on the load of trains. Down trains were limited to 160 tons, and Up ones to 180 tons, and goods trains had to be worked with a heavy brake van if one was available. If not, two lighter vans (with a guard in each) had to be used. Some official must have been haunted by the vision of trains getting out of control on this gradient, for when the junction was remodelled in 1953 trap points were installed to protect the level crossing and station (see diagram "D").

Looking from the level crossing towards Ottery St. Mary.   *photo: Lens of Sutton*

Although goods traffic survived on the branch until May 1967, facilities were withdrawn from Tipton in 1964. The sidings remained in use for the shunting of terminating passenger trains as previously described. Otherwise the station remained reasonably busy until closure, although the replacement of steam by diesel multiple units from 4th November, 1963 simplified the junction work to some extent. The main disadvantage of dieselisation was that it brought about the demise of the through Waterloo carriages on weekdays, although these continued as complete trains on Summer Saturdays until the end of the 1965 season.

All track and fittings were removed shortly after closure in 1967, but the main station building survived as a private house.

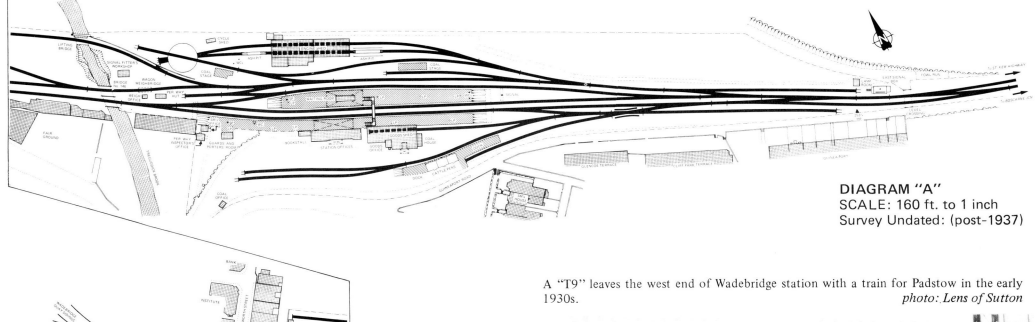

DIAGRAM "A"
SCALE: 160 ft. to 1 inch
Survey Undated: (post-1937)

A "T9" leaves the west end of Wadebridge station with a train for Padstow in the early 1930s.

photo: Lens of Sutton

Original station opened: 4.7.1834
Company: Bodmin & Wadebridge Rly. acquired by L & SWR 1847
Station on present site opened: 3.9.1888
Closed: 30.1.1967 (Passengers)
Closed: 2.9.1978 (Goods)

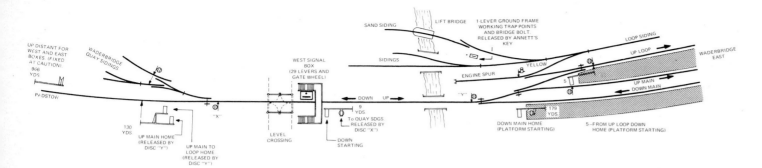

UP DISTANT FOR
WEST AND EAST
BOXES. (FIXED
AT CAUTION)
966 YDS

WADEBRIDGE
QUAY SIDINGS

PADSTOW

SAND SIDING

LIFT BRIDGE

1-LEVER GROUND FRAME
WORKING TRAP POINTS
AND BRIDGE BOLT.
RELEASED BY ANNETT'S
KEY

SIDINGS

WEST SIGNAL
BOX
(29 LEVERS AND
GATE WHEEL)

ENGINE SPUR

YELLOW

LOOP SIDING

UP LOOP

WADEBRIDGE
EAST

UP MAIN
DOWN MAIN

DOWN   UP

130 YDS

UP MAIN HOME
(RELEASED BY
DISC "Y")

UP MAIN TO
LOOP HOME
(RELEASED BY
DISC "Y")

"X"

LEVEL
CROSSING

9 YDS
To QUAY SDGS
RELEASED BY
DISC "X"

DOWN
STARTING

"Y"

DOWN MAIN HOME
(PLATFORM STARTING)

5

179 YDS.

5—FROM UP LOOP DOWN
HOME (PLATFORM STARTING)

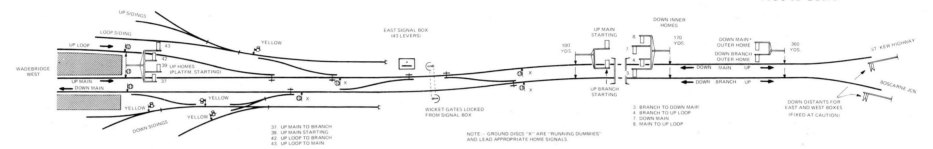

UP SIDINGS

LOOP SIDING

UP LOOP

43

WADEBRIDGE
WEST

UP MAIN

DOWN MAIN

42
39
37

UP HOMES
(PLATFM. STARTING)

YELLOW

YELLOW   YELLOW

YELLOW

DOWN SIDINGS

YELLOW

EAST SIGNAL BOX
(43 LEVERS)

X

X

WICKET GATES LOCKED
FROM SIGNAL BOX

NOTE:— GROUND DISCS "X" ARE "RUNNING DUMMIES"
AND LEAD APPROPRIATE HOME SIGNALS.

37. UP MAIN TO BRANCH
39. UP MAIN STARTING
42. UP LOOP TO BRANCH
43. UP LOOP TO MAIN

UP MAIN
STARTING

100
YDS.

UP BRANCH
STARTING

8
7
4
3

170
YDS.

DOWN INNER
HOMES

DOWN MAIN
OUTER HOME

DOWN BRANCH
OUTER HOME

DOWN   MAIN   UP

DOWN   BRANCH   UP

3. BRANCH TO DOWN MAIN
4. BRANCH TO UP LOOP
7. DOWN MAIN
8. MAIN TO UP LOOP

360
YDS.

ST. KEW HIGHWAY

BOSCARNE JCN

DOWN DISTANTS FOR
EAST AND WEST BOXES
(FIXED AT CAUTION)

Looking towards Padstow in July 1961. The extension to the goods shed is obvious in this picture.
photo: C.L. Caddy

One of the veteran "0298" class, No. 30586 shunts the Down siding on 19th July, 1961.
photo: C.L. Caddy

WADEBRIDGE

Early history of the Bodmin and Wadebridge Railway cannot be dealt with in this volume. The first station was on a slightly different site nearer to the sand dock, and was swept away when the L & SWR carried out deviation works in 1888 and erected the nucleus of the station illustrated by these plans. The original B & W sand dock and quay sidings remained. Diagram "D" shows this arrangement, the single platform being adequate for the traffic even after the North Cornwall line opened on 1st June, 1895. However, when the extension to Padstow was under construction in 1899 the station was considerably enlarged, an island platform 105 yds in length, complete with waiting room and generous canopy, being added. This work also involved considerable re-arrangement of the track layout and signalling, the original goods connection across Molesworth Street to the quay being upgraded as a passenger line. The original signal box was closed, and new "East" and "West" boxes brought into use. The section to Padstow opened on 27th March, 1899.

Initially the lines to Launceston and Bodmin respectively joined at an isolated signal box called "Wadebridge Junction", but in February 1907 the Launceston line was extended to run parallel to the existing single line right into Wadebridge station, where a new scissors crossing was provided to permit traffic off either line to run directly to any part of the station. The old Junction box was then abolished, and the lever frame in the East box was extended from the original 29 levers to 43, whilst that in the West box was increased from 20 to 27. This work was inspected and sanctioned by the Board of Trade on 7th June, 1907.

In February 1908 there were further alterations in connection with the introduction of rail-motors on the Bodmin line. A two-road "Motor Shed" was built onto the east end of the existing engine shed, the two tracks being extended to a new connection with the Loop line operated from the East box.

At first passengers using the island platform crossed the line by a sleeper crossing, but the wooden footbridge was provided by about 1910. The Southern Railway replaced this with one of their concrete structures c.1930, the goods shed being doubled in length at around the same time, the extension being at the west end. Unfortunately the SR precast concrete style did not blend happily with the original buildings of local stone! In 1937 the scissors crossing at East Box was taken out and replaced by the two separate crossovers shown in the plans.

Despite the extremely rural nature of all three routes that converged on Wadebridge, the station was surprisingly busy and shunting always seemed to be in progress. London passengers even had a choice of route; they could either travel "Southern" to Waterloo (there were several through daily trains), or catch the local to Bodmin Road for a connection to Paddington! Transfer to the Western Region in January 1963 foretold the end of the Waterloo service, all through trains being withdrawn in September 1966. The Launceston line closed on 1st October that year, leaving the station to be served solely from Bodmin Road for the last few months of the passenger service. Both signal boxes were abolished on 17th December, 1967, such points as were necessary to cater for the surviving goods traffic being fitted with hand levers.

Since complete closure in 1978 many of the buildings, including the large engine shed, have been demolished.

Activity at Wadebridge in the 1950s. A train for Bodmin stands in the Loop platform whilst one of the "0298" Tanks shunts the goods shed. *photo: R.C. Riley*

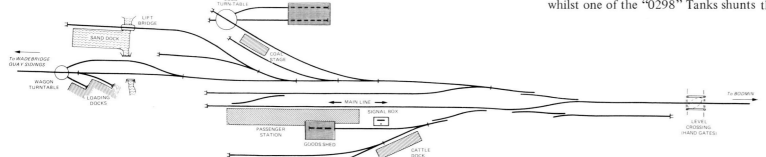

DIAGRAM "D"
Not to Scale
Sketch plan of layout in 1898, before extension of the station and opening of line to Padstow

WADHURST

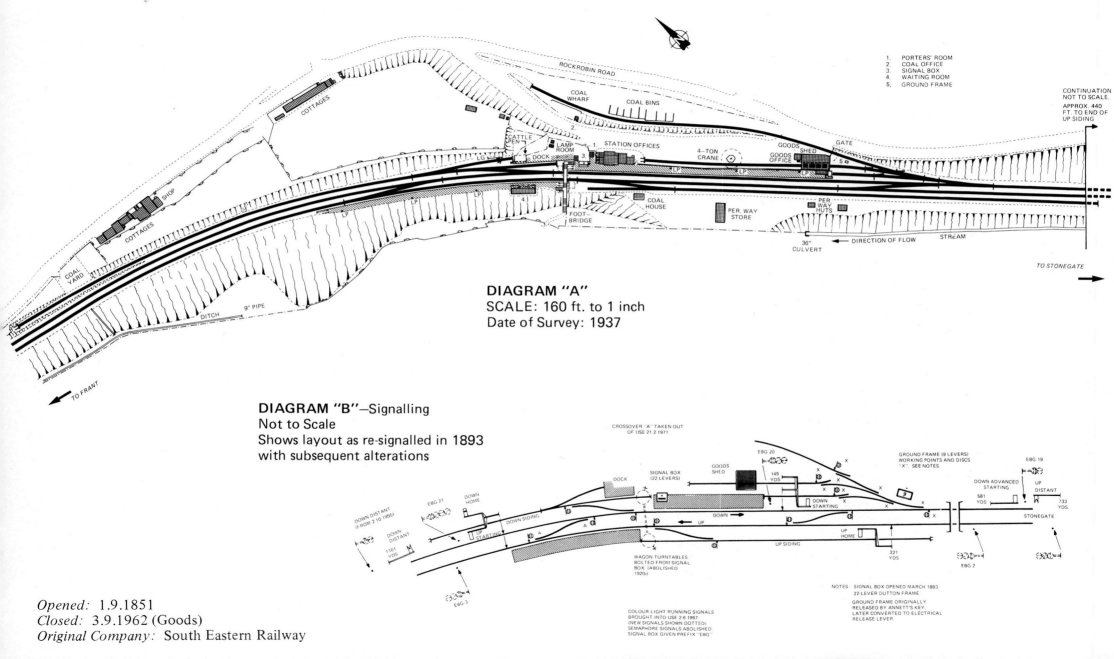

1. PORTERS' ROOM
2. COAL OFFICE
3. SIGNAL BOX
4. WAITING ROOM
5. GROUND FRAME

CONTINUATION
NOT TO SCALE.

APPROX. 440
FT. TO END OF
UP SIDING

ROCKROBIN ROAD

COAL WHARF

COAL BINS

COTTAGES

CATTLE
PEN

LAMP
ROOM

DOCK

STATION OFFICES

4—TON
CRANE

GOODS
SHED

GATE

GOODS
OFFICE

SHOP

COAL
HOUSE

PER.
WAY
HUTS

FOOT—
BRIDGE

PER. WAY
STORE

COTTAGES

COAL
YARD

36"
CULVERT

DIRECTION OF FLOW

STREAM

9" PIPE

DITCH

TO STONEGATE

TO FRANT

DIAGRAM "A"
SCALE: 160 ft. to 1 inch
Date of Survey: 1937

DIAGRAM "B"—Signalling
Not to Scale
Shows layout as re-signalled in 1893
with subsequent alterations

CROSSOVER "A" TAKEN OUT
OF USE 21.2 1971

EBG 20

GROUND FRAME (9 LEVERS)
WORKING POINTS AND DISCS
"X". SEE NOTES.

EBG 19

DOCK

SIGNAL BOX
(22 LEVERS)

GOODS
SHED

145
YDS

DOWN ADVANCED
STARTING

UP
DISTANT

DOWN DISTANT
(FROM 2.10 1955)

EBG 21

DOWN
HOME

DOWN
STARTING

DOWN SIDING

DOWN

581
YDS

733
YDS

DOWN
DISTANT

UP
STARTING

UP

9

STONEGATE

1161
YDS

A

A

UP HOME

UP SIDING

221
YDS

WAGON TURNTABLES
BOLTED FROM SIGNAL
BOX. (ABOLISHED
1920J

EBG 2

EBG 3

NOTES: SIGNAL BOX OPENED MARCH 1893.
22 LEVER DUTTON FRAME.

GROUND FRAME ORIGINALLY
RELEASED BY ANNETT'S KEY,
LATER CONVERTED TO ELECTRICAL
RELEASE LEVER.

COLOUR LIGHT RUNNING SIGNALS
BROUGHT INTO USE 2.6 1957.
(NEW SIGNALS SHOWN DOTTED)
SEMAPHORE SIGNALS ABOLISHED.
SIGNAL BOX GIVEN PREFIX "EBG".

Opened: 1.9.1851
Closed: 3.9.1962 (Goods)
Original Company: South Eastern Railway

View towards Frant c. 1880, before the construction of the new signal box. The original box, a tiny hut-like building, can be seen immediately below the signal.

photo: Lens of Sutton

The "new" Dutton signal box of 1893 as it appears today. When comparing this view to the older one (left), it becomes apparent that the station offices were extended by one bay at some time. Thankfully the same style was used.

photo: G.J. Bowring

WADHURST

Looking at the old photograph (above), one might be forgiven for mistaking Wadhurst for a station on a branch line! Not so, for it is situated on the Tonbridge–Hastings main line of the SER – a line which many people consider to pass through some of the most attractive scenery in the South of England. The stations are attractive too, this example being a masterpiece by the architect William Tress. The style can best be described as a restrained "Italianate" (although there are some Classical features) and the building remains in good condition at the time of writing (1979).

The South Eastern's use of staggered platforms is well known. Here at Wadhurst there was a direct connection across the main lines between the Up and Down Sidings. Originally there was no footbridge, and passengers also crossed the line by means of a sleeper crossing at the same point. These features were not uncommon on the SER, but most of the siding connections involving wagon turntables had gone by the mid-1920s.

The Up platform was only equipped with a small shelter. The goods shed was of brick and rather plain in style, bearing little resemblance to the main passenger building. The layout was entirely resignalled in 1893, a new wooden signal box being supplied by the well-known firm of Dutton.

For many years the station had a rather infrequent service, but with the introduction of diesel multiple units in 1958 a basically hourly service was introduced. Four years later the goods facilities were withdrawn and the sidings in the yard removed. In the motor age this was perhaps inevitable, but it is also a pity. Had full services been retained Wadhurst would have provided the perfect example of an SER wayside station, particularly since the original building of 1851 has not been obscured by a platform canopy as in so many other cases.

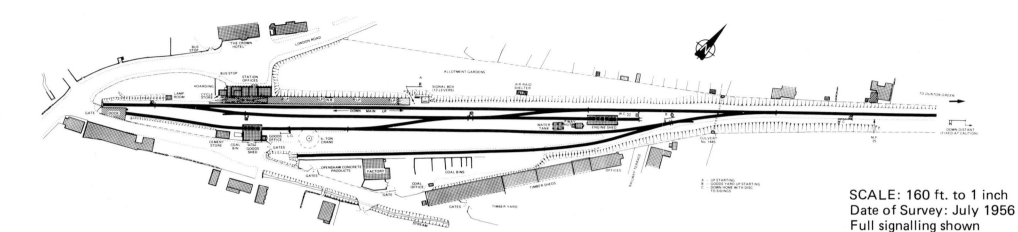

SCALE: 160 ft. to 1 inch
Date of Survey: July 1956
Full signalling shown

General view of station from near coal bins, August, 1935.   *photo: Lens of Sutton*

Opened: 7.7.1881
Closed: 30.10.1961 (Completely)
Original Company: Westerham Valley Railway, absorbed by SER
August 1881

OPERATING NOTES: Trains were authorised to run between Dunton Green and Westerham without a guard. A junior porter could accompany the train for the purpose of collecting tickets and sorting parcels. Some special and excursion trains were permitted to work over the branch with an engine at each end. Goods traffic for the intermediate station at Brasted could be worked as a trip, the brake van being propelled on the return journey.

View from the buffer stops around 1950.

photo: Lens of Sutton

WESTERHAM

Although initially the property of a local Company this line was very much a creature of the South Eastern, that Company constructing it and operating the service from the outset. This explains why the simple wooden buildings are so similar to those at many other SER stations of the period, some of which are covered in this volume.

One platform was sufficient to accommodate the traffic, and both the goods and engine shed matched the station offices by being of timber construction. The engine shed was closed around 1930 and was partially demolished to leave only the brick base, but the siding which served it continued to be used for watering and stabling engines until the closure of the line.

The layout of the yard was a little unusual, particularly in the position of the loading dock. This could only be used for side loading into wagons standing at the end of the main line! It was possible to run round fairly long trains, but the service generally worked as a "push-and-pull" shuttle from Dunton Green. During 1936 the Sentinel-Cammell steam rail bus was tried on the branch, but it was mechanically unreliable and lasted only a few months.

There had been plans in pre-Grouping days to electrify to Westerham using the 1,500 volts d.c. system, but neither this nor any subsequent scheme was carried out. In many ways this turned out to be the line's undoing, for once the neighbouring main lines were electrified it became inconvenient to operate this isolated section of steam railway. Although there was some commuter business to London, it was not enough to stave off eventual closure, particularly as part of the trackbed was in the path of the proposed motorway! A preservation society was formed but failed to realise its ambition, and very little remains on the site of Westerham station today.

Close-up view of the wooden station buildings.

photo: R.C. Riley 123

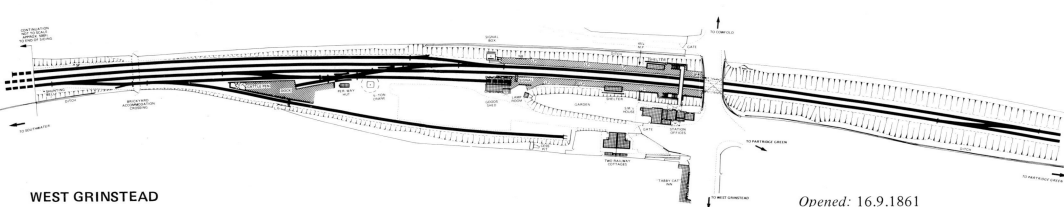

WEST GRINSTEAD

This station was situated on the line from Christ's Hospital to Shoreham, and is included as an example of a "typical" LB & SCR wayside station—not so much because of the position of its buildings, but because of their style. It was built at the point where the road crossed the railway in a deep cutting, the office buildings being placed at road level. Attached to the office block was a two-storey house for the Station Master, and a pair of cottages was provided for other staff. The station was in a somewhat isolated location, the nearest village being a good mile away. The line opened as single track and was doubled between 1877 and 1879, the Down platform and signal box being additions of that period.

The connection between the sidings and main line are interesting, and unusually complicated for such a small station. The Down Siding could accommodate a train of fifty wagons. It was useful for refuge purposes, but local instructions also insisted that any Down freight train stopping to shunt the yard was placed therein. Before work was commenced the front brake van had to be detached and "screwed down" at the south end of the station—a precaution against runaways on the falling gradient towards Partridge Green. There was no headshunt to the yard, but this was not a serious handicap on this comparatively quiet line.

In 1946 the Southern Railway announced their intention to electrify the line, but the outbreak of war caused work to be postponed and the scheme was never revived. However, the train service was improved in 1958 by the introduction of diesel electric multiple units running on an hourly interval basis.

All the goods yards between Horsham and Shoreham closed at the same time (September 1961), and in November 1963 there was a similar purge on signal boxes which left Steyning as the only intermediate block post. It was still possible to maintain the hourly service, as the double track was retained throughout.

The large goods shed was demolished prior to closure (c.1962), and most of the other buildings have now gone. The office buildings at road level survived until recently, albeit in very poor condition.

DIAGRAM "A"
SCALE: 160 ft. to 1 inch
Date of Survey: 1958

Opened: 16.9.1861
Closed: September 1961 (Goods)
Closed: 7.3.1966 (Passengers)
Original Company: LB & SCR

View from the footbridge with Down train arriving.   *photo: R.C. Riley*

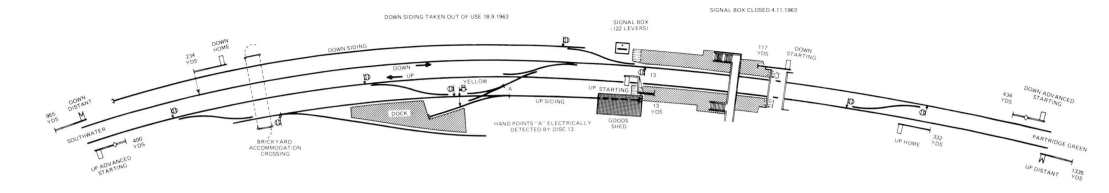

DOWN SIDING TAKEN OUT OF USE 18.9.1963

SIGNAL BOX CLOSED 4.11.1963

SIGNAL BOX
(22 LEVERS)

DOWN
HOME

234
YDS

DOWN SIDING

117
YDS

DOWN
STARTING

DOWN
DISTANT

DOWN

UP

YELLOW

434
YDS

DOWN ADVANCED
STARTING

965
YDS

A

UP STARTING

13

SOUTHWATER

UP SIDING

13
YDS

PARTRIDGE GREEN

400
YDS

DOCK

HAND POINTS "A" ELECTRICALLY
DETECTED BY DISC 13.

GOODS
SHED

UP ADVANCED
STARTING

BRICKYARD
ACCOMMODATION
CROSSING

332
YDS

UP HOME

1335
YDS

UP DISTANT

DIAGRAM "B"—Signalling
Not to Scale

Looking towards Partridge Green c. 1964. The station house and offices are at the higher level on the right.

photo: J. Scrace collection

View towards Southwater c. 1960. The nameboard, footbridge, shelters and signal box are all typical LB & SCR.

photo: J.H. Aston

WIMBORNE

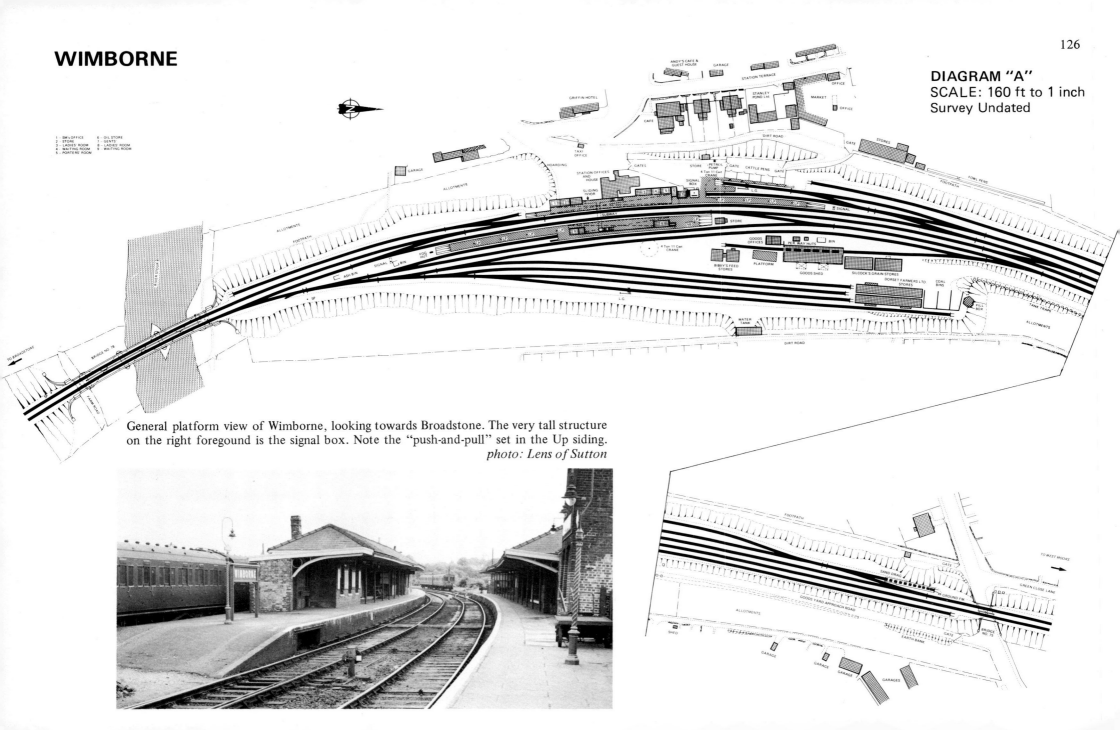

1 – SM's OFFICE   6 – OIL STORE
2 – STORE   7 – GENTS'
3 – LADIES' ROOM   8 – LADIES' ROOM
4 – WAITING ROOM   9 – WAITING ROOM
5 – PORTERS' ROOM

ANDY'S CAFE & GUEST HOUSE
GARAGE
STATION TERRACE
GRIFFIN HOTEL
STANLEY POND Ltd.
MARKET
OFFICE
OFFICE
CAFE
DIRT ROAD
GATE
STORES
TAXI OFFICE
GARAGE
HOARDING
STATION OFFICES AND HOUSE
GATES
STORE
PETROL PUMP
4 Ton 11 Cwt CRANE
GATE
CATTLE PENS
GATE
FOOTPATH
FOWL PENS
ALLOTMENTS
FOOTPATH
SLIDING DOOR
SIGNAL BOX
L.G
SUBWAY
STORE
SIGNAL
RIVER STOUR
SIGNAL
BIN
FOG HUT
GOODS OFFICES
PER WAY HUTS
BIN
4 Ton 11 Cwt CRANE
ASH BIN
BIBBY'S FEED STORES
PLATFORM
GOODS SHED
SILCOCK'S GRAIN STORES
DORSET FARMERS LTD. STORES
COAL BINS
SP
L.G
WATER TANK
PILL BOX
TANK TRAPS
ALLOTMENTS
TO BROADSTONE
BRIDGE NO. 78
FARM ROAD
DIRT ROAD

General platform view of Wimborne, looking towards Broadstone. The very tall structure on the right foregound is the signal box. Note the "push-and-pull" set in the Up siding.

photo: Lens of Sutton

WIMBORNE

FOOTPATH
TO WEST MOORS
SAND DRAG
GATE
GROUND FM
GREEN CLOSE LANE
ALLOTMENTS
GOODS YARD APPROACH ROAD
SHED
EARTH BANK
GATE
BRIDGE NO. 75
GARAGE
GARAGE
GARAGE
GARAGES

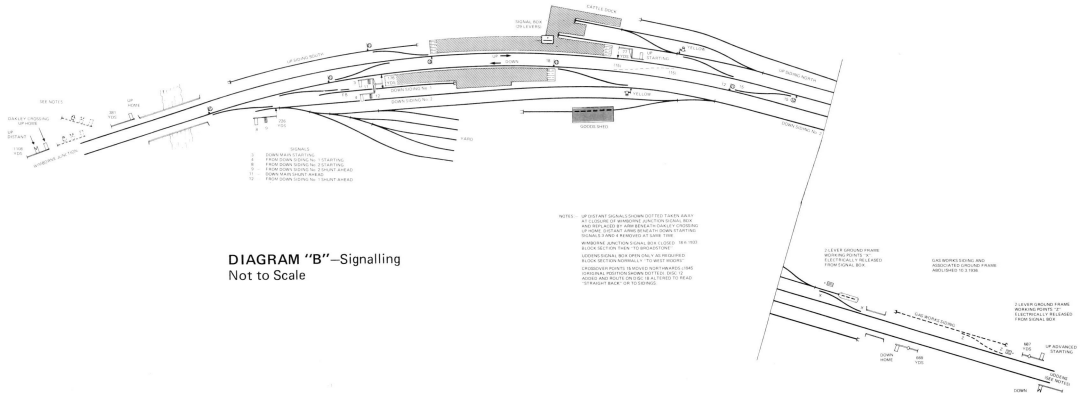

DIAGRAM "B"—Signalling
Not to Scale

SIGNALS

3	DOWN MAIN STARTING
4	FROM DOWN SIDING No. 1 STARTING
8	FROM DOWN SIDING No. 2 STARTING
9	FROM DOWN SIDING No. 2 SHUNT AHEAD
11	DOWN MAIN SHUNT AHEAD
12	FROM DOWN SIDING No. 1 SHUNT AHEAD

NOTES:— UP DISTANT SIGNALS SHOWN DOTTED TAKEN AWAY
AT CLOSURE OF WIMBORNE JUNCTION SIGNAL BOX
AND REPLACED BY ARM BENEATH OAKLEY CROSSING
UP HOME. DISTANT ARMS BENEATH DOWN STARTING
SIGNALS 3 AND 4 REMOVED AT SAME TIME

WIMBORNE JUNCTION SIGNAL BOX CLOSED 18.6.1933.
BLOCK SECTION THEN "TO BROADSTONE"

UDDENS SIGNAL BOX OPEN ONLY AS REQUIRED
BLOCK SECTION NORMALLY "TO WEST MOORS"

CROSSOVER POINTS 15 MOVED NORTHWARDS c1945
(ORIGINAL POSITION SHOWN DOTTED). DISC 12
ADDED AND ROUTE ON DISC 18 ALTERED TO READ
"STRAIGHT BACK" OR TO SIDINGS.

Opened: 1.6.1847
Closed: 4.5.1965 (Passengers)
Closed: 2.5.1977 (Goods)
Original Company: Southampton and Dorchester Rly. amalgamated with
L & SWR 1848.

Looking towards West Moors. The coal wagons on the extreme right are standing in what was once a short platform for the use of Somerset and Dorset trains.

photo: Lens of Sutton

WIMBORNE

This has been one of the saddest closures of recent years, (perhaps second only to Templecombe), for unlike many stations falling to the "Beeching Axe" which had never been more than moderately busy, Wimborne could once be described as the most important junction in Dorset! Originally it was just another intermediate station between Southampton and Dorchester, but the opening of the Dorset Central Railway to Blandford on 31st October, 1860 was the first step in enhancing its importance. The physical junction was on the Broadstone side of the River Stour viaduct, but Wimborne station became the exchange point for traffic.

Such a development was modest enough, but this branch was extended to join the Somerset Central three years later, thus forming the famous if impecunious "Somerset & Dorset", and the opening of that Company's Bath Extension in 1874 turned it into a valuable North-South route. Through trains from the S & D to Bournemouth had to reverse at Wimborne, and the activity must have been intense at some times of the day. In the meantime two more routes converging on Wimborne had been opened, Broadstone to Poole & Bournemouth West (1872), and Salisbury (Alderbury Jcn) to West Moors (1866), so that in 1875 one could leave Wimborne by train in any one of five directions and there was constant shunting in the yard as wagons were exchanged between the various lines.

The first blow fell on 14th December, 1885, when the S & D opened their direct cut-off line between Corfe Mullen & Broadstone to eliminate the tiresome reversals for through trains. Long distance traffic was diverted at once, but a sparse local service to Wimborne was retained and goods exchange arrangements were largely unaltered. Much more serious was the opening of the Holes Bay Curve in 1893, completing an alternative through route between Southampton and Weymouth (via Bournemouth) to which the Waterloo service was diverted. Thereafter the story is one of continual decline. The meagre S & D passenger service was withdrawn on 11th July, 1920 followed by milk and parcels in February 1932, the line being fully closed to freight on 17th June, 1933. Wimborne Junction signal box closed the very next day! The short bay platform on the Down side was retained as a siding, but the points were altered so that it formed part of the yard on 13th December, 1953 (compare plans "A" and "B").

Loss of the S & D left the station with only an infrequent "push-and-pull" service between Brockenhurst and Bournemouth West plus a handful of Salisbury trains, the only long-distance traffic appearing on Summer Saturdays when the route was used to relieve congestion at Bournemouth. In latter years there was a general air of neglect, although goods traffic remained quite heavy until sundries were concentrated on Bournemouth Central from 28th February, 1966. The passenger service had already ceased by this time, and some rationalisation of the track and signalling became possible. On 24th July, 1966 "Siding Working" was introduced, the Down line being put out of use and all trains using the former Up line. Signals were removed, but the box remained workable as a ground frame until 8th January, 1967, when all points were converted to hand operation. All traffic ceased between Wimborne and West Moors in May 1974, the track being removed in July of that year. Stop blocks were erected on the station side of bridge No. 75, which was demolished to allow road improvements.

Total closure came on 2nd May, 1977, but the previous day (Sunday) saw more traffic on the line than for many years, as a shuttle service from Poole was run for the benefit of enthusiasts. This was worked in "push-and-pull" fashion by a "Type 3" loco and TC stock. On Tuesday 3rd May an engine ran to Wimborne to clear the yard, and the return trip—consisting of just one wagon—was the last train to use the line.

A Bournemouth West—Brockenhurst train leaves Wimborne in the early 1960s. "M7" tanks worked this service in push-and-pull fashion, the van next to the engine being appropriately fitted. This was provided for the conveyance of prams. *photo: Lens of Sutton*

WINCHESTER CITY

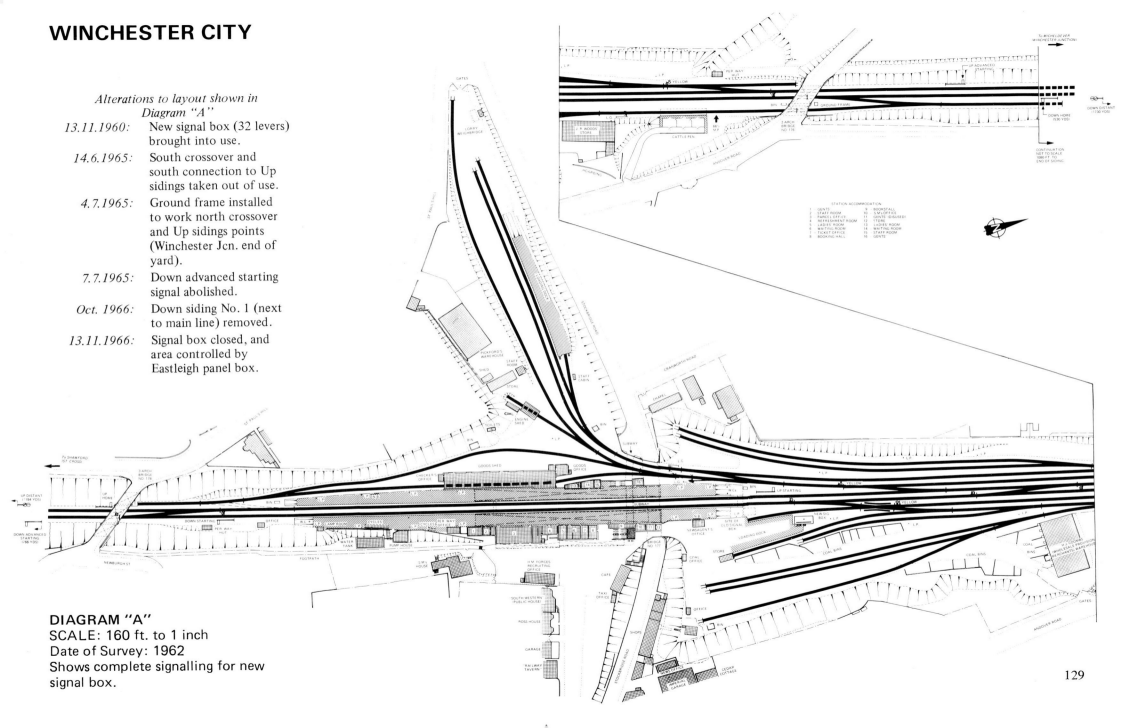

Alterations to layout shown in Diagram "A"

13.11.1960: New signal box (32 levers) brought into use.

14.6.1965: South crossover and south connection to Up sidings taken out of use.

4.7.1965: Ground frame installed to work north crossover and Up sidings points (Winchester Jcn. end of yard).

7.7.1965: Down advanced starting signal abolished.

Oct. 1966: Down siding No. 1 (next to main line) removed.

13.11.1966: Signal box closed, and area controlled by Eastleigh panel box.

DIAGRAM "A"

SCALE: 160 ft. to 1 inch
Date of Survey: 1962
Shows complete signalling for new signal box.

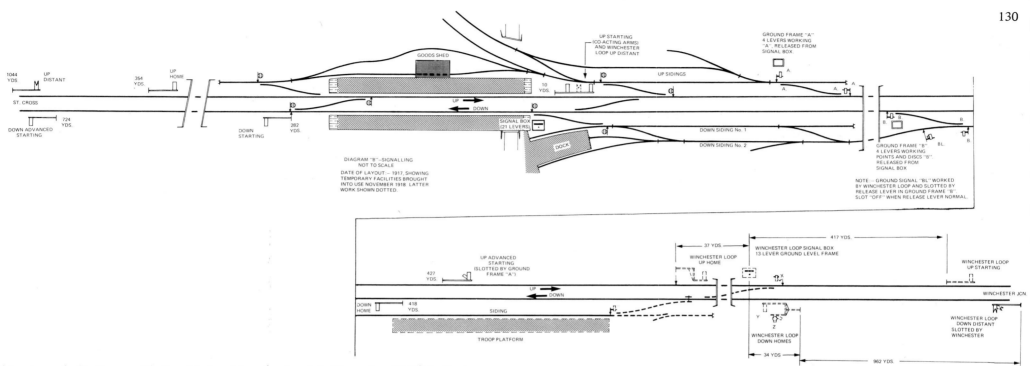

UP STARTING
(CO-ACTING ARMS)
AND WINCHESTER
LOOP UP DISTANT

GROUND FRAME "A"
4 LEVERS WORKING
"A", RELEASED FROM
SIGNAL BOX.

GOODS SHED

1044
YDS.

UP
DISTANT

354
YDS.

UP
HOME

UP SIDINGS

ST. CROSS

10
YDS.

UP

DOWN

724
YDS.

DOWN ADVANCED
STARTING

282
YDS.

DOWN
STARTING

SIGNAL BOX
(21 LEVERS)

DOWN SIDING No. 1

DOWN SIDING No. 2

DOCK

DIAGRAM "B"—SIGNALLING
NOT TO SCALE

DATE OF LAYOUT:— 1917, SHOWING
TEMPORARY FACILITIES BROUGHT
INTO USE NOVEMBER 1918. LATTER
WORK SHOWN DOTTED.

GROUND FRAME "B"
4 LEVERS WORKING
POINTS AND DISCS "B".
RELEASED FROM
SIGNAL BOX

NOTE:— GROUND SIGNAL "BL" WORKED
BY WINCHESTER LOOP AND SLOTTED BY
RELEASE LEVER IN GROUND FRAME "B".
SLOT "OFF" WHEN RELEASE LEVER NORMAL.

417 YDS.

37 YDS.

WINCHESTER LOOP SIGNAL BOX
13-LEVER GROUND LEVEL FRAME

UP ADVANCED
STARTING
(SLOTTED BY GROUND
FRAME "A")

WINCHESTER LOOP
UP HOME

WINCHESTER LOOP
UP STARTING

427
YDS.

UP

DOWN

WINCHESTER JCN.

DOWN
HOME

418
YDS.

SIDING

X

Y
Z

WINCHESTER LOOP
DOWN HOMES

WINCHESTER LOOP
DOWN DISTANT
SLOTTED BY
WINCHESTER

TROOP PLATFORM

34 YDS.

962 YDS.

Looking towards St. Cross, with the old signal box (replaced in November 1960) in the foreground.

photo: R.C. Riley

X — SHUNT FROM UP MAIN
(SLOTTED BY WINCHESTER)
Y — WINCHESTER LOOP DOWN MAIN HOME
Z — WINCHESTER LOOP DOWN MAIN TO
SIDING HOME. (SLOTTED BY WINCHESTER)

DIAGRAM "B"—Signalling

Not to Scale

Date of Layout: 1917

Shows temporary facilities as brought into use November 1918. Latter work shown "dotted". For signalling applicable to new signal box see Diagram "A".

Opened: 10.6.1839
Electrified: 3.4.1967
Closed: 6.1.1969 (Goods)
Original Company: L & SWR

Looking north in 1967, shortly after electrification.　　　*photo: B.L. Jackson*

WINCHESTER CITY

For its first few months this station functioned as the terminus of an isolated length of railway from Southampton, pending completion of construction through the difficult chalk country to the North. The line was opened as a through route on 11th May, 1840.

The main office buildings are on the Down platform, the central section being original and bearing a strong family likeness to others on the line designed by Sir William Tite. Extensions on either side, a canopy and a large clock case have considerably altered its original appearance. The site chosen for the station was convenient for providing road access but difficult in other respects, very heavy earthworks being necessary to enlarge the facilities. The goods yard soon proved inadequate and was extended by the cheapest means: by turning it up a side valley parallel to the Stockbridge Road. This largely solved the Civil Engineer's problem, but it created one for the Operating Department, as the resulting curvature was too sharp to permit the use of anything but the smallest tank engines. This made it necessary to stable a suitable locomotive at Winchester, a minute engine shed being provided for the purpose. At one time an ex-SECR "P" class tank did duty, but "B4s" ruled from 1950 to 1963, after which diesel shunters took over until the withdrawal of goods services.

The station's importance was enhanced on 2nd October, 1865 by the opening of the "Mid-Hants" line to Alton, which branched off the main line at Winchester Junction. Many of these trains ran through to Eastleigh or Southampton, but several started from or terminated at Winchester, and as there was no bay or loop line, the stock had to be smartly shunted. The First World War brought heavy Military traffic, and with the return of peace the City became a demobilisation centre. With thousands of troops descending on the station it was decided to segregate this traffic at a temporary wooden platform built beside the long Down Siding, which was converted into a loop in November 1918.

Diagram "B" shows the necessary alterations. After a few months of hectic activity the troop platform fell out of use, and Winchester Loop signal box and its associated connections were later abolished.

General passenger traffic is heavy, and has increased since electrification. There has been some modernisation of the booking hall and other station offices, and in 1965 the platforms were extended at the south end to accommodate twelve-coach trains. The old L & SWR signal box at the end of the Down platform was found to be in danger of collapse in the late '50s, and it was replaced by a new one on the end of the loading dock in 1960. Diagram "A" gives dates for this and subsequent alterations, and shows full signalling applicable to the new box. The points shown "dotted" were never connected to the later box, being taken out of use when the original one was closed.

The track layout and signalling have altered considerably in recent years following withdrawal of goods facilities and the introduction of colour-light signals are under the control of Eastleigh panel. All sidings on the Up side were taken out in September 1970, and the site is now a car park. Most other sidings have also been removed, but when the panel assumed control a facing slip connection from the Up Line to the Down Siding was provided for reversing a couple of local workings from the Eastleigh direction daily. This one long Down Siding is also used occasionally for berthing "Freightliners" or trains of "Carflats" awaiting acceptance at Eastleigh or Southampton.

The station has had two changes of name. Until nationalisation it was plain "Winchester", the "City" being added on 26th September, 1949 to distinguish it from the former GWR establishment on the far side of the City, which became "Chesil". When the GWR line was closed it was no longer necessary to make the distinction, and it became just "Winchester" again on 10th July, 1967.

WOOL

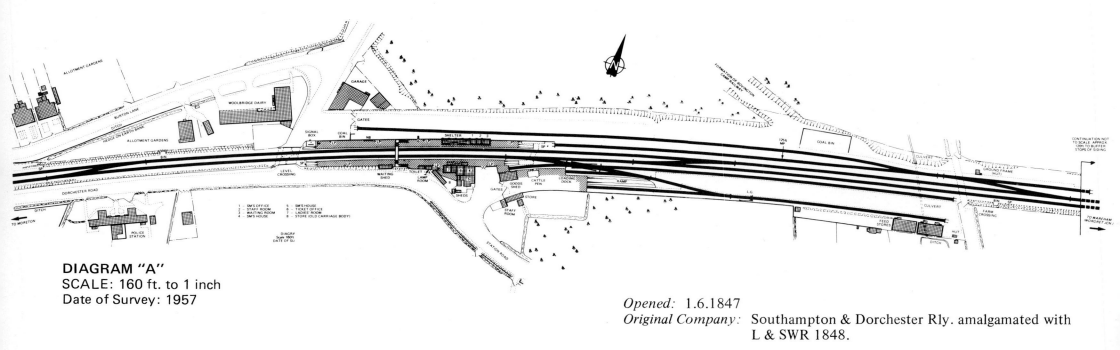

DIAGRAM "A"
SCALE: 160 ft. to 1 inch
Date of Survey: 1957

Opened: 1.6.1847
Original Company: Southampton & Dorchester Rly. amalgamated with
L & SWR 1848.

WOOL

Starting life as a peaceful country station set amidst the water meadows of the River Frome, later developments were to make it one of the most prosperous establishments west of Poole.

The original nameboard, (which lasted until the rebuilding of the station), proclaimed "Wool for Lulworth Cove", and although some visitors to this picturesque spot on the coast were quite numerous in the pre-motor age, they became very few in latter years. The 'bus connections were more often academic than real, and the walk much too long for modern tourists, so the new BR-style nameboards make no mention of the little resort.

Wool station became important, not because of tourists, but through the establishment of military camps at West Lulworth and Bovington. The latter is a Royal Tank Corps depot, and as such has generated a large quantity of traffic in heavy equipment. Today railborne loads are more occasional than regular, but during the First World War they reached such a pitch that it was decided to construct a line into the camp. The work was undertaken by prisoners of war, but in the event the branch, a little over two miles in length, was not opened until well after the end of hostilities on 9th August, 1919, despite

completion of the junction the previous year. It was purely a goods line, and connected with the Up Sidings at Wool station. Diagram "B" shows the extent of the new work. Like most creatures of war it was shortlived, being closed completely on 4th November, 1928, but the rails were not removed until 1936. Indeed, three "Well" wagons were left at Bovington for several years after closure to enable troops to practise loading and chaining armoured vehicles.

The station goods yard remained busy with military traffic, cattle feed and general merchandise, but all facilities except those for specified traffic in wagon loads were withdrawn from 1st March, 1965. Passenger traffic is well maintained, as the camps still exist and supply many long-distance travellers, and the village itself has become quite large with poor alternative public transport. The station was rebuilt in 1967, the original "cottage-style" buildings giving way to modern re-fabricated structure, and on 10th July that year the "push-and-pull" diesel service was inaugurated.

OPERATING NOTE: Bogie coaches prohibited from loading dock.

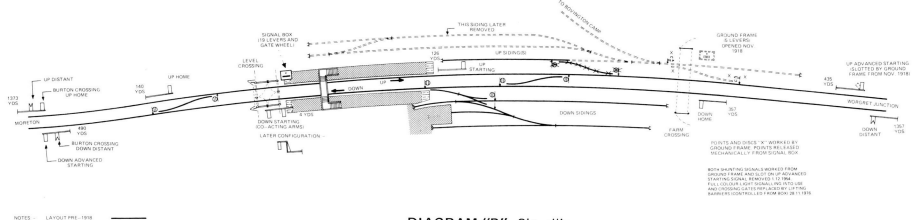

NOTES: LAYOUT PRE—1918
NEW WORK NOVEMBER 1918
POINTS AND DISCS SHOWN AS CROSSED OUT REMOVED WHEN NEW LAYOUT INSTALLED

DIAGRAM "B"—Signalling
Layout Date: 1918
Not to Scale

Wool station before the reconstruction of 1967, looking towards Wareham. Note the travelling crane in the yard for handling military traffic.
photo: Lens of Sutton

The station in rebuilt form, looking towards Dorchester.
photo: M.J. Tattershall

DIAGRAM "A"
SCALE: 160ft. to 1 inch
Survey Undated

Looking towards Wateringbury in 1870. This station was destroyed by fire in 1893. Note the very short and low platform of the period.
photo: Lens of Sutton

The same viewpoint a century later. Both station buildings and signal box date from 1894.
photo: J. Scrace

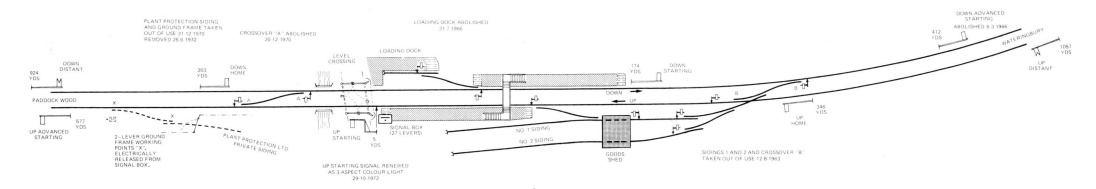

DIAGRAM "B"
Signalling
Not to Scale

Opened: 25.9.1844
Electrified: 12.6.1961
Closed: 27.5.1963 (Goods)
Original Company: South Eastern Railway

YALDING

Although the station at Yalding was opened with the Paddock Wood—Maidstone branch of the SER there were no proper facilities at first. Even platforms seem to have been beyond the Company's means, a wooden plank being provided to help passengers climb into the trains! Fortunately this crude arrangement was shortlived, but the original station was certainly no architectural gem. The older photograph shows it as a single-storey wooden structure with large and hideous chimneys, a small hut-like signal box being erected next to the level crossing gates. As diagram "A" shows, a house for the Station Master was built a little way down the road, and not immediately on the platform as was customary at the time. As things turned out, this was fortunate for the occupant, as the station was destroyed by fire in 1893. The platform, of course, staggered in true SER fashion, and a small wooden shelter was provided on the Down side.

After the fire the offices were rebuilt in brick to a somewhat better design, a short canopy now being provided. In 1894 the existing signal box replaced the primitive hut,

and the entire layouts both here and at neighbouring Wateringbury were re-signalled. The platforms were much lengthened at this time, and as the end ramps were no longer opposite each other, a trap in the surface of the Up platform was provided to give access to the sleeper crossing. The Board of Trade Inspector was rather unhappy about this — hardly surprising, since this was the only way passengers could cross between the platforms! A footbridge had been added by 1895.

The goods shed was rather unusual in that the opening farthest away from the running line had the space between the rails filled in so that is was available to both road and rail vehicles. A private siding for Plant Protection Ltd. (shown dotted on diagram "B") was added around 1950, and this remained in use after the withdrawal of the ordinary freight service, not closing until 31st December, 1970. Layout alterations in recent years are shown on diagram "B", but the station itself has changed very little.

"T9" on a Padstow–Okehampton train at Wadebridge.   *photo: R.C. Riley*

Veteran Adams' tank No. 30583 runs round its train on arrival at Lyme Regis.

photo: R.C. Riley

The **SOUTHERN RAILWAY'S** slogan
is still as true as ever:

"South for Sunshine"